(re)Aligning with God

(re)Aligning with
GOD

Reading Scripture
for Church and World

BRIAN D. RUSSELL

CASCADE *Books* • Eugene, Oregon

(RE)ALIGNING WITH GOD

Reading Scripture for Church and World

Copyright © 2016 Brian D. Russell. All rights reserved. Except for brief quotations in critical publications or reviews, no part of this book may be reproduced in any manner without prior written permission from the publisher. Write: Permissions, Wipf and Stock Publishers, 199 W. 8th Ave., Suite 3, Eugene, OR 97401.

Cascade Books
An Imprint of Wipf and Stock Publishers
199 W. 8th Ave., Suite 3
Eugene, OR 97401

www.wipfandstock.com

ISBN 13: 978-1-60608-551-6

Cataloging-in-Publication data:

Russell, Brian D.

   (re)aligning with God : reading scripture for church and world / Brian D. Russell.

   xiv + 190 p. ; 23 cm. Includes bibliographical references.

   ISBN 13: 978-1-60608-551-6

   1. Bible—Criticism, interpretation, etc. 2. Bible—Hermeneutics. I. Title.

BS476 R85 2016

Manufactured in the U.S.A.

To all who love the Bible and pray that the Scriptures will astonish our twenty-first-century world with their richness and power.

Contents

Acknowledgments

Introduction

1: Scripture and Conversion

PART ONE: (re)Engaging God's Story

2: The Old Testament Story: Creation, Fall, and Israel

3: The Old Testament Story: Israel's Life in the Land, Prophets, and Writings

4: The New Testament Story: Jesus the Messiah, the Mission of the Church, New Creation

PART TWO: Learning to Speak Human:
Reading the Bible for All People

5: Learning to Speak Human: Methodology and Missional Hermeneutics

6: Reading the Old and New Testament Missionally: Jonah and Philippians

PART THREE: Aligning Our Communities

7: Unleashing the Biblical Narrative: Implementing a Missional Hermeneutic in Our Communities of Faith

Bibliography

Acknowledgments

(re)Aligning with God represents the work of many years. I am pleased with its final form and hope that it proves helpful to you its reader. Thank you for picking up a copy.

Thank you to my good friend Eric Hallett for introducing me to the literature of mission and church planting. I am grateful for our breakfast conversations in 2004–2005 that opened a new world to me.

Thank you to Alex McManus of the International Mentoring Network for many stimulating conversations as well as for challenging me to become involved personally in church planting as an integral part of my preparation for teaching in a seminary. I remain grateful for the opportunities to share my ideas with your IMN cohorts.

I am grateful to my students at Asbury Theological Seminary for engaging my ideas rigorously. Teaching this material in courses in Old Testament and Inductive Bible Study helped to sharpen the material. It is a joy to study missional hermeneutics and its application to preaching and teaching with you.

Thank you to Alastair Sterne for reading an early version of the manuscript. I am grateful for Cheri Cowell for providing editorial and format help on the penultimate draft. Of course, any remaining imperfections are due to my own negligence.

Finally, thank you to my family for the support, encouragement, and love that you continue to provide for me. Te amo mi amor Astrid and much love to my daughters Micaela and Katrina as well as to my step-children: Julio, Astrid, Patricia, and Sarah. I am grateful for a family in which we can all aspire and grow into the people whom God created us to be.

Introduction

The art and craft of listening to Scripture today involves learning to operate simultaneously in two contexts: the Church and the World. Of course these are not mutually exclusive categories, nor should they be, but increasingly in our day these two entities coexist almost as foreign countries.

On January 8, 2009 an amazing convergence occurred between Tim Tebow, the Google search engine, and John 3:16. Tim Tebow, the former record-setting quarterback for the University of Florida Gators, was leading his team to victory over the Oklahoma Sooners in the 2009 National Championship game. Tebow is a Christ follower and as part of his public witness during that season he routinely painted "Phil 4:10" on the grease paint under his eyes so that when the camera focused on him, as it often did, the audience would encounter a reference to Scripture. Of course, this assumes that Tebow's audience could decode "Phil 4:10" as a reference to the Book of Philippians chapter 4 and verse 10. For the National Championship game Tebow switched from Phil 4:10 to John 3:16. This is where Google entered the picture. Amazingly, "John 3:16," and related variations of it, rose to become the number one search on Google from early in the game through the morning of January 9, 2009. Think about it. For more than twelve hours, John 3:16 was the most popular search on Google. Of all of the possible searches, Tebow drove searchers to the good news about Jesus. But before we say, "Praise the LORD!" too quickly, let's look at this story from a different angle. What does it mean that the #1 search on Google was John 3:16 in the United States, especially considering the main audience of the game were the fans of two universities located in the Bible Belt? If people living in the United States don't know John 3:16, what can we assume they know about the Scriptures? What does it mean to read the Bible for a world that no longer knows John 3:16, let alone any other

Introduction

biblical texts that have served as starting points for the proclamation of the Gospel?

The year 2009 also marked another profound shift in the world. Within a few months of Tebow's John 3:16 phenomenon on Google, human culture reached a new milestone. For the first time in history, the population of people dwelling in urban areas exceeded the number of persons living in rural areas. Large masses of people in small areas create unprecedented opportunities for the church of Jesus Christ in the United States. Of course there are opportunities for resourcing global mission in the major cities around the world, but large urban areas in the United States are likewise in need of the Gospel. John Wesley, the eighteenth-century founder of the Methodist movement, once proclaimed that the "world is my parish" and then spent a lifetime riding thousands of miles on horseback to preach the Gospel all over England as well as unleashing a corp of committed evangelists to follow in his footsteps. The growing urbanization of our world inspired missiologist Timothy Tennant to turn Wesley's dictum into "The world is *in* our parish." The mix of diverse cultures and religions in our urban areas creates challenges for existing churches because, in order to grow, historic churches must now learn to engage different demographic groups. What does it mean to read Scripture in our multi-cultural, multi-ethnic, and religiously pluralistic urban centers?

We humans value and desire *security* and we often experience fear in the face of new and unpredictable situations. The issues of biblical illiteracy and the need to engage a pluralistic urbanized world are daunting. The church of Jesus Christ can feel paralyzed and may even desire to retreat into and hide within the slowly deteriorating walls of its church buildings.

There is a way forward to an alternative and exciting future. I have written this book to help Christ followers reflect seriously on what it means to reengage the Scriptures for a World that no longer knows the Christian message and one that is increasingly urbanized. It is vital to recall that the Scriptures themselves emerged in the context of a pluralistic world. Ancient Israel existed in the midst of the nations. The New Testament church lived as a tiny minority in cities throughout the Roman Empire. The Bible narrates the story of God's missional outreach to a lost humanity and a broken creation. God engages humanity within their cultures as means of transformation and redemption. The Scriptures continue to beckon us all to the life that God created for us to live. Thus, the current missional realities of our present world may actually help us to regain the proper posture from which to read the Bible.

INTRODUCTION

In our churches many of us sense we are in a new day. We know the numbers of Christians are declining and our position of prominence in culture and society has slipped away.[1] But we struggle in the face of this emerging new reality with the temptation to hunker down and hold firm to some imagined glorious past. We often return to programs that proved successful in the past only to be disappointed by their failure in the present. Others choose the pathway of accommodation in which the Church merely serves as a mirror for the culture rather than as a window through which the culture may encounter the one true God. The Church flounders aimlessly in futile attempts at relevancy in an ever-changing cultural landscape. I have written this book for Christ followers who are returning to the Scriptures for a bold rediscovery of the power of the Gospel as the key to finding our way forward again.

Yet it is not enough to read Scripture for the world or for the church. We must learn the art and craft of reading the Bible simultaneously for both the world and for the church. We need to help persons who have grown up *inside* the church to recapture the missional vibrancy and confidence of the apostolic church of the first four centuries by reintroducing them to the biblical story. We must likewise introduce the life-changing message of Scripture to those on the *outside* of the church. Scripture is for both *insiders* and *outsiders* because God desires to bring healing, hope, restoration, and wholeness to all people. We thus must learn to speak human.

What does such a reading of Scripture involve?

Our argument will unfold in three parts. Part One "(re)Engaging God's Story" will present a broad overview of the Bible in terms of the rubric: Creation—Fall—Israel—Jesus the Messiah—Church—New Creation. As we engage this grand narrative we will rediscover that God's mission stands as the central thread that holds the biblical materials together and serves as the story that God invites all people to embrace as their personal story. Part Two, "Learning to Speak Human: Reading the Bible for All People," will focus on the craft of a missional hermeneutic and provide clear examples of reading the Scripture for Church and World through a missional perspective. Finally, Part Three, "Aligning our Communities," will look at how to implement a missional approach to reading the Scriptures in our

---

1. As of 2009, in the Western world, there are five thousand less Christians every twenty-four hours.

INTRODUCTION

local communities of faith. By realigning our faith communities with the missional center of the Bible, we are setting the stage for inviting the world to align itself with God's missional intentions for creation.

1

Scripture and Conversion

The goal of biblical interpretation is conversion. We must not forget this. The Bible may be read as a gateway to understanding the ancient world, or to encounter stories about God, Jesus, and an assortment of interesting characters. It can be read for spiritual formation. It can even be used as the basis for understanding the literature and culture of the Western world. But without a conversion to the Scriptural story, the reading and study of the Bible is incomplete.

Scripture must become our story. Most of us in the Church will eagerly cry out, "The Bible already is our story," and confess our belief in the authority and efficacy of the Scriptures. But how many of us really grasp the implications of it for living?

In John Steinbeck's classic, *East of Eden*, Liza Hamilton serves as the pillar of faith for her family. She is a staunch advocate of biblical morality and ostensibly reads the Scripture as the guide for her earthly existence. Yet, there are cracks in her pious veneer. Steinbeck describes her use of the Bible sublimely:

> Her total intellectual association was the Bible. . . . In that one book she had her history and her poetry, her knowledge of peoples and things, her ethics, her morals, and her salvation. She never studied the Bible or inspected it; she just read it. The many places where it seems to refute itself did not confuse her in the least. And finally she came to a point where *she knew it so well that she went right on reading it without listening.*[1]

---

1. Steinbeck, *East of Eden*, 42. Italics added.

To this day, the final line of this quotation haunts me. As I reflect and dream about advancing the Gospel in our day, I am convinced that, like Hamilton, we are missing out on the true riches and power of the Scripture not only to transform our lives but also our world. Even much of our biblical preaching and teaching misses the central theme of the Scriptures.

The goal of *(re)Aligning with God* is the unleashing of the Scriptures in all of their richness and complexity. This book is not merely a call to return to the Scriptures. It is an invitation to experience a conversion to Scripture. It is a summons to a rehearing of the core message of the Bible. It is a bold and daring reentry into the world of the text for there we find God's visions and dreams for humanity. In the Old and New Testaments we discover the *true* story of our lives as individuals and as part of the fabric of creation.

The Scriptures are the narrative about God's mission from Creation to a New Creation. They focus primarily on God's relationship with humanity and serve to call women and men to live as the people whom God created them to be. The goal of the Scriptures is our conversion to its viewpoint and way of thinking. Such a reading of Scripture seeks to shape us into the sort of people whom God desires for the purpose of the advance of God's mission in Creation.

In the following three chapters we will take a big-picture look at the narrative found in the Scriptures. The storyline may be summarized succinctly: Creation—Fall of Humanity—Israel—Jesus the Messiah—Church—New Creation.

In this chapter, we will start our journey through the Bible with the beginning of Jesus' ministry. Jesus Christ is the central figure of the Scriptural story so the life, death, and resurrection of Jesus is the foundation of the Christ following movement. Jesus launched his ministry with a provocative message: "Repent for the Kingdom of Heaven is at hand" (Matt 4:17).[2] In Jesus' opening proclamation, he announced the long awaited age of salvation. The Gospels use the synonymous phrases "Kingdom of God" and "Kingdom of Heaven" to express this reality. This language answered the longings of Israel who were hoping for the renewal of God's activity in their day. Jesus' words signify the inauguration of God's reign on earth. God's kingdom is the sphere in which God manifests his reign.

---

2. Mark's Gospel describes the launch of Jesus' ministry in similar fashion: "The time is fulfilled, and the Kingdom of God has come near; repent and believe in the good news" (1:15). Likewise, in Luke's Gospel, Jesus reads Isa 61 and announces the fulfillment of its promises in his person (Luke 4:16–21).

Jesus' words need unpacking for our twenty-first-century world. Why does Jesus begin his ministry with a call to repentance? What does repentance mean in this context? Who is Jesus' primary audience? Why all this talk about the Kingdom of heaven? Why do Jesus' words mirror those of John Baptist (Matt 3:2) from earlier in the Gospel as well as the message with which he entrusts his disciples later in his ministry (Matt 10:7)?

When we carefully observe Jesus' words, we notice that it consists of an exhortation "Repent," followed by the rationale for this call to action "for the Kingdom of Heaven is at hand." But let's first look at the context of Jesus' initial proclamation.

Who was Listening?

The question of audience is critical for understanding the missional force and model of Jesus' message. Jesus begins his public ministry on the margins. This is significant. Matthew (4:12–16) understands Jesus' move to the margins as a fulfillment of Isaiah's words about a coming Messiah who would pierce the darkness with light (Isa 9:1–2). Galilee was the region linked to the eschatological expectation of the renewal of God's kingdom. The reference to "Galilee of the Gentiles" is important. In Galilee, Jesus is nowhere near the religious epicenter of Jerusalem and the Second Temple. Instead, he is far to the north. This was Gentile country. Jesus proclaimed the message of the Kingdom to people who lived around the Sea of Galilee. This region was a mixture of Jews and Gentiles with Jews perhaps in the minority.[3] It was under the authority of Herod Antipas. This context is significant for understanding all of Scripture. If we are not careful we can easily misread the Bible as a story of God's preferential dealings with God's people. Rather, the Bible is the story of God's calling of a people for the sake *of God's mission to the nations.* It is fitting then for Jesus to locate his own ministry on the margins of Israel in the Galilee. Moreover, it is significant for understanding the movement of God to recognize the importance of the margins.

In the biblical narrative the Gospel moves repeatedly from the margins to the center. The first responders to Jesus' message were fishermen (Matt 4:18–22). The first recipients of Jesus' miracles were lepers, gentiles, and women (Matt 8:1–17). John the Baptist preached his fiery call for repentance in the wilderness (Matt 3). If we go to the Old Testament, Abram

---

3. France, *Gospel of Matthew*, 5–6 and 138–43.

was a wanderer in the world (Gen 11:27ff.; Deut 26:5) before God called him to be the eponymous ancestor of God's people. Israel's home in the hill country of Canaan was not the epicenter of the ancient world, but rather a "backwoods" region wedged between the dominant power centers of Egypt and Mesopotamia. Moreover, the history of God's people is rooted in servitude and slavery out of which God redeemed them (Exod 20:2).

The Gospel is not about power but about people—all people. Thus, the beginning of Jesus' ministry adumbrates the post-resurrection mission—the proclamation of the Gospel to all people everywhere. Moreover, Jesus' initial message is inclusive of both *insiders* and *outsiders*. He has come to save *his people* from their sins (Matt 1:21). It is easy to assume this meant *Israel*, but Jesus' actions in the Gospel of Matthew suggest a broader understanding. Jesus' people certainly include "the lost sheep of Israel" (Matt 10:6), but we must not miss the dynamic expansion of mission embodied in Jesus' ministry. Matthew reminds us in the initial verse of the Gospel that Jesus is the "son of Abraham." Abraham stands in the biblical story as the one through whose seed all peoples of the earth will be blessed (Gen 12:3). Jesus embodies this calling. This theme reaches its climax in the story of Jesus when in Matt 28:16–20 Jesus sends out his disciples to make disciples of all nations. Significantly, this sending out occurs when the disciples meet the resurrected Jesus in Galilee.

Rationale for (Re)alignment

Jesus' opening words are audacious and demand an immediate shift in the orientation of his audience. Jesus is declaring that the new age of God's salvation has arrived. It is a declaration that a new page in history is now being written. This new age is God's long awaited era of salvation. It had been originally envisioned in Israel's Scriptures. The Old Testament rings with anticipation. As we will see, Israel's prophets foresaw a future renewal and redemption for the nation on the other side of its experience of judgment and exile. Israel's prayers and songs celebrated the rule of God and hoped for a renewal of the Davidic monarchy. Those living in Palestine at the time of Jesus were languishing under the thumb of the Roman Empire. They were longing for a renewal of God's saving power. They hungered for a Messiah who would bring liberation from oppression and usher in God's new age of peace, wholeness, hope, and restoration.

In short, the people of God in Jesus' day were expecting a decisive climax to occur in history. This would be marked by the arrival of God's kingdom. The present evil age would pass away and a new age of justice, righteousness, peace, and salvation would replace it. What does the kingdom look like? In the LORD's Prayer Jesus helps us to unpack its core reality with the phrases, "May your Kingdom come. May your will be done, on earth as it is in heaven" (Matt 6:10). In other words, the Kingdom of God is dynamically present whenever and wherever God's *will* is being embodied and accomplished. In the Gospels, Jesus is the announcer of the Kingdom's arrival and its personal embodiment. Jesus models the ethos and values of the Kingdom in his earthly ministry. He demonstrates the reality of the Kingdom through his acts of power and miraculous works (Matt 11:4-6). In his life, death, and resurrection Jesus embodies God's Kingdom.

In his first-century context, Jesus' words are bold and daring. For he declares that God's long anticipated end-time rule is now present in his person. The announcement of the Kingdom is the core message of Jesus. Jesus' coming is not the start of a new religion; it is more radical. It is a full-blown declaration of the saving power and presence of God's Kingdom.

This puts Jesus' message in continuity with the prophets of old and with the future proclamation of the Church. In Matthew's Gospel, John the Baptist functions as the last of the prophets. Matthew records his message in 3:2 in identical fashion with Jesus' in 4:17, "Repent for the kingdom of heaven has come near." Likewise, when Jesus sends out his disciples for ministry, they are to proclaim the gospel of the Kingdom: "The kingdom of heaven has come near." In Jesus, God has arrived to usher in his end-time rule. This is the Gospel. But, there is a human response necessitated by Jesus' announcement.

(Re)alignment

What response is required given the reality of a new age of salvation? Jesus' message is simple. His exhortation is a single word, "Repent." Jesus is calling for a radical change and transformation in the face of the arrival of the long awaited age of salvation. It remains the work of God's people today to change and live out the Kingdom in their day.

Let me offer you my dynamic translation of Matt 4:17: "Continually (re)align yourselves [with the ethos and will of God] for the long awaited age of God's saving reign has arrived in the person and ministry of Jesus the Messiah."

Much could be said here, but I want to focus on my retranslation of "repent" as "(re)align." "Repent" is a competent and adequate translation of the Greek verb *metanoieo,* but in the emerging cultures of the twenty-first-century western world, I think that (re)align is an improvement on repent for several reasons. First, repent conjures up (rightly or wrongly) images of angry Bible thumpers ranting about hell from the pulpit, or street preachers accosting passersby with threats of divine wrath. For too long the call to repentance has been understood primarily as a word to those "outside" the Church. Yet, to whom was Jesus speaking in the Gospels? Was Jesus speaking to insiders or outsiders in 4:17?

Jesus was preaching in the context of the nation of Israel, but his message and acts were not limited only to those on the inside. As we will see, Jesus' harshest messages were reserved for those on the inside. He continually engaged persons on the margins with his saving words and deeds. He launched his earthly ministry from multicultural Galilee. He was in the borderlands of Jewish and Hellenistic culture. Moreover, there were no restrictions on who heard the message in Matthew's Gospel. Nowhere in Matthew does it suggest that only Jewish persons listened and responded to Jesus.[4] Jesus' call to realignment was proclaimed equally to both insiders and outsiders.

Second, "repent"[5] has been defined traditionally as "change one's mind." This is too limiting. "Repent" assumes a change in both *thinking* and *actions*. Most importantly, it involves shifting or reshifting to align oneself with God. It is a turning fully to God and away from any competing orientations.[6] Thus, *(re)align* best captures the meaning of *metanoieo* for our day. Jesus' proclamation of the kingdom is a call to (re)align one's thoughts, actions, and direction with the arrival of the kingdom of heaven. To (re)align is to experience *conversion* in light of the reality of the Kingdom of God.[7]

---

4. For example, in the context of Matthew 4, Matthew refers to Galilee as "Galilee of the Gentiles (4:15) and lists the following regions and cities as the home areas of Jesus' audience: Galilee, the Decapolis, Jerusalem, Judea, and from beyond the Jordan (4:25). In other words, Jesus' audience was a mixed one.

5. Greek *metanoieo*

6. The Greek *metanoieo* is a translation of the Hebrew *shub*. The latter focuses on turning or returning.

7. For sytlistic reasons, the remainder of the book will only occasionally use the parentheses in writing (re)align. Whether (re)align or realign is present, remember the

The core of Jesus' message was, and is, about realignment. It is a word both for insiders and outsiders. Followers of Jesus respond to the words of Jesus by realigning their lives to match up with the movement and teaching of Jesus; non-Christ followers join the movement by aligning their lives with the movement and teachings of Jesus. Thus, the goal of biblical interpretation (i.e., encountering the word of God) is conversion or realignment.

Last, realignment is not a one-time event. Conversion is more dynamic than this. It is not a one-size-fits-all proposition. It is continuous and ongoing. It is a process and a way of life. An initial alignment occurs at a crisis moment, but it assumes a process of continual realignment throughout the life of a Christ follower. Note that our translation includes the adverb "continually." This nuance is absent from major English translation. Yet, this key element of an ongoing, continuous conversion is implicit in the Greek verb behind "repent" or "realign."[8] The ongoing nature of realignment is critical for understanding the message of Jesus and of the Bible as a whole.

Realignment is the key stance we must take as we read the Scriptures. As we seek to become the people and communities God desires for us to be and if we wish to fulfill his mission, we will need to realign ourselves continually with God's kingdom. When we come to the Scriptures with this understanding, we open ourselves up to an ongoing conversion to live authentically as God's people as we eagerly await the full consummation of God's salvation. Life with God involves a moment-by-moment walk of faithfulness.

Jesus' call to realignment serves as an invitation to reread Scripture through this lens. The books of the Old Testament serve as "Act 1" to the New Testament's "Act 2."[9] When Jesus announces the kingdom of heaven, he explicitly links the launch of his ministry with the witness of Israel's Scriptures. This call to realignment means we, as readers of the Bible, must locate and understand Jesus' life and ministry within the broader context of the larger narrative of the Bible.

---

point: *insiders* hear the Scriptures as a call to realign; *outsiders* hear the Scriptures as an invitation to an initial aligning of their lives.

8. Present active imperative carrying durative force.

9. Goldingay, *Old Testament Theology*, 25–26.

Call to Missional Community that Reflects the Character and Ethos of God

Realignment involves the reconfiguration of life in light of the arrival of God's kingdom in Jesus. This includes a total recalibration in light of Israel's Scriptures and Jesus' life, death, and resurrection. It is profitable to read the remainder of Matthew's Gospel for details on what realignment looks like. But it is vital we don't miss the specific response in the context of Matthew 4:17–22.

Immediately following his initial proclamation, Jesus creates a new community by calling disciples. Jesus' call is clear and memorable: "Follow me and I will teach you to fish for people." But don't miss the core reality of Jesus' call to his first disciples. We often boil down the call to discipleship to be in a relationship with Jesus. Of course, this is true. But, it is a relationship with a broader purpose. Jesus calls disciples as a means of returning humanity to its original role as ambassadors for God to all Creation. Disciples serve as a vanguard for the work God desires to do in the world, and they are called to multiply by reaching others. We should also observe that Jesus embeds this calling into the fishing culture of his first followers. He contextualizes his message by grabbing hold of imagery that would resonate clearly and compellingly with his audience of fishermen. Jesus models incarnational mission from his opening words to his disciples. He uses language and illustrations that connect directly to his audience. He would not have called accountants or engineers to learn "to fish for people."

Discipleship can never be understood adequately apart from mission. Following Jesus means following Jesus into the world to carry the good news about the kingdom to new audiences in new places. This is a crucial paradigm for understanding a missional reading of Scripture. This is played out in Matthew's Gospel. Jesus teaches his disciples the ways of the kingdom through words and actions. He then sends them out on their own (Matt 10:1–48) to reach the "lost sheep of Israel." At the end of the Gospel, this earlier mission is expanded to include the nations. Jesus' final message in Matthew is a bold and daring commission to make disciples of all nations. This mission is to be contextualized for and multiplied in each person who receives the Gospel. The Gospel comes to us on the way to other places and people. An experience of God's graciousness is not an end in itself; it is a commissioning for mission.

But discipleship, likewise, can never be understood properly apart from community. There was never a moment in the Christ following movement where there was only one solitary disciple. From its beginning there has always been at least two.[10] The people of God are a missional community whose whole is always greater than the sum of its individual parts.

Jesus' call to realignment also involves a distinctive ethos. The Christ following movement is more than merely a missional community. It is a missional community that reflects God's character. The call to realignment involves a change in action and behavior. Jesus models the ethos and values of the kingdom in his life and ministry. We thus find that realignment involves a triad of key themes: mission, community, and holiness. Jesus calls a band of disciples to become a *missional community that reflects and embodies God's character to, for, and in the world.*

By beginning with Jesus' core message we root ourselves in the key premise of a missional reading of Scripture: *the goal of biblical interpretation is conversion.* The Bible seeks to call its readers or hearers to align, or realign, with God's purposes for humanity and for all. In our next chapter we will move back to the beginning of the Scriptural story to understand God's original purposes for humanity and all creation.

Introducing GPS

The triad of mission, community, and holiness lies at the core of our understanding of a missional approach to the Scriptures. We will trace these themes through the broader narrative of the whole Bible and find them in our study of its discrete passages. I now want to introduce a helpful rubric for remembering these themes using the acronym GPS.

Most readers will recognize GPS as short for global positioning system. The global positioning system (GPS) is a network of twenty-four satellites launched by the Department of Defense to be used by the United States military for pinpoint navigation around the globe. Each of the satellites orbits at roughly twelve thousand miles above the Earth's surface. The satellites move at over 7000 mph so each one completes two orbits around the earth each day. Since the 1980s GPS equipment has been available for civilian use. GPS navigational tools are precise and enable persons with receivers around the world to determine their exact location, as well as to

---

10. In the Scriptures as a whole this remains a key element. In the Genesis 2 Creation account, the principal problem in the Garden is the man's aloneness. When in his darkest moment, Elijah feels utterly isolated and marginalized. Yet God reminds him that he is part of a larger community of faithful worshippers of the LORD (1 Kings 19).

maintain correct course headings on land, sea, and in the air. Many of us can barely find our way to new places without making use of this technology. To work, the receiver must be able to lock into the signal from at least three satellites.

GPS technology greatly enhances the ability of its users to navigate unfamiliar territory. But it is not foolproof. Navigation requires the intelligent use of GPS technology. It is not as simple as obtaining one's starting position and charting a course to one's destination. As soon as movement ensues other variables come into play. If one is traveling by ship, currents, wind, waves, and storms constantly move the ship off-course. If one's position is not recalculated continually during the voyage, travelers will be surprised to discover that they end up far from their intended destination. In fact, a ship guided by GPS navigational tools is rarely perfectly on course. Instead, the GPS equipment continually monitors the ship's location and realigns the ship with the proper heading to reach the desired goal.

As we've described above, the core message of Jesus was a call for *continual realignment* in light of Jesus' announcement of the Kingdom. This realignment was understood in view of Jesus' call to his initial followers to follow him. We observed that Jesus' call was a call to mission, new community, and holiness. The realignment is continual because as we *follow* Jesus into the world on mission we will encounter new contexts and challenges. We will have to recalibrate our course and position as the Risen Lord shifts direction to lead his people to meet the challenges of the present rather than to maintain the status quo of the past.

As we seek to follow Jesus the Messiah faithfully, we, likewise, need GPS navigation so we remain constantly aligned with the Risen Lord. The three themes of mission, community, and holiness serve as a GPS triad for navigating our way through life, and the Scriptures, as Jesus' followers. If Scripture is the navigational tool for following Jesus, then the triad of mission, community, and holiness serves as the three orbiting satellites that triangulate and calculate our current position vis-à-vis God's mission embodied in Jesus through the power of the Spirit. As we will discover in our journey through the Bible, God created humanity to serve as a missional community that reflects God's character to the world, in the world, and for the world. God's new humanity, the Church of Jesus Christ, embodies God's purposes for humanity and participates in God's missional activity to reach the nations with the Gospel and to serve as stewards of Creation. This is a huge task. The Church must constantly realign itself as it advances.

Scripture and Conversion

Reading the Scriptures through the GPS navigational lenses of mission, community, and holiness allows the people of God to stay aligned with the heartbeat of God by continually realigning with the world of the text. Likewise, as the people of God engage the world with the Gospel, the lenses of mission, community, and holiness allow *outsiders* to the Gospel message to hear God's invitation to align themselves with the emerging new humanity created through the power of the Gospel of Jesus, the Messiah.

GPS can serve as a helpful acronym for the triad of mission, community, and holiness:

G = Global/local mission

P = Persons in community

S = Spiritually Transformed (Holy character)

(Re)aligning with God is, thus, a hermeneutic that involves reading the Scriptures as call to conversion using GPS. This approach brings our engagement of the text to new life and makes it possible to hear God's call for (re) alignment by persons in both the Church and the World.

But we are getting ahead of ourselves. Now that we have introduced Jesus' call to realignment around GPS, we must now move to a big picture review of the Scriptural story.

PART ONE

(re)Engaging God's Story

2

The Old Testament Story: Creation, Fall, and Israel

Jesus' call to realignment emerges out of the Scriptures of the Old Testament. From Genesis to Malachi, the Old Testament testifies about God's mission to return all Creation to a state of wholeness, justice, love, and peace. This vision of God's kingdom reaches its fulfillment in the coming of Jesus the Messiah. Jesus demonstrates the arrival of God's kingdom through his words and actions. The Gospels tell the story of Jesus' life, death, and resurrection as the climactic and decisive action of God's mission. The remainder of the New Testament narrates the movement of the good news about Jesus into the world through Jesus' followers empowered by the Holy Spirit in anticipation of the full consummation of God's mission in the New Creation.

However, to focus only on the New Testament message distorts the richness of God's story. A missional reading of the Bible must begin with an understanding of the overarching narrative. This chapter and the two following will briefly map the contours of the biblical narrative using this rubric: Creation—Fall—Israel—Jesus the Messiah—Church—New Creation.

A Very Good Creation (Gen 1–2)

Scripture opens by announcing that God (Heb: *elohim*) created the heavens and the earth (Gen 1:1). When God completes his work of creation, he declares his handiwork to be very good (Gen 1:31). From Gen 1:2–31 God guides his creation from undifferentiated matter shrouded in darkness

(RE)ALIGNING WITH GOD

(1:2) to a very good world teeming with potential and possibility. God establishes the framework for life in the cosmos and then fills it with vegetation, fish, birds, animals, and finally men and women. Humanity is the high point of God's creative work (1:26–31).

God is present and in control even in creation's chaotic beginning. Genesis 1:2 informs us of the darkness and formlessness of the pre-creative state but then decisively declares God's dynamic presence ready, willing, and able to establish very goodness as the abiding reality in his creation. God acts unilaterally in his work of creation and, profoundly, God accomplishes this work simply by speaking the various elements of the physical world into existence. The initial creation story reaches its climax with God resting in Sabbath (2:1–3). This movement from undifferentiated darkness to very goodness and to Sabbath is a powerful word for the world. The reader of Scripture immediately realizes that the God of Creation is a God who can bring order and wholeness to the most hopeless of situations. The Bible will prove to be a book for people desperate for deliverance, liberation, and salvation.

Genesis 2:4–25 follows with a second account of Creation. Genesis 2:4–25 complements the theology of Genesis 1:1—2:3 but does so in its own distinct style. If Genesis 1:1—2:3 portrays humanity as the high point of God's work and Sabbath as the climax, Genesis 2:4–25 focuses on the centrality of humanity and its relationships within God's world. Humanity enjoys productive and positive relationships with God, with creation, and between men and women. The climax of the second creation story (2:18–25) celebrates the intimate union and harmony between the man and the woman who enjoy life together at the center of God's creation while serving as caretakers and stewards of God's good world (2:15 cf. 1:28–29).

The biblical stories of creation exist to witness to the truth about reality and the Creator God. Israel's creation stories did not arise in a vacuum. There were competing claims and stories about the gods and the nature of creation. Likewise, today we find ourselves in a world awash with a multitude of understandings, sacred accounts, and claims about spirituality, life, God, and the universe. Genesis 1–2 use the creation stories as a vehicle to communicate to the world a message about a different kind of god and a new understanding of the cosmos. This God demonstrates his power and character as King of Creation.

Genesis' counter-testimony to the polytheistic and mythic worldview of the nations surrounding Israel is clear. First, Genesis is subtle in its

The OT Story: Creation, Fall, and Israel

introduction of the God of Scripture. Genesis 1:1—2:3 uses the Hebrew *elohim* thirty-three times. *Elohim* is translated "God" though grammatically it is a plural noun. It is Israel's way of declaring the prestige of its deity.

We get so use to hearing the word "God" that we forget Israel's god's personal name is Yahweh. The millennia old practice of saying "LORD" rather than uttering Yahweh obscures this personal dimension. Yet the Bible's consistent witness is that Yahweh alone is Israel's God (Deut 6:4–5). Why then doesn't the Bible open with an audacious declaration that Yahweh created the heavens and the earth? Perhaps it is the missional intent of Scripture at work. By using the more ambiguous *elohim*, Genesis opens its story of creation in a way that invites non-Israelites to listen or read more. The power, majesty, and prestige of *elohim* is clear in 1:1—2:3. In fact, one of the questions that this text begs asking is, "Who is *elohim*?" This is precisely the question that Genesis desires to answer. Genesis and all of Scripture will reveal an unprecedented portrait of a radical new conception of God that will contrast with and critique the gods of the nations.

The Bible opens with Genesis 1–11 to remind God's people that their purpose and mission is linked intimately with all people and all creation. Thus, Genesis 1–11 addresses not merely the prehistory of Israel, but the prehistory of all people and nations. The Scriptures invite a hearing by all interested parties. All that Genesis 1:1—2:3 asks of its hearer/reader is an openness to the divine. It then skillfully introduces its hearers/readers to a radically different god than its hearers may have experienced previously.

Second, unlike other ancient creation stories from Mesopotamia or Egypt, Genesis 1:1—2:3 presents an orderly account of creation. The Creation stories of the ancient world depicted the creation of the world as a battle between gods and goddesses. It is noisy and messy. For example, in the *Enuma Elish* from the Babylonian tradition, the gods craft the heavens and the earth out of the dead halves of the goddess Tiamat. Beyond the realm of even the gods was a force that threatened existence in the form of watery chaos. The act of creation for the ancients thus involved great struggle and conflict between primordial forces. To create was to demonstrate supremacy. In a polytheistic context, the various gods and goddesses battled each other as well as the primordial forces to bolster their claims to be the chief god or goddess.

In contrast, there is not a hint of polytheism in Genesis 1:1—2:3. Genesis 1:2 talks about undifferentiated and unproductive chaos-like matter cloaked in darkness. Yet it demythologizes it by affirming the dynamic presence of *Elohim* who hovers above it ready, willing, and able to shape the nothingness of 1:2 into the very goodness of 1:31. *Elohim* does not battle primordial forces or other deities. *Elohim* creates the cosmos quietly and orderly through his speech. The six days of creation demonstrate *Elohim's* power and sovereignty as he separates and fills creation. Elohim is the creator of the sun, the moon, the stars, the fish, the birds, all living creatures, and humanity. Thus, there is no being worthy of worship and service other than Elohim. The things that other nations worship as gods are merely part of Elohim's good creation.

Third, the biblical creation stories witness to the profound potential, dignity, and purpose of every human being. In Gen 1:26–31, God creates women and men in God's image (Latin: *imago dei*). In the ancient world, only the kings and the powerful in society possessed intrinsic dignity. The majority of men and women were considered the slaves of the gods and kings. The religions of the ancient world celebrated and solidified a suffocating status quo that favored the powerful and oppressed the vast majority of the population. There are references to humans created in the images of the gods in other literature, but such references focused on the king to raise his status and prestige over the average person. Thus, Gen 1:26–31 is remarkable because it proclaims audaciously for its time that all humanity bears the image of God. Moreover, this includes women. Such claims are unprecedented in the ancient world and lay the foundations for subverting all paradigms and worldviews that privilege the few over the many. Genesis 1:26–31 depicts the creation of humanity as the climax of God's creative work.

What does it mean to be created in the image of God (Heb: *tselem*)? In the ancient world, gods and kings projected their power by erecting images of themselves for their subjects to see. These images came in the form of idols or statues. The later Roman emperors issued coinage stamped with their images. Thus, an image is a visible representation of something or someone. According to Scripture, this is the role that women and men serve. Humans are to be visible representations of the invisible Creator God to the rest of creation. This points to the purpose and mission of people. God created humanity to serve as a missional community that reflects and represents the Creator God to/for/in the Creation. God designed humans to function as priests and priestesses who will fill the earth.

Fourth, the general nature of Gen 1:1—2:3 and 2:4–25 functions to set the Bible within an *international* context rather than only a parochial one. With the call of Abraham in Genesis 12, Israel's Scriptures will focus on God's calling of a special people to serve his mission, but this calling is set intentionally within God's creational intentions for *all* people and *all* creation. The story of Creation is the story of humanity. This is critical from a missional perspective because it invites the World to read the Bible as its story and not merely as the story of Israel and the Church.

Fifth, the biblical accounts of creation present *Yahweh Elohim*[1] as the Creator of a beautiful and inviting world. There is no violence. There is no discord. It is a world of abundance and order. We see a move in Gen 1:1—2:3 from undifferentiated matter to very goodness. But ultimately there is something even better than a state of very goodness. This higher state is called Sabbath. Even the very good work of creation is purposeful as it moves to the rest and harmony of Sabbath.

Last, the climax of Gen 1:1—2:3 is God's Sabbath rest. Work ends at Day 6 and the Creator God intentionally rests. This is an important witness. Creation is God's cosmic temple and humanity serves as God's visible representatives in it. The power of Israel's opening creation story lies in its movement from undifferentiated disorder (1:2), to a finished product that is very good (1:31), and finally to a Sabbath rest (2:1-3). The implication is that Sabbath sits on the other side of very goodness. It is a gift of God that is woven into the fabric of the created world. Sabbath is the goal of God's creation. This is something to be celebrated whether we are Iron Age Israelites or twenty-first-century Americans because the opening page of the Bible declares that the purpose of creation is rest rather than work.

Genesis 2:4–25 continues this good news by focusing on the central role of the divine human relationship in the world. Genesis 2:4–25 offers a portrait of a small part of the creation: the Garden of Eden. It is an idyllic setting filled with beauty, animals, and plenty of good food. Genesis 2:4–25 affirms humanity's role in preserving and enhancing God's creation (2:15). These verses also emphasize the relational aspects of human life. Humanity walks and talks with God. The Divine-Human relation is central to the biblical story. As we move deeper into the Scriptures, we will find that our lives can be understood broadly through two expressions of love: love for God and love for neighbor. Humanity's relationship with the earth is also clear. Humanity functions as caretakers and stewards of creation. This includes both the physical world as well as the animal world. The latter is implicit in humanity's naming of the animals. The climax of Gen 2:4–25 is the creation

---

1. After using *elohim* only in 1:1—2:3, the narrator skillfully identifies *elohim* with *Yahweh* by combining the two beginning in Gen 2:4.

of the first woman as a partner for man (2:18–25). The relationship between man and woman is intimate and joyous.

The takeaways from Genesis 1–2 are rich. Yahweh is a powerful God who unilaterally created an orderly and harmonious world of peace. Humanity exists to serve as God's ambassadors of his abundance to all creation by serving as a missional community that reflects his character and ethos. They make visible the invisible king of creation who invites all to experience sabbath as the defining purpose of life. Creation is very good. Relationally there is mutuality and goodness between God and humanity, creation and humanity, and men and women. This is a powerful witness to the present age of what God originally intended and a portrait of the salvation that God ultimately is working to consummate again in his coming New Creation.

The Fall and Fracturing of Humanity and Creation (Genesis 3–11)

The very good world that God created was lost long ago. With the advent of human rebellion, brokenness, and sin, the very goodness of God's creation morphed into something much less than God intended. The actions of humanity corrupted creation. All human beings find themselves lost and broken. Sin infects and infests all people and all human institutions. As Paul will later write in Romans, even creation groans and longs for redemption (Rom 8:18–23). The materials in Genesis 3–11 explore the tragic brokenness and alienation caused by the entrance of sin and rebellion into the human story.

A missional reading of these iconic stories (Eve and the Serpent, Cain's murder of his brother Abel, Noah's Ark, the tower of Babel) recognizes the complexity of engaging these narratives in the modern world. On one hand, these stories are woven deeply into the fabric of Western culture and literature. Their deep truths speak to the human experience. On the other hand, these narratives rarely show up in sermons or Christian education settings except for children's Sunday school where much of the theological richness is lost.

The richness and potential of Creation is matched by the tragedy of the human response to God's work. The stories of Genesis 3–11 portray the undoing or loss of the "very good" creation. These stories boldly assert the fundamental problem present in our world: *every person has ridiculously overestimated his or her own goodness by an infinite degree.* Or as the Apostle Paul would write much later, "All have sinned and fallen short of

God's glory" (Rom 3:23). The brokenness of Creation including all people is a given for understanding the biblical story. Sin has wreaked havoc on the created world and sin has infected every human being who has ever lived and infested every human institution.

These stories remain in the same *international* framework of Genesis 1–2. The narratives of Gen 3–11 are descriptive of the global human condition. There is still no Israel. We will find a few faithful followers of God, but we have not yet reached the moment when God will call a new humanity into his service to begin the narrative thread that will culminate with the life, death, and resurrection of Jesus and the unleashing of the Church through the power of Holy Spirit. It is vital to recognize this international context. The Bible is the story of all humanity. The Bible will soon narrow its focus for a time on the descendants of Abraham, Isaac, and Jacob as the human lineage through whom Jesus Christ will emerge, but the first eleven chapters of Genesis set the backdrop for the biblical story as a whole and assume its relevance for every people, language, and nation.

The Watershed Moment: Eve, Adam, and the Serpent

Genesis 3 marks the watershed moment in humanity's walk with God. Before Gen 3, men and women enjoyed endlessly open and free relationships with God, the created world, and one another. They lived in the world described and assumed by Gen 1:1—2:25.[2] Genesis 3:1–7 narrates the disastrous conversation between Eve, Adam, and the serpent. The German theologian and pastor Dietrich Bonhoeffer calls this encounter the "first conversation about God."[3] This is a sublime observation. The root of humanity's rebellion is the idolatrous objectification of God. In Genesis 2, humanity freely conversed with God. In Genesis 3, God moves from subject to object. The serpent *tempts* Eve and Adam.[4] At issue is the trustworthiness of God. The serpent denies that God can be trusted. The serpent suggests that humanity needs to eat from the tree of the knowledge of good

---

2. Note that the actual subdivisions in Genesis are 1:1—2:3 and 2:4—4:26. We are simply observing that Genesis 1–2 describe the world as God had intended. It is however crucial for the reader to understand 2:4—4:26 as a unit. In particular, the stories of Adam/Eve in the Garden and Cain/Abel outside of the garden are in parallel.

3. Bonhoeffer, *Creation and Fall*, 111.

4. Although he does not talk, it is clear that Adam is present in 3:6–8. Why is Adam silent? Genesis does not answer the question.

and evil because God is intentionally withholding something good and desirable from humanity. In essence, the existential question faced by Eve is this one: *Do I trust that God has my best interests at heart?* This is the fundamental question that all people face. In the context of Genesis 1–3, God has demonstrated his trustworthiness and care for humanity by providing a pristine setting in Eden, abundant food, authentic relationships between men and women, purposeful vocation as keepers of creation and regents of the Creator, and unfettered access to himself. God has gifted humanity with access to all sources of food *except* for the tree of the knowledge of good and evil (2:16–17). This exception serves as the only prohibition that God gives to humanity. Otherwise, humanity is endlessly free to fulfill God's creation affirming mandates. Yet, it is the prohibition against eating the fruit of a single tree that serves as the impetus for the decision facing Eve and Adam. Thus, from the beginning humanity's sin and rebellion against God are illogical and astonishing given God's kindness and grace to humanity. Humanity was supposed to exercise dominion over the created world, but instead allows the subtle questions of a talking serpent to lead the first man and woman away from the Creator God.[5] In the conversation with the serpent, God becomes an object rather than the subject of a moment-by moment-relationship. Trust is broken. Apart from dependence on and trust in God, humanity goes its own way and eats the forbidden fruit. The effects are tectonic. Adam and Eve feel the breech immediately. Their new knowledge illuminates their own nudity for which they feel shame. They hide from God.

In the aftermath of their decision, God comes looking for his prized creation. God does not hide from humanity; humanity hides from God. This is the profound irony of sin. Adam and Eve attempt to reach beyond their creaturely status and tragically fall well below the potential for which they were crafted. Their decision to eat from the tree causes immediate fractures in their relational web. They have already experienced their own nakedness, which now comes between their once intimate relationship with one another. Their unfettered access to God becomes a liability as they are now fearful at the sound of God's approach. Yet, the first words out of

---

5. Christian tradition following the lead of later biblical reflection identifies the serpent as Satan. This is foreign to the text and introduces an unnecessary dualism and diminishes the culpability of humanity's rebellion. The serpent is merely one of the animals that God created—albeit the "most crafty." For a fascinating close reading of Gen 3:1, see Stone, "Soul," 57–59.

the Creator's mouth are "Where are you?" (3:9).[6] God's response to sin is an immediate attempt to re-engage humanity relationally. God's initial words demonstrate God's continued engagement with humanity despite their disobedience. God doesn't withdraw from Creation—he goes looking for his lost people. The verb used for God's pursuit of humanity is *qr'* "called." The Lord calls out to a humanity that has alienated itself through its actions.

Humanity's rebellion has consequences (Gen 3:14–24). God draws out of Adam and Eve the details of their conversation with the serpent and their actions.[7] The serpent is downgraded from its high place in the animal world to a creature, which will henceforth crawl on its belly. Adam and Eve will face a daunting new world. Their vocation of filling the earth will now be complicated by painful childbirth and the relational brokenness. Genesis 3:16 describes a new power dynamic between the sexes. No longer will the relationship be rooted in mutuality. Men and women will focus on issues of power and attempt to dominate one another.[8] Humanity also will experience the created world as an adversary. Humanity will toil over the earth to maintain life. Easy access to food and sustenance ends. The climax of sin's consequences is humanity's expulsion from the Garden of Eden. Access to the tree of life and immortality ends for all people from Adam and Eve onwards. As Paul will pen years later, ". . . through one man sin entered into the world and through sin came death. Thus death spread through all humanity because all have sinned" (Rom 5:12).

A missional reading recognizes the devastating effects of human sin on God's creational design. However, it also highlights the character of God in response to Adam and Eve's transgression. We have already observed that God pursues humanity in the aftermath of the garden. God does not speak words of condemnation, but rather calls out to humanity, "Where are you?" One of the distinctive features of the divine-human relationship is the capacity for verbal communication. This does not end with the entrance of sin. The relationship between God and humanity has changed, but *verbal* revelation remains.[9] Moreover, Gen 3:21 records an additional

---

6. Perhaps God even addresses the man by name, "Adam, where are you?" Or even "Humanity, where are you?" These are all possible translations of the Hebrew.

7. Humanity's willingness to externalize blame is evidence of their brokenness.

8. The word *desire* in 3:16 is not about sexual desire as though a woman is overcome by a longing for her mate. Rather the word suggests a *desire to control* or *exercise power* over another. See the parallel phrase in God's conversation with Cain (Gen 4:7).

9. This is crucial. We are not left to our own ends. God continues to speak to us even today through his Word. God makes himself known to us even in our sinful state.

act of God's grace and mercy. The immediate result of Adam and Eve's consumption of the fruit of the forbidden tree was the sudden realization of their own nakedness. This marks the irony of their disobedience. They were seeking wisdom and instead discover nakedness through their folly. They move from "naked and unashamed" (2:25) in chapter two to "naked and ashamed" (3:7) in their heightened awareness. Yet, instead of leaving them exposed and humiliated, God kindly provides a suitable covering for the man and woman. God's love and compassion for humanity, even when men and women are at their worst, will remain a hallmark of God's character and actions. It serves as a model for God's people as we seek to engage the world with the Gospel.

Reading Genesis 3–11 Missionally

Moreover, these are not merely past-historical reports. The stories of Adam and Eve, Cain and Abel, Noah's Flood, and the Tower of Babel take on a mythic import.[10] By this I mean that these narratives are the stories of all humanity and not merely limited to the original characters. We live daily in the reality of Gen 3–11. Paul instinctively captures this in Rom 5:12–21 and 1 Cor 15:20–22 where he finds the death of all people rooted in the sin of Adam and Eve in the garden.[11] Yet, we don't want to short-change the remaining chapters of Genesis 3–11. Reading the Fall through a narrow Pauline lens has served to marginalize the stories of Genesis 4–11. Our contention is that Genesis 4–11 serve with Genesis 3 as vital witnesses of the problem of sin and rebellion in our world today.

1) God's saving actions for humanity reach their climax and fullest revelation in the incarnation, crucifixion, and resurrection of Jesus. But God begins the movement that will culminate in Jesus as soon as sin enters the world. God reaches out to Adam and Eve. God expels Adam and

---

10. By mythic, I am making no judgment on the inherent truthfulness or historicity of Genesis 3–11, but rather am asserting their significance beyond their original context. For an up to date review of the various understandings of technical understanding of myth as a genre, see Oswalt, *Bible Among the Myths*, 29–46. Oswalt argues cogently that the Bible is wholly distinct and different from the mythic worldview of Israel's neighbors by its insistence on the discontinuity between God and creation.

11. Of course, Paul is principally concerned in contrasting the first man Adam with the ultimate human Jesus the Messiah. If the Adam is the figure responsible for the death of all, so Jesus as the ultimate human is the one responsible for life and recreation.

The OT Story: Creation, Fall, and Israel

Eve from the Garden, but he clothes them and gives them the gift of children. God attempts to intervene before Cain kills Abel by pointing to a better way (4:6–7). After Cain murders Abel, God protects Cain from the wrath of others.

The genealogy of Genesis 5 serves as a testimony to God's kindness and mercy as he permits humanity to multiply despite its ongoing sinfulness. The genealogy repeatedly reminds us that in the midst of extraordinarily long lives the end arrives—"and he died." There are two exceptions that point to a brighter future: Enoch does not die (5:23–24) and the birth of Noah raises expectations for good (5:28–29).

In fact, Noah becomes a point of light and hope for all creation. He walks with God in the midst of creation-wide wickedness (6:9–13). God saves Noah's family and representatives of the animal kingdom from the flood. God cuts the first explicit covenant in the Bible with Noah (Genesis 9:1–17)[12] and promises to never again destroy creation. In the aftermath of the Flood, humanity increases exponentially. It again falters at Babel, but God uses the ongoing rebellion of humanity to advance the mission by scattering them from Babel to fill the earth in fulfillment of God's creational intentions for humanity (1:26–31). This sets the stage for the calling of Abraham (12:1–3). The God of the Bible works to advance his mission and continues to engage humanity.

2) God's mercy and grace in response to human sin serves as a missional model for the community of faith. Sin is not taken lightly and its grave effects are clear, but God continues to reach out with hope and love to His fallen world. In fact, God takes the initiative to redeem humanity. God's first response is to call out: "Adam, where are you?"[13] God makes the first move. Yes, sin is profoundly tragic, but it does not alter God's desire for relationship with humanity.

3) These texts give no warrant for a knee-jerk withdrawal from engagement with the world. The community of faith, if faithful to God's missional model, will remain engaged in the world rather than seek to separate and build a bulwark around itself to keep the world out. Genesis 3–11

---

12. Some scholars argue for an Adamic covenant. In my opinion, this is a theological construct rather than something that the Bible clearly articulates. By explicit, I mean that the language of covenant (Heb: *brt*) is present. Noah's covenant is the first of five in the Pentateuch: Noahic, Abrahamic, Sinaic, Phinehic, and Moab. See below in footnote 23.

13. Gen 3:9.

offers a snapshot of the world that we inhabit. It is not merely some far off place from a far distant time. The Noahic covenant establishes our world as the context for all ministry this side of the New Creation. Since God continues to engage our lost world, this remains our mandate as well.

4) There are persons who will respond to God's *missional* actions. God shows great patience and acts broadly in search of those who will respond to his grace. This suggests that followers of Christ should practice a consistent and persistent witness of loving service and clear communication of the Gospel to as wide a population as possible. As God's missional work in Genesis 3 and 4 involved both words and deeds, so should ours. The only tangible response to God in these chapters is the action of Enosh in 4:26. A person in the line of Seth began to call upon God's name. The word call (Heb *qr'*) brings to mind God's call to Adam in 3:9. Finally, with Enosh God's invitation for relationship is again heeded. God's people must commit to offer a clear and persistent witness to the Gospel. There is no guarantee of a response from everyone, but this text reminds us that there will be *some* who will indeed hear God's call and respond to the grace offered to them.

Why the Fall Matters?

1) The biblical witness offers a basis for understanding the presence of both good and evil in humanity. Genesis 1–11 describes both the potential and the pitfalls of women and men as persons created in the image of the Creator God. God crafted humanity as the pinnacle of the creation and as the center of the myriad of relationships built into the created order by God. God created women and men to serve as a missional community that reflects God's character to/for/in Creation. But now in the aftermath of the sin and rebellion described in Gen 3–11 God's creational intentions for humanity stand shattered, but the potential remains. People still intrinsically long to be the people that they were created to be and women and men still commit astonishing acts of goodness and generosity. The biblical story can thus account for the goodness and kindness in our world based on the vestiges of God's image in humanity. Yet the final verdict on humanity is its lostness. Every single human

being whom we will ever meet (including ourselves) has overestimated his or her own goodness by an infinite degree and is hopelessly lost apart from God's grace.

2) Creation itself is marred. Humanity was created to serve as stewards and caretakers of the created world. Post-Genesis 3, there now exists an enmity between humanity and the earth God commanded it to keep and fill. One of the hot button issues of our day is concern over the depletion of the earth's resources and abuse of the environment. These texts call us to remember humanity's original mandate of dominion over the earth. The environment should neither be worshipped or abused. Biblical faith is a worldly one in the sense that the focus of the biblical story is our present world in anticipation of its recreation. Salvation is not an escape from the earth, but rather it is a return to the realities of Eden.

Paul reminds us of God's intention to redeem even the world in Rom 8:18–23:

> I consider that the suffering of our present time is not worthy with respect to the glory, which is about to be revealed to us. For the deep longing of creation awaits eagerly the revelation of the children of God. For the creation was subjected to futility not willingly but on account of [God] who subjected it, in hope that the creation itself will be fully released from the bondage to decay for the purposes of the freedom of the glory of the children of God. For we know that all creation has been groaning and suffering labor pains until the present. But it is not only creation, who suffers, but we ourselves who have the first fruits of the Spirit are groaning inwardly as we await our adoption, the redemption of our bodies.

God's people testify to the saving work of God when they participate in creation affirming practices.

3) All life and ministry on this side of the final consummation of history in the creation of a New Heavens and a New Earth will occur within the reality described in Gen 3–11.[14] The biblical narrative assumes this. We lose sight of this reality at our own peril. There is room for a profound optimism because of the life, death, and resurrection of Jesus, but every person has the capacity for the destructive and life-denying patterns

---

14. This statement is not denying the infusion of God's grace into the world nor is it limiting the power of the Holy Spirit. I am merely asserting the lostness of every human person apart from God's actions and affirming the brokenness of Creation.

witnessed to in Gen 3–11. There is no room for a naïve hope that the "good in people" will have the last word. We can't simply "be good for goodness sake" out of our own strength.[15] We need a solution outside of ourselves.

4) God's mission recalibrates in response to the rebellion of humanity and brokenness of the "very good" world. God's mission shifts to work for the salvation of a fallen world and of a lost humanity. If there is to be a continuance of God's mission that began in Creation, God will be the driver. Humanity on its own has shown itself to be incapable of serving as the missional community that God created women and men to be. In these chapters, God sets in motion the initial reverberations of his desire to redeem creation. As we reflect on mission in the twenty-first century, it is vital to affirm the need to reach lost people with the Gospel of Jesus Christ, but likewise a fully robust biblical missiology will work for the good of the creation as a whole. There is no dichotomy between personal evangelism and social justice. The Old Testament affirms the importance of the created world, and missional thinking in the twenty-first century must return to a full biblical understanding of mission. Likewise, we must not make the opposite mistake of emphasizing social justice to the neglect of reaching lost people with the Gospel. Beginning in Genesis 3 God's mission entails the redemption of humanity in all of its individual and social dimensions and of creation itself.

5) The "good news" of Gen 3–11 is that God the Creator of the "very good" heavens and earth commits to the redemption of creation rather than the option of uncreation. The Flood Story is about partial uncreation but ends with a renewal of creation. Even in the judgment on humanity's sin, God saves Noah, his family, and enough species of animals to replenish the earth post-Flood. The first explicit biblical covenant serves to guarantee the future of Creation, presumably regardless of humanity's potential for ongoing wickedness. The future is secure because God guarantees it. God's love for humanity and the world that he created is not stated explicitly, but it is surely implicit here. The beginnings of

---

15. Contra an advertisement observed on public transportation in the Washington, DC area during the 2008 holiday season portraying a woman in a Santa Claus suit with the caption: "Why believe in God? Just be good for goodness sake." If only this were possible!

The OT Story: Creation, Fall, and Israel

God's mission to bring salvation adumbrate the ultimate demonstration of God's love in the sending of the Son into the world.

6) Genesis 3–11 ends with hope that God will indeed achieve his creational aims. The Tower of Babel does not end in the destruction of humanity. Instead, humanity has now filled the earth. This is ironic because humanity on its own terms had chosen to converge on a single location to build a tower to the heavens, but God scattered them around the globe.[16] Thus, God responds to human sin by partially fulfilling his creational intentions for humanity. God now has creatures created in his image scattered throughout the world. This is good news. But how will humanity ever function as God's visible and tangible representatives? This will involve the creation of a new human community: the people of God. This lineage will begin with the call of Abraham (Gen 12:1–3).

7) Psalm 8 serves as a provocative counter narrative to Gen 3–11. It is clear from the beginnings of the biblical narrative that humanity is lost and has failed to achieve the potential latent in being formed in God's image. Yet, a text such as Psalm 8 reminds us of the profound potential of humanity even in the aftermath of the Fall. Psalm 8 is a hymn of praise to the LORD. The psalmist is astonished for the high place in creation that God has given to people. Psalm 8:5–8 echo the themes of Gen 1:26–31. On the surface, Psalm 8 reads as though the psalmist knows nothing of humanity's sinful ways. But on a closer look the psalmist is simply reminding humanity of its truest vocation under God. The effects of sin have not removed the fact that every man and woman was born with the potential to serve in God's creational plans. It is not surprising that the New Testament reads Psalm 8 through a Christological lens. It is the Son of God who lived as God incarnate in Jesus of Nazareth who brings the potential of Psalm 8 to its fullest light. Jesus came to make it possible to live fully as the human beings whom God created us to be. Thus, the writer to the Hebrews sees Jesus as the human person described in Ps 8:4–6.[17] This reality serves as an encouragement to evangelists in the twenty-first century. There are pre-Christian people who are living

---

16. Genesis 10 records the "Table of Nations." It indicates that humanity has populated the planet. How did humanity fill the earth so quickly following Noah's story? Well, Gen 11:1–10 informs the readers that God scattered humanity across the earth against its will in response to the Tower of Babel.

17. Heb 2:5–10; cf. 1 Cor 15:27.

apart from the saving grace of God, but who, nevertheless, due to their creation in the image of God, are participating in creation affirming activities. The wise Christian will see such persons as women and men who may be open to the Gospel due to their movement toward what it means to be human. Jesus came to restore our truest humanity. Readers of Scripture will use this reality to reach out to those on the perimeters of our communities who instinctively are seeking out a loving and compassionate way of living. The values and good news of the Kingdom are precisely for what seekers are longing even if they've never heard the name Jesus previously.

If Genesis 1–2 opens the Bible with a portrait of Creation and life as God intended, then Genesis 3–11 describes the world as we find it today: a lost humanity and a broken creation. Babel ended with humanity dispersed globally as God intended, but women and men were not serving as images of God, but rather as projections of brokenness. How will God advance his mission given this reality? The rest of the Bible tells this story.

Israel: God's New Hope

Out of the ashes of Genesis 3–11, God calls one family through whom God will bless all peoples and nations (Gen 12:3). God's response to the fracturing of creation and the spread of human disobedience is the commissioning of a new hope for creation: a missional community that embodies and reflects God's character to/for/in the nations and all creation. This missional paradigm remains true for God's people today.

Israel's Ancestors

The locus for this new beginning is the family of Abraham.[18] In an act of grace, God calls Abraham out of the world of Genesis 3–11 to a new world of hope and blessing. Abraham has deep roots in southern Mesopotamia. His family lived in the ancient city of Ur. God calls Abraham out of idolatry to follow him (Josh 24:2). In the immediate context of Abram's call (Gen

---

18. In Genesis, Abraham is known as "Abram" until Genesis 17. In Genesis 17, God enters into covenant with Abraham and marks this occasion by giving the rite of circumcision and a new name "Abraham" to Abraham. For ease, we will use Abraham from the beginning of the story.

11:27–32), we learn that Abram's father, Terah, decided to emigrate with his family from Ur to Canaan, but instead settled in Haran (roughly half-way between Ur and the land of Canaan).

God commissions Abraham to move his family from Haran to Canaan (Gen 12:1–3). The election of Abraham is critical for understanding God's mission for humanity and all creation. God makes lavish promises to Abraham. This will be a recurring theme throughout Genesis 12–50. God grounds the calling of a people for God's mission in *promises*. In Genesis 12, God promises to increase Abraham by making him into a great nation, by protecting him, by granting him the land of Canaan, and by using him as an agent of God's blessing. Genesis 12:3b is critical for reading the Bible missionally. In Gen 12:3b, God declares to Abraham, "all peoples on earth will be blessed through you." God's people exist as conduits of God's blessings to all people. God promises to bless Abraham so that he can live as a blessing to the nations of Genesis 1–11. The story of Israel from Genesis 12 until the coming of Jesus the Messiah is the narrative of God's calling of one people to serve as a new humanity through whom God will extend blessing and salvation to the lost world of Genesis 3–11. If we lose sight of Israel's missional calling, we will misread the Old Testament. It can easily become the story of God against the nations and for Israel instead of God for Israel for the sake of extending God's blessing to all nations.

Genesis 12–50 tells the story of the emergence of Abraham and his family as the hope of all humanity. God's promises ground the book of Genesis in *grace*. God's promises and kindness serve as the foundation for the relationship between God and God's people.

1) God calls a new humanity to serve as his missional community that will reflect God's character to/for/in the nations. We saw that God embedded mission into the essence of humanity (Gen 1:26–31). The calling of Abraham and his family is a relaunching of humanity's role in God's mission following the tales of lostness, chaos, and alienation in Genesis 3–11.

2) God's mission begins in the borderlands rather than in the centers of power. God does not call Abraham to live in Babylon or Egypt. He calls Abraham from the power center of southern Mesopotamia to the land of Canaan. Canaan had a significant population and walled cities during Abram's day, but it was peripheral to the main power bases of Egypt,

Mesopotamia, and the land of Hittites (modern Turkey). This is significant for understanding God's mission and some of the unexpected detours that the biblical narrative takes.

The Bible consistently affirms that in God's economy the weak become strong, the poor become rich, outsiders become insiders, and the tail becomes the head. God advances his mission through his power and not merely through the common structures and ways of humanity.

Reading the Bible missionally involves hearing Scripture's critique of human power constructs and its desire to tear down our strongholds of self-determinism and superiority. Two themes emerge in Genesis to remind God's people that God's power (and not ours) fuels the advance of God's mission. First, God promises descendants to a childless couple. Abraham and Sarah are well advanced in age, and they do not have any biological children of their own. God's mission will advance through their line because of God's kindness and not through their own natural reproductive power. One of the central narrative threads of Abraham's story is the fulfillment of God's promise of descendants. Ironically, the greatest threat to this promise is the human action that Abraham and Sarah instigate as a means of overcoming their childlessness. Following the accepted practice of their day, Sarah gives Abraham her slave girl Hagar and Abraham has a son named Ishmael with Hagar (Gen 16). Ishmael is Abraham's firstborn, but Ishmael is a son born out of human power and ingenuity and not the child of promise. This tension resolves in the birth of Isaac through Sarah (Gen 21:1–6). As we move into the next generation, Isaac and Rebekah will likewise face childlessness until God gifts them the twins, Esau and Jacob (Gen 25:19–26). The theme of God advancing God's mission apart from human channels of power will continue to recur through the Bible with key leaders such as Samson (Judges 13), Samuel (1 Sam 1), and John the Baptist (Luke 1:5–26) all coming into the world through formerly childless couples (cf. Isa 54:1–5). Jesus will experience the most unusual birth of all: a virgin conceives without the help of any human male (Matt 1:18–25).

The tension between Isaac and Ishmael (Gen 21:8–21) also points to a second theme that reminds readers of God's grace and power in the advance of God's mission. This is the consistent selection of the younger over the older. Ancient cultures privileged the firstborn son. This allowed families to maximize assets by concentrating them on one member of the family. In contrast, God demonstrates his ability to bless the nations apart from this common cultural practice. Thus, Isaac, the second born, is the son of promise. When Isaac and his wife Rebekah receive twin sons, it is the younger, Jacob, through whom God will extend God's promises.

3) God's mission in Genesis 12–50 advances through God's faithfulness to his promises. God extends God's promises from Abraham to the subsequent generations: Isaac, Jacob, and Jacob's twelve sons. The initial promises to Abraham in Gen 12:3 recur in Gen 18:18; 22:16–18; 26:3–5,;and 28:13–15. These promises ground God's mission in grace and raise the expectation of God's ongoing goodness to God's people for the sake of blessing all the nations of Genesis 1–11.

4) Genesis 37–50 provide witness to God's grace and kindness in watching over and preserving God's people. Through the miraculous story of Joseph and his brothers, God's people survive a famine and enjoy the hospitality of the Egyptians. This migration to Egypt during Joseph's day sets the backdrop for the story of the Exodus. Genesis ends with the anticipation of God's people returning to Canaan (50:24–25).

Exodus

The Exodus from Egypt serves as God's principal act of salvation in the Old Testament. God delivers God's people from illegitimate bondage and unjust service to Pharaoh in Egypt for creation honoring and enhancing service in God's mission to/for/in the nations.

Exodus 1–15 reveals to the world the power of God to save God's people. At the beginning of the book of Exodus, God's people are thriving and multiplying in fulfillment of God's creational designs for all humanity (Exod 1:6–7 cf. Gen 1:26–31). The Egyptians, led by Pharaoh, view the large numbers of Israelites as a threat rather than as a blessing. This moves Pharaoh and all Egypt to engage in a systematic attempt to suppress and destroy God's people through harsh slave labor and ultimately through the murder of all male Israelite children. It is critical to understand the Exodus as God's response to Pharaoh and all Egypt's anti-creational actions. These actions serve as an attempt to thwart God's mission to bless the nations and heal creation. Pharaoh is more than a cruel unjust leader. He takes cruelty and injustice to a cosmic level by actively attempting to destroy God's human agents of salvation for all creation. Thus, the struggle between God and Pharaoh is high stakes. Nothing less than God's mission that will culminate with the life, death, and resurrection of Jesus hangs in the balance.

In response, the God of Creation and of Abraham, Isaac, and Jacob reveals himself as the God who saves and rises up to deliver God's people from Egyptian oppression. This act serves as the decisive witness to the identity and nature of the LORD. The God of Scripture desires for all creation to know him. In response to the tragedy of Genesis 3–11 God called a new humanity into existence. In the book of Exodus God delivers this new humanity for the sake of all humanity as a means of making God's name known in all the earth (Exod 9:16). Thus, the exodus from Egypt is missiological in scope and intention.

The witness of Exodus is profound. Often we read the Old Testament from our own dominant position as citizens of a Western power. At the time of the Exodus, Egypt was the superpower in the ancient world. Egypt extended its power and prestige far beyond its borders. God's people were powerless to rebel or fight against the dominance of Egypt. The only way for Israel to gain its release was for God to confront and subdue the might of the Egyptians.

Pharaoh himself raised the stakes of the engagement in Exod 5:2. God had sent Moses and Aaron to demand the release of God's people. Instead of acquiescing to God, Pharaoh foolishly asks, "Who is the LORD that I should listen to him. . . ? I do not know the LORD. . . " From this point in the narrative until the destruction of the Egyptian army at the Red Sea (Exod 13:17—14:31), there will be no doubt about the identity of the LORD. The book of Exodus becomes a showdown between the alleged king—Pharaoh with the true king and Lord of all Creation—the LORD (Exod 15:18).

The deliverance of Israel unfolds as a series of ten signs that God sends through the hand of Moses to gain the release of God's people (Exod 7:8—13:16). Each of these signs is a direct confrontation with the ideology and worldview of the Egyptians. Exodus 12:12 describes the Exodus as a judgment of the gods of the Egyptians.[19] This includes Pharaoh whose principal role as a divine-king was to maintain order and harmony for Egypt. Each of the ten signs disrupts a key element of Egypt's understanding of order and reveals the supremacy of the LORD over Pharaoh and the gods of Egypt. Yet, Pharaoh stubbornly refuses to submit to God. God uses the hardened will of Pharaoh as a vehicle for declaring God's name to all the

---

19. Currid, *Ancient Egypt*, 104–20.

earth (9:16). The book of Exodus uses the theme of Pharaoh's stubborn will as a means of demonstrating God's power. The LORD of the Bible is greater than even a living "god" of a Near Eastern superpower. Pharaoh may not "know" the LORD (Exod 5:2) and may attempt to assert his will against God's mission, but this is no obstacle for the God of Creation who will use Pharaoh's intransigence as a means of declaring and revealing himself as the incomparable God who saves his people. This is good news indeed for those desperate masses of humanity who need what only this kind of God can provide.

Passover

In response to Pharaoh's steadfast refusal to release God's people into the unrestricted service of God, God unleashes a final sign that will take the life of the firstborn of all Egypt (12:1—13:16). Passover commemorates this sign.

Passover is the climactic act that delivers God's people from the land of Egypt. The book of Exodus embeds the narrative of the original Passover into the liturgical instructions for future celebrations (12:1—13:16). This invites us to read the Passover account as though we were present in Egypt when God delivered his people from slavery. The dominant theme is *remembrance*. God's people are called to reflect and remember God's actions on their behalf.

Having liturgy embedded in a narrative has implications for our reading of this text. This is not merely *history* as testimony about the past. This is a narrative that uses past *history* to invite its hearers/readers into the events themselves so that they can be *experienced anew* by the present generation who will then embody this Mosaic *ethos* for the world.

This mix of historical narrative and liturgy reminds us that an event *as it really happened* cannot be strictly separated from the event as *memorialized* subsequently in the worshipping community. The Scriptures serve to draw us into its story so that the Scriptural story becomes our story. The God who destroyed the firstborn of Egypt and spared the firstborn of Israel is the same who saves us today. The question of historicity does matter in all of this, but more pressing is the question of its significance in the present. Passover is not recorded for antiquarian reasons. It is *kerygma* that seeks to shape a community. Reading a text missionally involves allowing the text to invite us into its world. The Passover narrative does this explicitly by combining narrative and liturgy seamlessly.

1) Passover as *Proclamation*. The Passover is a form of proclamation and witness to the world by the people of God. It is kerygmatic. As we will see, Israel will be called to serve God as a "kingdom of priests and a holy nation" (Exod 19:4–6). Passover becomes a yearly festival in which the nation shuts down for a time to *remember* and *reenact* God's deliverance of God's people from Egypt. Of course, the celebration of the Passover impacts the community of faith, but it also serves as a *witness* to resident aliens and workers who are present. In the New Testament, there is a missional dimension in the celebration of the Eucharist. The Apostle Paul picks up this thread in 1 Cor 11:26 "For every time you eat this bread and drink out this cup, you are announcing and proclaiming the Lord's death until he comes again." In other words, God's past actions matter. God's people believe that God's saving actions in the past guarantee that God will continue to save them in their present and future.

2) Passover as a *ritual of conversion*. By the time that the readers of the book of Exodus arrive at Sinai with the original generation and hear the words, "You have seen what I did to the Egyptians and how I carried you on eagle's wings and brought you to myself" (Exod 19:4), they have been *converted* to the people of God through *participation* in the Passover liturgy in which past, present, and future generations are intermingled into a one people of God. Circumcision is a precondition of participation but it is the Passover that creates the people of God. For future generations, joining in the Passover (Exod 12:43–48) testifies that they are now Israelites.

3) Passover as *ritual of confirmation*. Participation in the Passover celebration *confirms* and *renews* persons into a new reality—life as God's missional people for the sake of the world. God's saving power as demonstrated in the Exodus serves as the foundational act for the past, present, and future of God's people. Embedded in the narrative at key points are hypothetical questions (Exod 13:8; 14–16) that future generations will ask. The text provides answers. Listen to the language of v. 8 "On that day, tell your son, 'I do this on account of what the LORD did for me when I left Egypt.'" The liturgy preserves a first person answer. The

power of this narrative is the way in which it is *inclusive* of subsequent generations. There is no "Exodus" generation. All God's people in all times are members of the *Exodus generation* through participation in the community's celebration of Passover. The use of the first person language makes every subsequent generation who passes on the Exodus story *the Exodus generation*.

Red Sea

If the Passover gained Israel's initial release from Egypt, the dramatic crossing of the Red Sea and destruction of the Egyptian army declares God's victory and guarantee's the future for God's people. At the Red Sea the LORD demonstrates his supremacy over the military of the superpower of the ancient world.

God uses the waters of the Red Sea as a weapon. What does it mean for the LORD to vanquish the power of Egypt using creation itself? To the ancients there was only one possible inference to make. The LORD is incomparable to any other god. In fact, the LORD is the only god worthy of the title "God."[20] In the hymn of Exod 15:1b–18 Israel testifies to this truth in its worship of the LORD in response to their salvation at the Sea. Exodus 15:11 asks, "Who is like the you among the gods, O LORD? Who is like you, mighty among the holy ones?"[21] God's people declare the only legitimate response to God's incomparability: "The LORD will reign for ever and ever" (Exod 15:18).

The Exodus from Egypt and deliverance from the sea serve as signifying actions for God's people and for the world. For God's people, these actions serve as the foundation for their relationship with the LORD. As witnesses to the work of God, God's people fear and believe in the LORD (Exod 14:30–31). What is it that God's people believe? They believe in God's power to save them from their enemies and lead them into relationship with him. Exodus 15:1b–18 serves as an anthem for God's people in which they sing and celebrate God's saving actions in the Exodus (15:1–12), and his gracious guidance to God's sacred mountain (15:13–17). The LORD demonstrates by his mighty actions his identity as the true King of Creation. There is no other god or goddess who can do or has done what the LORD has done—take the side of the oppressed against the powerful rule

---

20. Wright, *Mission of God*, 136–88.
21. For discussion of this translation, see Russell, *Song of the Sea*, 11

of Pharaoh, defeat the strong, and guide the freed slaves to God's own holy mountain to forge a relationship (Exod 15:13, 17; and 19:4–6).

So the God of Israel is beyond compare. Although our world is full of idols and competing claims to deity, Exodus demonstrates decisively that there is only one being worthy of the title of God—the LORD. The deliverance from Egypt is the Old Testament's preeminent display and pronouncement of God's saving power and character. No other deity in the ancient World or modern world alike can make the claims that the God of the Exodus can. Thus, there is no basis for idolatry. All competing gods must be placed user the Lordship of the God of the Exodus.

God can even use human intransigence and rebellion to reveal his character and power. The core struggle in Exodus is the showdown between Pharaoh, king of Egypt, and the LORD, god of Israel. Pharaoh asserts his authority and steadfastly refuses to recognize the LORD's. But God reduces the most powerful "king" in the world to the status of a puppet as a means of declaring God's name in all of the earth (Exod 9:16). This is an important word because it reminds the people of God that God can achieve his purposes even in the darkest moments when God's people are facing the most stalwart of opponents.

The Exodus announces to the world that the *status quo* does not have to be the final word. The future will not be shaped by oppressive and suffocating religious expressions that attempt to sanctify injustice, nor by mere human power where might and cruelty makes right. There is a new kingdom emerging from the chaos of the Genesis 3–11 world, and it is not the kingdom represented by Egypt and its Pharaoh. This new kingdom has a king unlike any king ever known to humanity. The LORD sides with the weak and oppressed against all forces representing an unjust *status quo*. Moreover this LORD is able to control creation itself and use it as a tool to defeat the powers of darkness that Egypt represented in a climactic battle at the Red Sea. God's use of the Sea to defeat Egypt was a powerful symbol to the world of the ancient Near East. To ancients, the Sea represented the power of uncreation. For a god to harness such power meant only one thing: this was a god like no other. This witness went before God's people as they migrated from Egypt to Canaan.[22] In the Song of the Sea (Exod 15:1–21) the Israelites sing of the fear and trembling experienced by the peoples in and around Canaan. News of God's victory over Egypt goes before his people as they move toward the Promised Land. In Exod 18:8–11

22. Russell, *Song of the Sea*, 96–97.

Moses recounts to Jethro, his father-in-law, all that God had done for Israel. In response Jethro rejoices in God and says, "Now I *know* that the LORD is greater than all other gods because he delivered the people from the Egyptians." In Joshua, Rahab announces to the Israelite spies that the news of what God has done has preceded them, "I know that the LORD has given you the land and that terror has fallen upon us, and that all who inhabit the land melt in fear before you. For we have heard how the LORD dried up the Red Sea when you came up from Egypt. . ." (2:9–10). As God promised in Exod 9:16, his name is resounding throughout the earth.

God's deliverance is inclusive of outsiders. God acts for God's people against Egypt, but this must not be interpreted as God against the world. Egypt and the Egyptian people experience divine wrath because they attempted to thwart God's mission for all people by oppressing God's people and acting murderously toward them. This does not mean that God is *against* Egypt simply because they are not Israelites. When Israel leaves Egypt, a mixture of people follows them out (Exod 12:38). The message is subtle but important. Membership in God's people is rooted in grace and not in race. The text does not tell us anything more about the identity of these people, but the implication is clear: *outsiders* are welcome to become *insiders*. The inclusion of outsiders reminds God's people of the mission given to Abraham (Gen 12:3). God's people exist to serve as blessings for all peoples. This includes future Egyptians.

The liberation of Israel is for the world. God's actions in the Exodus have creation-wide implications. God frees God's people from bondage and oppression so that God's mission in and for the world can advance. The emphasis in Exodus is not merely Israel's liberation *from* Egypt but on Israel's liberation *for* God's purposes of blessing and redeeming the nations.

God's victory over the forces of Egypt at the sea has cosmic implications for creation. In ancient lore God's victory using the waters of the sea represented much more than a spectacular Hollywood-style miracle. By defeating Egypt through the means of deploying the sea (Heb *yam*) the LORD demonstrates that he is the incomparable God who wields the primordial power of creation. In Near Eastern mythology, the god Yamm bore the titles "Prince Sea and Judge River." Yamm was the god of watery chaos and posed a threat to the created world. It is astonishing to reflect that in Israel's Gospel the LORD directs Israel's salvation in such a way as to subvert any claims of Yamm to sovereignty by splitting both Sea (the Red Sea) and River (the Jordan). In both cases, the waters are only instruments for the LORD to wield as in the case of the Red Sea or as an obstacle in the pathway of God's people as they prepare to enter the Promised Land (Josh 3–4). God's actions, thus, proclaim the LORD's sovereignty, prestige, and power over the "gods" of the nations. Don't miss this truth: even the means that God uses to deliver Israel serves to advance God missional purposes.

Sinai Covenant (Exod 19:1—Num 10:10; Book of Deuteronomy)

The goal of the Exodus is relationship. God desires for the world to know him. God delivers God's people from bondage in Egypt to be in a dynamic relationship with him as a means of unleashing God's people to serve as a missional community. The forging of the Sinai covenant formalizes this relationship. Covenant is a legal structure drawn from the culture of the Ancient Near East. It establishes the framework for a relationship between a great king and a people. It teaches God's people to respond to God's grace with *faithful obedience*.

Covenant

In the Pentateuch there are a series of five covenants that provide a shape and vision for the life and mission of God's people. The Sinai Covenant is the third explicit covenant in the Pentateuch. Frank Moore Cross and his student S. Dean McBride Jr. have observed that the authors of the Pentateuch embedded five explicit covenants[23] (Noah, Abraham, Sinai, Phinehas, and Moab), which give these books an even greater interconnectedness. These five covenants form a chiastic structure that provides a literary shape for the Pentateuch and centers the focus on the covenant forged between God and his newly redeemed Israel at Sinai:

A   Noahic Covenant (Gen 9:9–17)

   B   Covenant Grant to Abraham (Gen 17:1–14; cf. Gen 15:1–21)

      C   Sinai Covenant (Exod 19:1—Num 10:10; esp. Exod 19:1—34:28)

   B'   Covenant Grant to Phinehas (Num 25:11–13)

A'   Covenant in Moab (Deut, esp. 29:1—32:47)

---

23. I.e., the presence of the word for "covenant" *brt*. Some scholars argue for an Edenic covenant. See Cross, *Canaanite Myth*, 295–300; and McBride, "Perspective and Content," 47–60.

The OT Story: Creation, Fall, and Israel

The outer bracket (A and A') focuses on the issue of stability. The Noahic covenant is with all living things and guarantees the stability of the heavens and earth. The covenant in Moab is made between God and Israel and serves to sustain Israel's life in the land without Moses through the authoritative instruction of God in the Torah. The inner bracket (B and B') focuses on issues of land and priesthood. God's land grant to Abraham guarantees Israel land, whereas God's grant to Phinehas (the savior of Israel at Baal-Peor) provides for a perpetual priesthood for Phinehas's children during Israel's life in the land. The Pentateuch then centers on the Sinai Covenant, which focuses on faithfulness in loving God/Neighbor and the institution of the proper worship of God.

God uses covenant as a rubric to communicate his vision for God's people's life and work in the world. The idea of covenant is not unique to Israel. It is drawn from the wider Near Eastern culture of the day.[24] The use of covenant is another example of the way that God incarnates himself into the culture as a means of communicating to humanity and redeeming discrete human cultures. God borrows an element common to a culture and deploys it as a platform for communicating the divine will for humanity. Covenant teaches God's people the true nature of reality—in particular the transcendence of God and the high value and worth of all human beings, including women and other persons whom cultures tend to marginalize. At the center of the covenant's portrait of God stands God's holiness. The Sinai covenant also reveals God's desire for men and women to live in an exclusive relationship with God rooted in trust and faithful obedience. God is holy and desires his people to likewise reflect his character in their corporate life together and in their engagement with the nations.

In particular the Sinai covenant and its recapitulation on the Plains of Moab in the book of Deuteronomy offer God's people a polity for shaping life according to God's will.[25] In Gen 12:3, God called Abraham to lead a family that existed as agents of blessing for the nations. The Torah as a whole details this way of life. It is crucial to read the various laws, lore, and instructions for worship within the missiological framework provided in Genesis. The goal of the Sinai Covenant is not merely obedience, as if God were a self-centered tyrant in need of validation, but the creation of

---

24. The critical question turns on whether Israel's covenants are more similar to Hittite treaties from fourteenth to thirteenth centuries BC or to Assyrian treaties from the seventh to sixth centuries BC. See discussion in Kitchen, *On the Reliability*, 287–91.

25. See McBride's seminal essay "Polity of the Covenant People," 229–44.

(Re)Aligning with God

a missional community that would reflect God's character in the world, to the world, and for the world.

Covenant and Mission

God delivers God's people for the purpose of mission rooted in relationship. Exodus 19:3–6 sketches this out in a programmatic manner. These verses serve as a summary of God's calling on his people. Verse 4 grounds Israel's call in *grace*. God delivered Israel. God's people were witnesses to and recipients of God's actions. Verse 4 reminds God's people that they stand because God lifted them from slavery and oppression and brought them to Sinai. The emphasis is on God's power to save and God's desire for relationship. The power dynamic is easy for us to see, but the relational element needs emphasis. In the ancient Near East, gods and goddesses lived on sacred mountains. Sinai was God's mountain (Exod 3:1). In the modern world, we tend to *assume* that God desires to be in relationship with us. In the ancient world, gods and goddesses did not invite humans to their mountains. Instead, they *only* invited other divine beings to their mountain. For example, in the Baal epic, Baal builds a house on mount Zaphon. He throws a party to celebrate his kingship and rule, but he only invites divine beings. There are no humans present.

Verse 5 explicitly invites Israel into a covenant relationship. Notice the language used: *if you truly listen to my voice and keep my covenant*. Listen and keep. These words echo the language of Gen 26:5 where God passes the promises from Abraham to Isaac by reminding Isaac of Abraham's faithfulness in *listening* and *keeping*.

What does it mean to listen to God's voice and keep God's covenant? The Mosaic Torah as a whole from Genesis to Deuteronomy serves as authoritative instruction for God's people, but more specifically the Sinai materials contain prescriptive and normative laws. The content of the Mosaic legislation articulates a dynamic vision for God's people that creates an ethos in which the nation reflects the character of God through its service to the Creator and Redeemer, its faithfulness and justice in its interactions with God's people and with the nations, and in its care for creation. The core of Israel's call is to live a life of love for God (Deut 6:4–5) and neighbor (Lev 19:18).

The Ten Commandments (Exod 20:1–17; cf. Deut 5:6–21) illustrate clearly the vision for God's people in the Mosaic Torah. These commandments begin by grounding *obedience* in *grace*. The God who commands is the God who first delivered God's people from bondage in Egypt. The initial commands focus on articulating a framework for *loving* God. This includes issues of allegiance ("no other gods"), relationship between God and creation ("no images"), honoring God's essence ("not speaking God's name in vain"). The second half of the Ten Commandments establishes an ethic for *loving* others: honoring parents, no stealing, no adultery, no killing, no false testimony, and no coveting. The Sabbath commandment serves the sublime role of connecting love for God and neighbor in the Creator/Creation honoring practice of Sabbath. The Sabbath is communal and assumes that its blessings will be extended to all people within Israel's community (insiders and outsiders alike, including service animals).

The remainder of the Pentateuchal legislation serves to describe in more detail the *particulars* of obeying the general principals of loving God and neighbor in specific situations.

The Torah also envisions God's people serving in the mediating role of priests for the nations (Exod 19:6 "kingdom of priests"). This involves God's mission to bless the nations (Gen 12:3b), and it also captures the Pentateuch's vision of loving God through worship.

Covenant and God's Presence

God created humanity in God's image to serve as God's priests for all creation (Gen 1:26–31). Men and women were God's visible hands, feet, and mouthpieces functioning as priests and priestesses in God's Cosmic Temple of creation. Sin shattered this. In the book of Exodus and the rest of the Pentateuch, this original vision is recreated in microcosm. In Exodus 25–31 and 35–40 God's people receive instructions for a portable tent shrine known as the Tabernacle, and then construct it. God's glory visibly descends and dwells within the Tabernacle (40:34–38). The presence of God guides God's people as they travel to the land of Canaan, and it abides with God's people wherever they encamp. The theme of God's presence continues throughout Israel's story.

How then will God's people live with the Holy Creator God abiding in their midst? The book of Leviticus establishes the cultic protocols for living as God's holy, missional people for the sake of the world. They include Israel's sacrificial system (Lev 1–7), priesthood (Lev 8–10), regulations governing clean and unclean practices (Lev 11–15), the Day of Atonement

(Lev 16), and laws for holy living including sexual practices, ethical living, and key community celebrations (Lev 17–27).

Threat to God's Covenant: The Golden Calf

While God revealed to Moses the plans to build the Tabernacle (Exod 25–31), God's people enlisted Aaron to build an image to worship (Exod 32:1–6). The irony here is rich. God had just delivered Israel from Egypt, audibly spoken the Ten Commandments (Exod 20:1–17), and established the covenant (Exod 24). Yet, God's people quickly turned away to the crafting and worship of a golden calf image. This action put in jeopardy the *relationship* between God and God's people that is critical for the advancement of God's mission in the world. Exodus 32–34 narrates a series of conversations between Moses and God as well as between Moses and God's people. Moses' role as mediator is forged in this cauldron. He repeatedly engages God and works to guarantee a future for God's people in God's mission.

The Golden Calf and its aftermath (Exod 32–34) serves a critical role in a missional reading of Scripture. It highlights the crucial role of *faithfulness* or *faithful obedience* as the response of God's people to the salvation of God. One of the foremost threats to faithfulness is *idolatry*. This will be a recurring theme throughout Scripture. The Old Testament will continually testify to the failures of God's people to live in fidelity with the LORD. Idolatry can involve turning away fully from the God of the Exodus to worship other gods, or it can be a syncretistic religious practice in which God's people combine the worship of the LORD with the worship of other gods and goddesses. Both are equally idolatrous because the LORD is the only one worthy of the title and honor of God.[26]

Idolatry threatens the relationship between God and God's people, but it is equally damaging to the mission of God to make himself known to the nations. Whenever God's people worship or serve any god other than the LORD, God's people misconstrue the nature and character of the true God to the world, and the good news of God is muted.

Stunningly, it is in the aftermath of the Golden Calf that Scripture for the first time definitively declares that *love* is the core internal characteristic of God (Exod 34:6–7). God has announced that God will accompany God's people to the Promised Land and that he will renew the covenant. In response to Moses' request to see God's glory, God declares his name and

---

26. Wright, *Mission of God*, 136–88.

reveals the true essence of the LORD. The love of God is infinite; the wrath of God is finite. Who is the God of the Exodus? He is a God who acts out of love, radical faithfulness, and mercy. This means that the God of Scripture *forgives sins*. There is always a future with God. The LORD is not petty, finicky, or random. God's people can trust the LORD fully because of who the LORD is (the God whose essence is *love*) and what the LORD has done (the God who saves God's people).

The profound revelation of the true nature of the LORD at Sinai (Exod 34:6-7) is critical for a missional reading of the Bible. It demonstrates the unity of the Old and New Testaments. It is not a *new* revelation in Jesus Christ that indicates God's love. Rather, Jesus expresses fully and powerfully the extent of God's *love* and *power* to save through his life, death, and resurrection. The Old Testament story is just as much a testimony of God's love for the world and God's people as the New Testament is.

Wilderness (Exod 15:22—18:27; Num 10:11—36:13)

Israel's journey through the wilderness (Exod 15:22—18:27; Num 10:11—36:13) forms a literary bracket around the Sinai materials (Exod 19:1—Num 10:10). The wilderness narratives highlight God's graciousness and faithfulness while serving as a witness against the *unfaithfulness* of God's people.

Israel's experience at Sinai occurs in the middle of Israel's time in the Wilderness. God's people journey from Egypt to Sinai through the wilderness (Exod 15:22—18:27) and then from Sinai to the Promised Land of Canaan (Num 10:10—36:13).

Throughout the wilderness narratives God demonstrates his power and willingness to provide sustenance for God's people. God continues to guarantee an abundant supply of food and water during their entire forty-year stay in the Wilderness. Exodus 15:22—18:36 narrates God's gracious and diligent care of God's people as they journey through the desert to God's mountain of Sinai/Horeb. As soon as God's people cross through the Red Sea, God begins to sustain them. In the initial three wilderness narratives, God miraculously provides fresh water (Exod 15:22-27; 17:1-7) and food in the form of manna and quail (16:1-36). God also protects God's people from enemies such as the Amalekites who threaten them *militarily* (Exod 17:8-16). God does for God's people what they were unable to do for themselves.

If the Wilderness narratives show the resolute faithfulness and kindness of God, they also point to the frailties of faith and the resulting foibles of God's people. In Exod 15:22—18:27 God acts often in response to the complaints of the people against Moses (e.g., 15:24; 16:2; and 17:2). The irony is that the people complain in the aftermath of the miraculous actions of God in delivering them from Egypt. The complaining begins as soon as they cross the Red Sea. A key theme in Scripture is the ability of people to complain to God and call for help. In Exod 15:22—18:27 the people have a legitimate *need* (i.e., food and water). In these occasions God meets these needs and does it with gusto!

The wilderness, however, also marks a time of failure for God's people. In Numbers 13–14 God's people steadfastly refuse to enter Canaan out of fear of the Canaanites. This points to a lack of *faith* on the part of God's people. They simply do not trust God. This decision to rebel against God is disastrous for the Exodus generation. They will spend the rest of their lives wandering through the wilderness (forty years). They witnessed God's powerful deeds to deliver them from Egypt, they heard the voice of God on Sinai declaring the Ten Commandments, and they received God's kind and faithful care in the wilderness. But they failed to *trust* and practice *faithfulness*. This is a warning to future generations of God's people, and it also demonstrates that powerful experiences of God's gracious actions do not guarantee future faithfulness. The Exodus generation serves as a warning (1 Cor 10:1–13) for God's people today to practice a faithful walk with God *moment-by-moment*.

Only Joshua and Caleb enter Canaan from the generation that God led out of Egypt. Even Moses and Aaron disqualified themselves in the Wilderness (Num 20:12). The story of the Old Testament is a testimony to the faithfulness of the God of Creation to work toward the redemption of all humanity as well as Creation itself. This mission involves God's people as God's agents, but as episodes such as the Golden Calf or Israel's time in the Wilderness demonstrates, the *unfaithfulness* of God's people serves as an obstacle to the world.

The Pentateuch ends with Moses recounting the need for faithfulness and reminding God's people of the Covenant (book of Deuteronomy). The next phase of God's missional story is the narrative of the life of God's people in the land of Canaan.

3

The Old Testament Story: Israel's Life in the Land, Prophets, and Writings

The Torah sets the stage for Israel's life in the Land. If the Torah describes Creation, Fall, and the beginnings of God's missional people, then the remainder of Israel's Scriptures (Joshua to Malachi) describes the possibilities and snares of living as God's missional people among the nations. This includes theological reflection on Israel's history, the writings of the Prophets, and the wisdom of Israel's poets and sages.

The Land: Settlement, Kingship, Exile, Return

The land of Canaan serves as the epicenter of God's mission through God's people to the nations of Genesis 1–11. Canaan sat between the major power regions of the biblical period (Egypt, Mesopotamia, and Asia Minor [homeland of the Hittites]). This places the beginning of God's mission to the nation in a borderland region. Canaan existed on the margins of the power players of the ancient world rather than at the center. As we saw in the Torah, God often uses the unexpected and hidden to advance the Gospel rather than those means common and obvious to humanity.

Israel's life in the land assumes the *faithfulness* of God's people. The Mosaic Torah provides authoritative instruction for living as God's missional people in the world. Israel's life in the land is a gift that God gives to God's people by *grace*. Israel's anticipated response to this *grace* was faithfulness. Israel was to live as a "light to the nations"[1] from the land of Canaan. God's people were to practice faithfulness as a means of living out their calling as a missional community that reflected God's character to/for/in the nations. Israel's life in the land illustrates the possibilities as well as the threats of living as a missional people in the midst of nations who do not yet know God.

There are two broad narratives that describe Israel's time in the land. These narratives are complementary; though, each one has its peculiar interests. First, the books of Joshua through Second Kings tell the story of God's people from Israel's entry into the land until the exile of Judah to Babylon. It ends with Israel still in exile but with the hopeful announcement that Jehoiachin, a living son of David in the thirty-seventh year of Exile (ca. 550 BC), was still alive (2 Kings 25:27–30). The implication of this ending is that God's people have a future on the other side of exile.

The second historical narrative (the Chronicler's history) includes the books of Chronicles, Ezra, and Nehemiah. The Chronicler's history traces the story of the Davidic monarchy through the Exile and includes the return of God's people to the Promised Land in which they rebuild the Temple and the walls around Jerusalem while also recommitting to faithfulness under the leadership of Ezra and Nehemiah.

The Tale of Two Generations: The Books of Joshua and Judges

The Faithful Obedience of Joshua's Generation

The book of Joshua models the fruits of faithfulness in the story of God's people. In Joshua, God's people succeed in inheriting the land promised to Abraham, Isaac, and Jacob because they practice faithful obedience. The LORD appears to Joshua in Josh 1:1–9 and exhorts Joshua to a courageous faith. The bedrock of this courage is a tenacious commitment to attentiveness to God's Torah and the faithful living out of its commandments. This will be the key to success in advancing God's mission and enjoying life as God intended for God's people. Joshua is not a military master; he is a spiritual leader. God's people succeed during Joshua's day because of Joshua's commitment to the Torah of Moses and its influence on the totality of life of God's people (Josh 23:5–10).

---

1. Isa 42:6 and 49:6.

The only exception to the faithful obedience of Joshua's generation was a man named Achan (Josh 7:1–26). When Israel had destroyed Jericho, they were not to plunder the city. But Achan disobeyed and kept several items of silver and gold. This solitary act of unfaithfulness caused God's people to fail in their attempt to capture the city of Ai. Israel had to purge this sin from its midst before moving forward in mission. The point of this episode is to emphasize the crucial role of faithful obedience in achieving God's mission. Human savvy and power are insufficient. Joshua and his generation succeeded because they followed the instruction of the LORD completely.

If Joshua and his generation serve as the golden era of God's people by modeling the successful advance of God's mission, then the book of Judges serves as a witness to the ongoing danger of unfaithfulness. Israel's Scriptures continually warn against turning away from the LORD. Later in the New Testament, Paul will warn the Corinthians, "Now these things happened as examples for us so that we may not desire evil as they did" (1 Cor 10:6). In fact, Joshua's generation stands out. The preceding generation of the Exodus died in the wilderness because of their unwillingness to practice obedience. The generation following Joshua, likewise, turned away from God's instructions.

This back and forth movements of unfaithfulness and faithfulness between generations points to a couple of key insights for missional readers. First, witnessing and/or receiving profound experiences of God's grace and saving power are no guarantee of faithfulness by people. God's people must respond to God's grace with a moment-by-moment walk of obedience. Second, each new generation must learn to practice faithfulness as part of its life with God regardless of the actions of the previous generation. Joshua's generation embraced faithful obedience despite the failure of its parents' generation. The generations of Judges were unfaithful despite the powerful witness of Joshua and his generation.

The Disobedience of the Generations of the Judges

The book of Judges paints a portrait of the chaotic years between the entrance into Canaan under Joshua and the rise of the Monarchy under Saul and David. From the beginning of Judges there is a clear contrast with the events of Joshua. If the generation of Joshua was almost completely successful in fulfilling God's mission, the generations described in Judges (including the generation immediately following Joshua) fail. Judges moves forward with a cyclical pattern (cf. 2:6—3:6) of disobedience, then oppression by outsiders, followed by cries for help, and finally deliverance by a Spirit-empowered deliverer known as a judge. But to reduce the period of the Judges to this static pattern misses the biblical witness. The book of Judges serves a missional reading of Scripture by testifying to the danger of disobedience. Disobedience does more than merely trap God's people into a recurring cycle; it actually causes de-evolution. As the book progresses the judges shift from being bold and daring leaders such as Othniel, Ehud, and Deborah to ambiguous ones, such as Gideon, to morally/missionally questionable figures such as Jephthah and Samson. In other words, the cyclical pattern of disobedience is better understood as a de-evolutionary spiral in which God's mission through his new humanity stalls and then begins to slide backwards into the chaos reminiscent of the Genesis 3–11 world out of which God called his people. By the time of Samson and Jephthah, even the judges, whom God sends as deliverers, are closer to being rogues than to the types of leaders who will inspire God's people to return to their missional calling.

The book of Judges points forward to a way out of this debacle—a godly leader (a king) who, like Joshua, will lead God's people to practice faithful obedience. Judges 17–21 contains a series of disturbing narratives that serve to reinforce the dark overtones of the book of Judges. A recurring refrain binds these stories together: "In those days Israel did not have a king, everyone did what was right in his or her own eyes" (17:6 and 21:25 cf. 18:1 and 19:1). The book of Judges represents a sustained period of unfaithfulness in which God remains faithfully committed to his unfaithful people.

The period of the Judges lasts until 1 Samuel 12. Samuel serves as a godly judge who functions as a transitional figure in the story of God's mission. Samuel guides Israel into its period of kingship. The godly Samuel contrasts with the ungodliness of the priestly family of Eli and with Samuel's own sons. God uses Samuel to anoint Saul as the first king and later David as Saul's replacement.

Kingship

Readers of the Bible often struggle to understand the role of kings in Israel. Scripture can appear ambivalent about kingship because it is critical of human kings. But God permitted his people to have a king. In fact, the Mosaic Torah provided regulations about kingship (Deut 17:14-20). The foundation for understanding Israel's distinct understanding of kingship is its proclamation that Yahweh (the LORD) is Israel's true king (Exod 15:18). The Creator is king of all creation, and God's kingdom, following the debacle of Genesis 3-11, begins to spread and manifest through his new humanity—Israel.

Human kings create law. What the king says goes. In other words, the king is the law. For Israel, there will always be a higher authority than its human king. Actually, there are two authorities above Israel's king: King Yahweh and the written law of King Yahweh (the Mosaic Torah). Thus, in Israel's polity, the law is king. The Israelite king serves merely as God's human agent to administer God's kingdom. According to Deut 17:14-20, the king's chief function was to create a copy of the law and read it all the days of his life. He was to avoid finding security/meaning in military power, political alliances (through marriages to foreign women), or wealth. The Israelite king would succeed through *faithfulness* because God is trustworthy and faithful to keep his promises. Israel's king was to serve principally as an exemplar of faithfulness for God's people.

This perspective is vital for understanding the Bible's negative statements about kingship. For example, Samuel gives a scathing warning to God's people in his final public speech as judge (1 Sam 12). Samuel stresses God's past gracious actions and warns against the dangers of idolatry and syncretistic practices. God's people were wrong for requesting a king because they did so out of a lack of trust in God to guide and protect them rather than out of a need for a leader to model faithfulness.

Saul and David: Contrasts in Faithfulness

Saul's kingship fails because of his inability to obey the clear instructions that Samuel provided (1 Sam 13:7-14 and 15:1-35). Instead of Saul, God identifies David and calls him a "person after God's own heart" (1 Sam 13:14). In this context, a heart for God means that David's mind, will, and intentions are attuned with God's desires and mission, which is in alignment with the commandment to love God (Deut 6:4-5). This becomes the mark of *faithfulness* and the key standard for judging future kings over God's people. David becomes king after Saul's death at the hands of the Philistines (2 Sam 1:1—5:5). He quickly succeeds in defeating the enemies

(RE)ALIGNING WITH GOD

of God's people, establishing Jerusalem as his capital, and moving the Ark and its shrine to Jerusalem (2 Sam 5:6—10:19).

Davidic Covenant

David functions as the model king for all others in terms of faithfulness and commitment to God's purposes. God seals this with a profound gift to David and the world. In response to his faithfulness and his desire to build a house (temple) for God, God sends the prophet Nathan to inform David that, instead, God will build David a house. 2 Sam 7:8–16 is a key text for understanding God's mission. The LORD offers an unconditional covenant with David and his descendants. David's family will rule forever as a dynasty to lead God's kingdom. God's promise to David and his descendants secures the future both for David and for God's people. This does not mean that there will not be trying times. There will be seasons of discipline and correction in response to unfaithfulness, but the bottom-line is this: *David's house and kingdom will be forever* (2 Sam 7:16). The Messianic hope of Israel's Scriptures finds its roots in this passage. God's people always have a future because of God's promises to David. The Prophets will witness to this as will the history of God's people.

Jesus' opening words about the Kingdom of God's arrival in his person (Matt 4:17; cf. Mark 1:13–15 and Luke 4:16ff.) are nothing more and nothing less than a declaration of the fulfillment of God's promises to David. Jesus, as son of David (Matt 1:1–17), acts to announce and restore God's kingdom. Jesus' life, death, and resurrection fulfills the Messianic vision first articulated by Nathan to David.

Temple

The temple in Jerusalem is another key development in Israel's story. King Solomon (David's son and successor) builds a temple for the LORD on the site secured by David. The temple encompasses the full theological implications of the Tabernacle that God gifted Israel at Sinai (Exod 25–31, 35–40). The book of Exodus reached its climax in Exod 40:34–38 with the glory of the LORD filling the Tabernacle. In the Tabernacle the God of Creation enthrones himself in the Holy of Holies and resides over the Ark of the Covenant. The God who demonstrated his holy love and power by delivering Israel from Egypt remains *present* in the midst of his people who then mediate his presence by embodying his character to/for/in the nations as a "kingdom of priests and a holy nation" (Exod 19:6). The original Tabernacle sat at the center of the camp of God's people and always led Israel as they processed toward the Promised Land.

The Tabernacle gains a permanent location in Jerusalem early in David's reign. The Solomonic temple represents the permanent home for the Tabernacle. The center of God's Kingdom becomes Jerusalem from where God's anointed king serves as the leader of God's missional people for the sake of the world.

At the dedication of the temple (1 Kings 8), Solomon reminds God's people of the implications of God's presence among them. Solomon's message offers a theology of the Temple. First, Solomon articulates the reality that a physical temple cannot contain the totality of who God is (8:27). The Old Testament proclaims the LORD as God of all creation (Gen 1:1). The earth is the LORD's (Ps 24:1). The temple is merely a visible witness and microcosm of God's reign and presence in all of the earth. Second, the temple is a center for mercy and forgiveness. It is a visible reminder of these core characteristics of God and thus invites all people to find forgiveness. Last, Solomon's words connect the temple to the mission of God to bless the nations. The temple is a place of prayer for all nations (8:41–43). Solomon asks God to listen to the prayers of all peoples so that the nations may know the LORD (8:43 and 8:60). This reminds God's people of the centrality of the mission to the nations.

Thus, the completion of the Jerusalem temple brings to a high point God's desire to abide among his people. This had been threatened by human disobedience in Genesis 3–11, but through God's actions, God's kingdom is slowly re-emerging from the wreckage of human sin and lostness. The Tabernacle represented a portable sanctuary and now the Jerusalem Temple gave God a physical focal point in the Promised Land. The presence of God at the center of God's people serves God's missional purposes. These purposes will be realized most fully in the mission of the Church in which the Holy Spirit fills each believer so that he or she lives as a temple of the Spirit (1 Cor 6:19) as a moving and living witness to the watching world. In the New Testament, a permanent temple will morph into God's presence being lived out in the lives of every follower of Jesus as they move into the world on mission.

(RE)ALIGNING WITH GOD

Exile

Solomon's Apostasy

Sadly, the vast majority of the kings of God's people fail. Solomon, David's son, moves from being the wise ruler who successfully builds the temple in Jerusalem to serving as the textbook example of a disobedient king by breaking injunctions against great wealth, many wives, and military weaponry of Deut 17:14–20 (1 Kings 9:1—11:13). After the death of Solomon, the United Kingdom of Saul, David, and Solomon splits into two pieces: the northern Kingdom of Israel and the southern Kingdom of Judah. Both kingdoms had the opportunity for success, but the books of First and Second Kings trace their slow but steady slide toward destruction.

First Kings 12—2 Kings 25 narrates the story of the rise and fall of the kingdoms of Judah in the south and Israel in the north. Due to Solomon's unfaithfulness, the United Kingdom of Saul, David, and Solomon divides in two. The southern kingdom of Judah (ca. 922–587 BC) remains under the kingship of the house of David, whereas the northern kingdom of Israel suffers through multiple dynasties during its tumultuous existence (ca. 922–722 BC).

The Fall of the Northern Kingdom

The Northern Kingdom lives under the shadow of its founding king, Jeroboam, son of Nebat. God had chosen Jeroboam to lead the northern kingdom and sent the prophet Ahijah to anoint him as well as to give him careful instructions about practicing *faithful obedience* in order that he might secure his reign (1 Kings 11:26-40). However, Jeroboam quickly turned away from God's clear instructions. Jeroboam lost trust and turned to his own instincts as well as those of his advisors (1 Kings 12:25-33). Rather than allowing his people to travel to the southern kingdom's capital of Jerusalem to visit the temple, Jeroboam constructed shrines in Bethel and Dan and erected golden calf idols for each shrine (cf. Exod 32:1–6). These idols led Israel down the pathway of idolatry and syncretism. Every king that followed after Jeroboam perpetuated his idolatrous practices.

Second Kings 17 offers a devastating critique of the northern kingdom's unfaithfulness in loving God and neighbor and indicts God's people in the north for their own downfall at the hands of the Assyrian empire in 722 BC. God mercifully sent prophets to call God's people back to their roots to serve as a missional holy community, but to no avail. It is a testimony to God's grace and patience that the north lasted as long as it did.

The Fall of Judah

The kingdom of Judah did not fare significantly better than the north, but there are a number of high points where its kings functioned as God intended: Asa (1 Kings 15:9–24), Hezekiah (2 Kings 18–20), and Josiah (22–23). These three kings acted faithfully. In fact, Josiah models closely the ideal king of Deut 17:14–20 because Josiah roots his actions and reforms in the Book of the Law.

However, too many of Judah's kings practiced unfaithfulness or permitted unfaithfulness to flourish during their reigns. In the end, Judah met its fate at the hands of the Babylonians. Babylon had defeated the Assyrians and taken over their empire by 612 BC. The power of Babylon quickly reduced Judah to a political puppet state. The last years of Judah were lived in tension between the desire for autonomy and the practical necessity of obeying the Babylonians. In 587 BC, after Zedekiah, Judah's last king initiated a move for independence, the Babylonians retaliated by invading Judah, and King Nebuchadnezzar sacked Jerusalem destroying the temple (2 Kings 25:1–21). The Babylonians exiled key members of God's people to Babylon as a means of destroying God's people as a nation. The reign of David's sons came to an end, or had it (2 Kings 25:27–30)?

Restoration

Unfaithfulness and exile are not the final words in the history of God's people. The LORD of Creation and God of the Exodus remains the same God who revealed at Sinai that He embodies love, mercy, and forgiveness at the core of God's internal character (Exod 34:6–7). Sin is serious and has consequences, but God's mission cannot be defeated by the mere unfaithfulness of humanity. God used the exile as a means of purifying God's people for a new future. God's people remained in Babylonian exile until 538 BC, but they were not excluded from God's plans and work (Jer 29:1–23). God sent prophets to speak to them and fill them with hope for deliverance. Ezekiel, Jeremiah, and Isaiah all envisioned a return from Exile and renewal in the land.

(RE)ALIGNING WITH GOD

In 539 BC, the Medo-Persian Empire under Cyrus defeated the armies of Babylon and expanded to control all of the former holdings of the Neo-Babylonian Empire. This regime change was pivotal for the Jews. In 538 BC, Cyrus issued an order that permitted the exiled Jews to return to their homeland under the leadership of Zerubbabel and Joshua. They led a group of God's people back to Judea and began the reconstruction of the Jerusalem temple (Ezra 1–4). The construction stopped for reasons that are not completely clear in the book of Ezra, but it was presumably because of intense opposition from the people who lived in the area.

The reconstruction of the Temple resumes under the guidance of the prophets Haggai and Zechariah (521–516 BC). God's people reorganize themselves as a temple state under Ezra and Nehemiah who serve during the fifth century BC. Ezra and Nehemiah are responsible for realigning God's people with the Mosaic Torah (Ezra) and for rebuilding the walls of Jerusalem (Nehemiah). The Old Testament story of Israel's life in the land ends with God's people replanted in Canaan and organized around the new Temple, seeking to live faithfully as a missional community that reflected God's character to/for/in the nations. But God's people will live under the authority of a series of human kingdoms until the coming of Jesus the Messiah. It is not surprising that Jesus' initial words announce the arrival of God's kingdom.

Missional Lessons from Israel's Story

1) God's answer to the chaos and tragedy of Genesis 3–11 is to call a new humanity to serve as his missional people to reflect his character to the world.

2) God is faithful to his promises and powerful to save. This theme reverberates throughout God's interactions with Abraham, Isaac, and Jacob, the Exodus from Egypt, protection from enemies, and the return from Exile.

3) God's faithfulness and grace is the final word. God's people act unfaithfully but this does not negate God's ability to advance his kingdom in advance of the arrival of Jesus the Messiah. Exile was well deserved, but it was a longtime coming as God's mercy and patience delayed its arrival.

Even when exile deservedly came, it lasted only fifty years (slightly more than a forty-year generation).

4) Israel's story demonstrates the potential and snares of living as God's people among the nations. The key takeaway is the necessity of *faithfulness* so that God's people may embody a missional holiness for the nations.

5) Idolatry and injustice are the key impediments to faithfulness. God's missional people must be vigilant against all practices that negate their witness by obstructing their love for God and love for neighbor.

The Writings: Psalms and Israel's Wisdom Literature

Psalms

The book of Psalms is the prayerbook for God's missional people. A missional reading of the Psalms focuses on the meaning of the prayers and hymns of the psalter for shaping the identity and ethos of God's people.

The book of Psalms takes its reader on a journey. Psalms 1–2 serve as a hermeneutical introduction to the rest of the book.[2] Psalm 1:1 begins with the word "Happy" and Ps 2:12 ends with "Happy." Psalm 1 focuses on the individual; Psalm 2 focuses on the nations. These two Psalms ground God's missional people into several core truths. First, Psalm 1 calls for each person to allow the words of Scripture to permeate his or her being as the path to success. Success for the psalmist is the achievement of God's will. Scripture shapes each individual in the ways of God and prepares him or her for the inevitable challenges that arise during one's journey through the world. Poignantly, Psalm 1 views life in stark terms. Depending on one's ground source, an individual becomes either a fruitful tree or dried up chaff. The person whose intake is a steady diet of Scripture connects himself or herself with the living waters flowing from the Temple itself (Ps 1:3). This person knows God, but most importantly God knows and guides the life of this righteous person (1:6). Second, these psalms ground security in God who has secured the future of the kingdom through God's Messiah. This is the message of Psalm 2, which expands the individual focused view of Psalm 1 to include an all-encompassing view of the world including the

---

2. Russell, "Psalms 1–2," 1–4.

nations that do not yet know or worship the LORD. Psalm 2 recognizes the challenges of living as God's people in the world, specifically acknowledging that the powers of this world may resist and oppose the movement of God's kingdom. The good news of God's missional people is that the power of God is greater than all the gathered strength of the nations. In response to the antagonism of the nations, the LORD laughs and announces that he has appointed his Messiah as King to serve as his human agent for administering God's kingdom. By the time of the Psalter's compilation, there was no longer an Israelite monarchy.[3] Thus, Psalm 2 becomes a bold and audacious prayer and a reminder of God's promises to David and a confident statement of trust in God's good future. Psalm 2 also reminds God's people of God's missional plans for the nations. Psalm 2:10–12 concludes with an invitation for the nations to find happiness and blessing in the service of God's Messiah and mission.

Now let's jump ahead to the climax of the Psalter in Psalms 146–150. These five psalms demonstrate that the Psalter moves from issues of security (Pss 1–2) to an all creational praise of the LORD, for who God is, and what God has done in achieving God's missional aims. Psalm 146:5 includes the same "happy" language with which the Psalter began (1:1; 2:12). This is a crucial word for God's people. God's blessing is indeed on God's people. This is the essence of happiness. It is not giddiness or some ephemeral joy. It is the state of blessedness that is the gift of a faithful God to his people through all of life. Remarkably, Ps 146:5–9 detail the character of God and how this influences human life. As the Psalms witness, God is powerfully present to save God's people in all circumstances. The Creator God is more than a God of the status quo who props up the powerful and prosperous. The LORD is the God who extends justice, mercy, love, and blessing to the oppressed and lowly. In fact, one of the key takeaways from the Psalter is that suffering is not a sign of shame and God-forsakenness. God's missional people will suffer from time to time, but God is present to save and advance God's missional purposes.

It is vital to understand the beginning and end of the Psalter in order to grasp the missional message of the rest of the psalms. Psalm 1–2 and 146–150 frame the remaining 143 psalms with a confidence in God. The future of God's people is secure so God's people can serve faithfully on God's mission in the present. When life's challenges come (and they inevitably will), God's people have a rich resource of trusting prayers to sustain

---

3. This assumes that the final form of the Psalter derives from the post-Exilic period.

them in advance of God's future abundance. Notice that life according to the Psalter begins with a faithful moment-by-moment walk with God that is fueled by Scripture (Ps 1) and anchored in the hope of a future secured by the true King of the Nations (Ps 2). The end of the Psalter affirms this reality. "Happiness" is found in the LORD (146:5). Human history is moving toward an all-Creational praise of the LORD. This points to the ultimate success of God's mission.

Psalms 3–145 trace and shape the journey of the life of God's people. Despite the positive grounding of Psalms 1–2, the Psalter's editors were keenly aware of the realities of living in a Genesis 3–11 world. God's people were to live as a missional people as clues to the good future that God has promised. Yet, God's people live in *anticipation* of this and so face the realities of a broken world. The Psalter provides prayers and hymns for a dynamic worship that takes into account the full spectrum of scenarios that God's people will encounter this side of the New Creation.

Let's now explore the types of prayers that we encounter in the book of Psalms:

First, laments or prayers for help dominate the landscape of the Psalms. They are the most common type of prayer found in the Psalter. Readers encounter the initial lament in Psalm 3. Remember the stability and security described in Psalm 1–2? It's gone in the opening words of the Psalm 3, "O LORD, how many are my adversaries!" Laments provide words for God's people when they find themselves in times of danger, suffering, illness, and death. The lament is a prayer for help. The assumptions of a lament are that the pray-er's present circumstances do not line up with the abundant life of God's kingdom and that God can do something about it. These complaints arise from a deep trust and faith in God; but this faith is matched by the desperation of the pray-er's circumstances. God's missional people need laments because our Genesis 3–11 world remains broken and lost. Jesus himself turned to the lament in Psalm 22 to find words to express his needs and anguish to God during his crucifixion. Missional communities need to reflect deeply on the reality that laments heavily dominate the initial eighty-nine psalms in the Book of Psalms. Learning to rely on God by remembering to bring all needs and even all complaints to the God who loves his people is critical for a dynamic and missional faith.

Second, through hymns, the Psalms also teach God's missional people how to praise God for who God is and what God has done. If a lament at its core is the simple prayer: "Help me/us God!" then the hymn is the jubilant cry of "Praise the LORD." Examples of hymns include Psalms 8, 66, 98, 100, and 146–150. The praises of the psalter reach profound heights and the images and phrases of the psalms have inspired the lyrics of Christian hymns and songs for millennia.

Third, psalms of thanksgiving synthesize praise and lament by praising God and giving thanks for the resolution of issues afflicting the community of faith. They are more specific than praise songs because they worship God by highlighting particular acts of deliverance that the psalmist has experienced. The thanksgiving psalm is the fitting and faithful response to the God who invites God's people to bring laments whenever needed. Psalms of thanksgiving include Psalms 118 and 136. The psalms teach us to pray to God in our times of need and to praise him, but they likewise instruct missional communities to practice gratitude openly as part of their worship of God. Thanksgiving psalms are important because they teach God's people that they do not have to wait for the New Creation to experience God's deliverance. It is available in the present and must be celebrated.

Lament, praise, and thanksgiving are three of the main types of prayers and songs collected in the Psalter, but there are several other types that are important for understanding the Psalter as the prayer book for God's missional people.

The Psalms remain filled with hope for God's victory and growth of God's kingdom. This hope centers on God's people's recognition that the LORD is the true king of Israel and of all creation. As we noted earlier, the Psalter ends with a call for all creation to praise the LORD: "Let everything that has breath praise the LORD" (150:6). What is the means of this hope? It is not in humanity or humanity's institutions. For example, Psalm 89 laments the loss and failure of the Davidic monarchy. The hope of the Psalter focuses on the kingship of God over God's kingdom (see especially Pss 90–99). This hope is epitomized by the expressions "The LORD is king" or "The LORD reigns" (93:1; 95:3; 96:10; 97:1; and 99:1). These psalms remind God's people that security and the future depends on God's power and leadership.

As we saw in our review of Israel's kingship, it is critical to understand YHWH's lordship, but there remains a human element in Israel's hope. Psalm 2 introduces the idea of the LORD's messiah as the human agent of God's kingdom. The hope for the messiah as God's agent of renewal and restoration remains alive throughout the Psalter. God is king, but God will reign through the hand of God's messiah. Royal psalms about Israel's kings such as Psalm 2 or 110 became audacious prayers for God to renew David's kingdom by raising up a new king to deliver them from the oppression of the nations and usher in a new age of salvation. The hymns of God's kingship as well as the songs about Messiah maintain God's people in a hopeful expectation for a good future despite any challenges or difficult circumstances faced in the present. In the New Testament, the Book of Psalms is one of the most frequently quoted of Israel's Scriptures. One of the main reasons for this is that the New Testament writers understand Jesus as the fulfillment of the Psalter's messianic expectations.

The Psalter is anchored by three Torah psalms that extol the authority of Scripture and a continual meditation on it as the way of life. The three Torah Psalms are Psalm 1, 19, and 119. Their location is critical. As noted above, Psalm 1 serves as part of the Psalter's hermeneutical introduction by articulating the happy life for the individual through the constant reflection on the Torah. Book 1 (Pss 1–41) is made up principally of laments, but about halfway through, the Psalter's editors provide another psalm (Ps 19) that reminds its readers of the crucial role and power of the Torah for transforming the lives of God's people. Lastly, in Book Five (Pss 107–150), Psalm 119 serves as a massive reminder of the importance of Scripture. The Psalter is steadfast in its affirmation and confession of God's kingship, but Scripture is the means of shaping Israel's king and all God's people into a holy and missional community that will serve Creation's true king. Psalm 119 with its 176 verses about the power of Scripture anchors Book 5 in preparation for the Psalter's concluding symphony of praise hymns (Pss 146–150).

A missional reading of the Psalter reads the interplay of these various psalm types as a means of shaping and securing God's missional people as they live among the nations as a witness to the true God. The God who created the world and called a people to him to serve as his ambassadors provides God's people with the gift of the Psalms to give them prayers for all occasions (both messy and magnificent).

Wisdom

Israel's Wisdom traditions (Job, Proverbs, Ecclesiastes, Song of Songs) connect God's people to the wider world's interest and reflection on the nature of the good life. Wisdom literature is a common feature of the ancient Near

East.[4] Like creation stories and flood narratives, wisdom was a transcultural phenomenon. There are extant extra-biblical Wisdom texts from Syria–Palestine, Mesopotamia, and Egypt. In fact, Israel's Wisdom traditions draw from the well of this wider pool of wisdom. For example, in the Book of Proverbs, most scholars believe that "The Words of the Wise" (Prov 22:17—24:22) show the direct influence of an Egyptian text called *Instruction of Amenemope*.[5]

Of course, Israel's Wisdom traditions are not mere imitations of older material. Instead, Israel's wisdom offers a distinct perspective for God's people. Wisdom literature serves to guide God's people on how to live well and prosper in the world. A successful life is one that fulfills God's will and mission. For God's people, the foundation for wisdom is a resolute commitment to the Creator God, the LORD. The good life flows from a correct positioning of the self in relationship to the Creator God. This is the core biblical distinctive. Iconic texts such as Prov 1:7, "The fear of the LORD is the beginning of knowledge; fools despise wisdom and discipline," and Eccl 11:13, "Fear God and keep his commands for this is all that humanity must do," summarize the key takeaways for the wise. Wisdom must be rooted in the recognition of the Creator God as the source of all wisdom. Wisdom points to God, and a life rooted in God is the epitome of the good life. Thus, it follows that an unwise person is one who lives foolishly (i.e., failing to follow the wise instruction that comes from God).

A missional reading of wisdom immediately sees the value of Israel's wisdom tradition. Wisdom is not only an ancient practice, but collections of the sayings of the wise as well as a burgeoning literature of success continues to this day. The Bible's wisdom literature invites God's people to interact with a world hungry for insight on how to make it through life, but to do this by listening to worldly wisdom through God-centered and Bible-centered lenses. God's people have the opportunity to become the "go to" experts on living well.[6]

---

4. Wisdom remains popular in the modern world. A simple perusal of any social media platform will reveal a flood of quotations about personal development, leadership, and the good life.

5. E.g., Clifford, *Proverbs*, 17–19 and 199–216.

6. Twenty-first-century missional communities are taking this possibility seriously by teaching life skills. Churches are helping people learn to manage finances and live debt free. They offer recovery ministries for people dealing with life traumas such as divorce and addiction.

A missional reading of the wisdom literature also sketches out an understanding of missional holiness. Wisdom is worldly in the sense that it teaches its readers how to live in *this world*. Life skills shaped by God are crucial. Living lives of excellence, ethical purity, virtue, and purpose serve as a potent witness to the watching world. The apostle Paul will remind Christ followers in Philippi that their true citizenship is in heaven (Phil 3:20), but this does not mean that God's people are supposed to live lives detached from the surrounding culture. It simply means that God's people are to live distinctively for God within the cultures of their day. Biblical wisdom is God's gift to God's people to guide them in this critical practice.

Prophets

The writings of the Prophets serve to call Israel back to her Torah roots while simultaneously envisaging a future act of God that will usher in a new age of salvation. God sent the prophets in response to the unfaithfulness of God's people. As we saw from our reading of the Torah, God desired for his people to serve as a missional community that reflected God's character to/in/for the nations. Instead, God's people reflected more the character of the nations by practicing syncretism, idolatry, and social injustice. When God's people lost sight of their true identity, God sent his messengers, the prophets, to deliver a reality check.

The Torah's distinct ethos of love for God and neighbor was at stake when God's people lapsed into the episodes of unfaithfulness to which the biblical narrative from Genesis to 2 Kings testified. God's people were unfaithful in their love for God through their practice of syncretism and out right idolatry.

The Old Testament is adamant about Yahweh's uniqueness and incomparability (e.g., Exod 15:11; Isa 45:22) in the midst of nations who were polytheistic. There may be other entities that men and women worship and that serve as "gods" and "goddesses", but in reality, only One is worthy of the title God, and that is Yahweh the Creator God and LORD of all.[7] Thus, any turning away from this core affirmation by God's people (no matter how small) is a massive misstep and endangers God's mission to reveal himself to the lost world of Genesis 3–11.

---

7. Wright, *Mission of God*, 136–88.

(RE)ALIGNING WITH GOD
The Prophetic Critique of Idolatry and Syncretism

The most insidious form of idolatry practiced by God's people was syncretism. Syncretism occurs when two or more religions are mixed to form a hybrid. In a polytheistic context, syncretism is the rule. The allegiance of God's people to the LORD alone was challenged continually by contact with the nations who recognized, worshipped and served many gods. The nations had no problem in recognizing the LORD as a god, but such recognition is not the same as full allegiance to the LORD apart from all other religious commitments. The temptation for God's people was to add certain practices to their obligations to the LORD. For example, the Old Testament is full of testimonials about the allure of Baal and/or Asherah (sometimes Astoreth). Baal was the Canaanite storm deity. Asherah was Baal's consort. In the mythology of Canaan, their union produced a fertile harvest of much needed food. God's people suffered times of drought. If an Israelite family was living in a rural area far from the LORD's shrine in Jerusalem, it is easy to imagine the family mixing in an occasional trip to a high place dedicated to LORD that included in its liturgy elements of the Canaanite fertility cult as a means of securing a sufficient harvest to feed the family for another season. This is not to excuse this behavior but rather to make it understandable. As we read the prophetic critique of idolatry and syncretism, it is crucial for us as missional readers to reflect on the plurality of religious expressions in our day and how easy it is to create syncretistic variants that ultimately lead us far from the biblical portrait of creation, God, and life. The missional reading of the Prophets calls God's people to elevate the LORD alone above all competing gods and goddesses as the first priority for faithfulness in our lives and witnesses.

The Book of Hosea is a poignant testimony about God's love for his people despite their unfaithfulness. Hosea served as a prophet in the early to mid-eighth century BC. God's people had adopted syncretistic practices and had lost their way. In response, God called Hosea to live out a flesh and blood dramatization of the relationship between God and Israel through the unfaithfulness that he experienced in his marital life with his wife Gomer. In this remarkable book, Hosea woos Gomer back to faithfulness (Hos 1–3). The book of Hosea does not sugar coat the costliness of idolatry and syncretism. These sins tragically mute the witness of God's people, but Hosea's message serves as a testimony to the love of God and for God's desire for God's people to turn away from unfaithfulness and realign with God and God's mission to the nations (Hos 3:5; 6:1–3; and 14:1–9). Hosea's message is a desperately needed one in the tweny-first century. Our world runs rampant in syncretism and idolatry. Yet God loves Creation with a love that will not let go and continues to offer hope to all with ears to hear and hearts to realign with God's mission.

Hosea and the prophets have a simple message that is foundational to loving God: *Trust God alone.* Faithfulness flows out of this commandment. It is indeed the great commandment (Deut 6:4–5; cf. Matt 22:34–40). The Prophets are adamant that the allegiance of God's people lies solely with the LORD. Moreover, the only true hope for all humanity and creation is the LORD. Isaiah declares this most directly: "Turn to me and experience deliverance, all the ends of the earth. For I am God, and there is no other" (Isa 45:22).

The Prophetic Critique of Injustice

But there is a second commandment that must be lived out: Love for neighbor. In Creation God envisioned a harmonious interplay between himself and humanity but also within humanity and between humanity and the created world. The Torah envisaged a new humanity of which God's people served as ambassadors and witnesses. Israel lived, breathed, and worked among the nations, but it was to be distinctive among the nations rather than like them. Its relationship with God was not a status quo religion that accepted and blessed the inequities of the present or one that recognized and elevated the superiority of certain humans, notably males but especially those who were wealthy, politically powerful, or religious professionals. As we saw, the Torah radically democratized the notion of God's image by declaring that God created all people in the image of God. Thus, it recognized the inherent equality of all members of the community. The Torah steadfastly held together spirituality and ethical living. To live as the human beings that God intended for us to be we have to learn that these elements cannot be compartmentalized. The prophets will remind God's people of these truths and insist that one does not love God apart from the practice of justice for others. Moreover, true justice cannot be defined or understood apart from the character of God.

The book of Amos famously trumpets justice as the core ethos of God's people. In Amos, the LORD "roars" forth from Zion (1:2) in an indictment of God's people for acts of injustice. God's people have forgotten their roots. So far in the Scriptural story, God has demonstrated that his mission advances through the margins and not through the status quo of human power. In God's kingdom, the second born can prove more significant than the firstborn; the childless couple can become parents; and the enslaved, alienated, and marginalized can be unleashed for the good of God's mission. Tragically, during times of plenty, God's people forgot their roots as liberated slaves who were freed to serve God as a missional community that reflected and embodied God's character (Gen 12:3; Exod 19:4–6 and 20:2). Essential to this witness is a commitment to practicing justice for all people as well as for the creation. Amos epitomizes the prophetic critique of injustice. Amos recognizes the hypocrisy and mixed messages sent by God's people when they attend to formal religious activities while abusing the poor and marginalized among them.

Recognizing the need to work for justice in the world is a logical inference from reading Israel's prophets. The missional movement has caught this stream and has emphasized it as part of getting local communities of faith outside of the "four walls of the church."[8] This is vital and a traditional part of the evangelical witness.[9] Yet, this emphasis has to be held in dynamic alignment with the prophetic critique of idolatry. The context for Amos's proclamation is at Bethel. Amos was from Judah, and Bethel was right across the border separating the kingdoms of Judah and Israel. Bethel was one of the two key shrine sites for worship in the northern Kingdom of Israel. Dan in the north was the other. This is important. Amos speaks the word of God in the *religious* center of the kingdom of King Jeroboam II. Amos's words decry the lack of justice in the kingdom. This is an affront to royal power. The ethos of Jeroboam's Israel is out of alignment with the values of the true kingdom, the kingdom of God. The worship of the LORD is corrupt in the north because it mistakenly has separated love for God and love for neighbor.

Amos's most famous words are those quoted by Martin Luther King Jr., "Let justice roll down like waters and righteousness like an everlasting stream" (5:24). This sums up Amos's devastating social critique of the north for its sins against the poor and marginalized (e.g., 2:5–8; 4:1–5). The message of Amos is clear. The worship of the LORD must be combined with justice and love for neighbor. Sacrifices and the attending to religious services are hollow apart from faithfulness in practicing justice for the

---

8. McNeal, *Missional Renaissance*, 41–88.

9. See profiles of historical figures in Dayton and Strong, *Rediscovering an Evangelical Heritage*.

community. Yet, even the worship of the LORD is compromised according to Amos through syncretistic practices that include other deities alongside the LORD (e.g., 5:26, 8:14).

The Prophets as Foretellers of God's Future

The prophets move beyond calling for a return to a conservative past. The prophet's are conservatives in the sense that they are adamant of the need for God's people to preserve their roots and ethos as God's liberated people for the sake of the nations, but the prophets also understand the realignment of God's people to involve future dynamic and game-changing acts of God. This future era of salvation will be the kingdom that Jesus announces. The Prophets understand God's future in light of the core story of Israel. In other words, the prophets see God's future in light of the ideals of the past. Examples from the Prophets include the following: a New Exodus (e.g., Isa 40–55), a New Covenant (e.g., Jer 31), a New Temple (e.g., Ezek 40–48), and a New King or Messiah (Isa 61).[10]

Thus, a missional reading of the Prophets recognizes their poignant call for (re)alignment by God's people with God's mission and their optimistic vision for the future age of God's salvation. This dual focus is essential for reading the Prophets wisely and well. Without this perspective, we run the risk of reducing the Prophetic message merely to a series of proof-texts about the later arrival of Jesus, rants against the sinfulness of the world around us, or data for prophecy "experts" to mine in order to construct guides to the future. The writings of the prophets are purposeful. They seek to reawaken God's people and shape them to serve as a missional community to reflect God's character to/for/in the nations.

Understanding the Balance Between Judgment and Salvation

Reading the prophetic books closely also challenges the reader with the amount of judgment texts within their pages. The profound visions of future salvation are only a small portion of the prophetic message. The prophets were not feel-good preachers. They brought biting critiques of the unfaithful practices of God's people. A faithful reading of their words

---

10. All of these themes are worthy of a full book length study and are illustrative of how the Prophets envision the future. The precise nuances require a full exegetical treatment of each of Israel's prophets.

will challenge Christ followers today to continuous (re)alignment with the mission of God. However, there is an abundance of good news. This abundance is not in terms of the amount of space given to the promises of salvation, but in the astonishing lavishness of these visions. This interplay of judgment and salvation occurs throughout these books. For example, the prophet Amos proclaims a powerful message against God's people for their injustice, idolatry, and unfaithfulness throughout most of the nine chapters of his book. He envisions the destruction of the northern kingdom and the imminent exile of its population. Yet, at the end of Amos (9:11–15) when all hope appears to be gone, the prophet sees a new day in which God will restore the fortunes of David and replant God's people in the Promised Land where they will rebuild their cities and prosper.

The Prophetic Visions of Salvation and God's Mission

In fact, it is the prophetic visions of salvation that provide a direct pathway to the Good News of God's kingdom that Jesus announces in the Gospels. A missional reading recognizes the hope that God's salvation sits just over the horizon of God's judgment on God's people. This is good news as it reminds us that human brokenness, alienation, and sin does not have to serve as the final word in human history. God's mission is a testimony to God's movement of human history toward God's victory in the life, death, and resurrection of Jesus.

Isaiah 40–66: A Suffering Messiah

Isaiah 40–66 clearly portrays God's desire for his people to fulfill a mission for all creation. But there is a problem. Israel, God's people, is to be God's servant nation to the world, but Israel has been unable to live up to this calling due to its sin (Isa 42:18–20).

Israel is God's servant, yet Isaiah also portrays an individual servant through whom God would transform the nation of Israel and ultimately the world. These texts are found in 42:1–9; 49:1–6; 50:4–9; 52:13—53:12; and 61:1–3. These passages portray a servant of God who will erase the nation's sins and extend God's justice and peace to all creation.

It is crucial to recognize the mission to bless the nations in Isaiah's servant songs (e.g., 42:6; 49:5–6). How will this blessing be accomplished? The fourth servant song (52:13—53:12) tells of the personal suffering and death of the servant for the sins, injustices, and healing of God's people. The New Testament clearly invites us to read this text in light of Jesus' ministry of healing (Matt 8:17), and his death and resurrection (Acts 6).

Israel's servant offers a Messianic vision of a different kind of king. The other prophets offer more traditional royal imagery. For example, Micah 5:2 sees the Messiah as arriving in the line of David from Bethlehem. Zechariah envisions the king riding into Jerusalem on a donkey (9:9). The New Testament will deploy these images as well for its understanding of Jesus, but Isaiah's "suffering servant" serves as a prevailing metaphor that shapes how we read the rest of Jesus' characterization in light of the Prophetic witness.

A missional understanding of the Scripture recognizes that God's mission advances through the suffering and death of the Messiah. It is not about traditional forms of royal power. Jesus' life will bring salvation through God's power alone, and it witnesses to the victory of love and justice over hatred, violence, and all forms of injustice. A careful reading of the prophets also serves as a critique of any modern understanding of the church or pastoral leadership that imports kingly images apart from the metaphor of suffering servant.

The story of Israel in the Old Testament, however, is not one of victory. Israel struggles to live in light of its calling and turns repeatedly to its own ways. It is clear that God will have to do another, even greater work, in order to accomplish the mission. This work will involve the coming of the Messiah, the Christ, who will embody and fulfill the mission of Israel. What is hinted at in Isaiah (and in other texts across the Old Testament) becomes a reality with the birth of Jesus.

The New Work in God's People

Jesus' proclamation of the kingdom finds its roots in the expectation for God's new age of salvation. Israel's prophets called God's people back to their roots as a missional community, but they also anticipated and announced a future work of God to facilitate this. The Israel envisioned on the other side of judgment is a transformed Israel. This transformation included a restoration from exile, but it included the inner spiritual renewal of individuals. We will now explore some specific examples in the Prophets.

The book of Deuteronomy had already anticipated this move with its talk of a circumcised heart (Deut 30:6). External attempts at obedience were never sufficient to guarantee faithfulness. The LORD promised this new work. The Prophets used a variety of metaphors and descriptors to capture this dynamic promise.

Jeremiah 31:31–34 announces a New Covenant for God's people on the other side of Exile. This declaration is stunning and vital for a people wondering if they still had a future with God. Jeremiah proclaims an abundant vision. Yes, God's people broke the Sinai covenant and, hence, God exiled them to Babylon. But there will be a New Covenant, and God will transform God's people from the inside out to empower them for faithfulness. The language of Jeremiah is reminiscent of Deuteronomy. God will write the Torah on the inner volitional center of each person. This work on the hearts of God's people creates a personal and direct knowledge of God. Faithfulness will flow from inside each person. The focus of Jeremiah's promise is the abundant future that exists and that will arrive for the good of God's people.

Ezekiel speaks of a spirit driven renewal. The LORD will do a new work inside of each member of God's people. Through the spirit, God will change hearts of stone into hearts of flesh (Ezek 11:19; 36:22–36). In other words, the stubborn willfulness that leads to unfaithfulness will be softened as a means to empowering faithfulness. This portrait of personal renewal hits a memorable highpoint in Ezek 37:1–14. Ezekiel envisions the re-enlivening of God's people metaphorically by describing a valley full of dry bones, which God raises up to new life. Ezekiel affirms that this restoration of God's people serves as a witness to the nation of the identity and power of the LORD. This is again a vital reminder that God's people exist to extend God's blessings to the nations. They function as a conduit through which the nations encounter the Living God.

The climax of Ezekiel's vision is a full restoration of the temple (Ezek 40–48). God's temple points to the future New Creation where God will be eternally present with God's people. We already saw in Israel's story that the theme of divine presence manifested in the form of tabernacle and temple. These physical places served as visible markers of God's presence that adumbrated the future when all creation will again serve as the temple of the LORD.

Ezekiel's vision of the temple is expansive. The temple will offer waters that will replenish the earth and offer a bounty of nutritious and healing foods for all. In the New Testament, a physical temple that offers borders limiting the perception of God's presence shifts to a new profound understanding of presence in which the indwelling Holy Spirit in the lives of Christ followers transforms the body of Christ in the world into a temple that bears witness to the true God wherever the feet of God's people carry them (1 Cor 6:19-20; cf. Rom 12:1-2).

Joel 2:28-32 prophesies the universal outpouring of God's spirit on all people. The spirit is present in the Old Testament but only certain key figures received the spirit such as Israel's judges and kings. Joel sees a new day when the spirit indwells *all flesh. All* means *all.* There is no discrimination in terms of gender, age, and status as even slaves receive the spirit. Joel's vision of the coming of the spirit prepares readers for the dawn of the Church. In Acts 2, Peter will interpret the arrival of the spirit on Pentecost as the fulfillment of Joel's vision. Moreover, the universal availability is crucial for understanding God's restoration of God's people and the mission of God's New Testament people. God's mission post-Jesus will be a spirit-drenched and spirt-driven mission.

Prophetic Visions of Salvation and the New Testament

The Protestant canonical order places the Prophets as the final section of the Old Testament. This is theologically important and justified as the future visions of God's new era of salvation serve as a direct point of connection between the Testaments. It is significant that the New Testament opens with Matthew's Gospel. Matthew's Gospel begins with a genealogy that ties the birth of Jesus specifically to key characters (Abraham and David) and to one pivotal event (Exile). The early sections of Matthew (1:1—4:16) rehearse a few significant events in Jesus' life before he begins his public ministry: his birth (1:1—2:12), flight/return from Egypt (2:13ff), Baptism (Matt 3), and temptation in the Wilderness (4:1-11). References to the fulfillment of Old Testament Scripture run through these stories and set the stage for Jesus' initial proclamation of the Kingdom of God (heaven).

In the next chapter, we will continue the Scriptural story by returning to Jesus' announcement of the Kingdom and the unfolding of God's mission through the Church in anticipation of New Creation.

4

The New Testament Story: Jesus the Messiah, the Mission of the Church, New Creation

Jesus the Messiah: Embodied Hope (Matthew to John)

Reading the Gospels

The four Gospels tell the story of Jesus as a means of announcing the kingdom and of shaping disciples for the kingdom building mission of God in light of Jesus' life, death, and resurrection. A missional reading emphasizes the centrality of Jesus' announcement and embodiment of the Kingdom of God. The Jesus of the Gospels did not come to start a religion but rather to unleash the Kingdom of God in words and power. The core of Jesus' call was the exhortation to realign continually in response to the manifestation of the Kingdom. Jesus' life, death, and resurrection incarnate the ethos of the kingdom in ways that subvert human claims to power, wisdom, and influence. The message of the Kingdom is good news because the way of Jesus is the fullest and final expression of hope and love. It is only through Jesus' life, death, and resurrection that men and women can live fully as the human beings whom God created them to be.

Jesus the Messiah begins his public ministry by announcing the arrival of the Kingdom of God in fulfillment of the Old Testament story. Jesus embodies, lives out, and brings to a climax Israel's story. God's sending of the Son into the world fulfills the promise and expectation of Israel's Scriptures. In the Synoptics, Jesus is born in Bethlehem as a descendant of David. He flees to Egypt in a time of distress and God brings him back to the land of Israel. Before his public ministry in Israel, he spends forty days in the wilderness, but unlike Israel whose forty years in the wilderness was a time of failure, Jesus prevails over temptation. His baptism confirms his role as God's Son (i.e., God's royal earthly representative through whom the Kingdom will be established).

Jesus models the authentic human life of mission, community, and holiness. As we saw in our reading of the Old Testament, this was Israel's mission post-Genesis 3–11. To embody a missional community, Jesus calls and shapes a band of disciples to serve as a newly constituted and restored people of God (Matt 4:18–22). Through his life, he embodies and fulfills all that Israel, as a nation, was to accomplish. He lives out the Torah perfectly (Matt 5:17–20). Through his twelve disciples he reconstitutes the people of God in microcosm by modeling Israel at its grandest. But Jesus is more than merely the ultimate expression of Israel. His sacrificial death on the cross and his resurrection on the third day secured the victory of God over death, sin, and evil for all creation.

Jesus' vision of the kingdom contrasts with that of his contemporaries. The study of the first century CE context demonstrates that there were multiple understandings of Judaism or perhaps better, there existed competing Judaisms. Some expected a militant Messiah who would overthrow Rome; some longed for the earthly restoration of the Davidic monarchy in Jerusalem; and others believed that the Messiah would lead God's people to fulfill the Mosaic Torah through strict adherence to its dietary and holiness laws.

Jesus embodies the kingdom vision of the Isaianic servant (Isa 61:1–2; cf. Matt 11:2–6 and Luke 4:16–21). He suffers (Ps 22:1). Jesus is radically on the side of the excluded and marginalized in society. Jesus is *for* the other. This includes lepers, the servants of Roman centurions, and women (Matt 8:1–17). In his ministry, Jesus challenges the religiously connected and politically powerful by lionizing a Good Samaritan, by including tax collectors as disciples and friends, and by shocking listeners with plot twists such as a father who willingly loses face in an attempt to reconcile with his shameful sons.

Jesus does take on the trappings of Messianic expectations by enacting prophetic expectations of a future king from Bethlehem (Micah 5:2) who will ride into Jerusalem on a donkey (Zech 9:9). His triumphal entry at the beginning of the Passover week was a powerful symbol of identity. But Jesus subverts any claims to human power by willingly submitting to humiliation and death on a cross.

Jesus' mission of announcing the kingdom and signifying its presence through his words and deeds involves challenging the religious status quo and breaking down boundaries between insiders and outsiders within Israel. Thus, the Gospels share the good news about Jesus for the purposes of transformation. Each Gospel in its own way seeks to transform its hearers into profound people who find themselves in the story of Jesus and open themselves to a reshaping or a realignment into a new humanity that exists for God's mission. Thus, a missional reading of the Gospels understands the Gospels as manuals of discipleship that invite all people into the story of the Scriptures. We read the Gospels not to learn facts about the life, death, and resurrection of Jesus but so we become disciples true to the name (i.e., we become men and women whose way of life manifests the deep magic of Jesus' life, death, and resurrection).

Jesus, the Kingdom, and Discipleship

Discipleship as Good News

To put it simply—Jesus did not come to initiate a new religion or some political program. He came to announce the in-breaking of God's future. The Gospels call this the "Kingdom of God" or "Kingdom of heaven." To miss this is to misunderstand fundamentally the message of Jesus.

The Kingdom language is coded speech that announced the inauguration of God's end-time reign or rule over creation. This spoke to the expectation of God's people in the first century. By announcing the Kingdom, Jesus was alerting those with ears to hear that God's long-awaited era of salvation had arrived. This connects the Gospels with Israel's story in the Old Testament. Jesus fulfills the expectations raised in the Prophets and offers the fullest answer to the problems raised by the Exile and its aftermath.

We must never lose the power of the "Good News" of the Gospel. In his words and actions, Jesus proclaims the Good News of the Kingdom. In Matt 11:3–5, John the Baptist questions whether or not Jesus is truly the long expected Messiah. Jesus responds provocatively with a thick theological statement rather than a mere "yes" or "no." What is Jesus' answer? He says to John's followers, "Go and tell John what you are seeing and hearing: blind people are receiving their sight, lame are walking, deaf people are now able to hear, dead are being raised up, and poor people are having the good news proclaimed to them." Jesus is using the language of Isa 61:1–2 to describe his activities. In other words, Jesus answers John's question with an unambiguous "Yes!" by appealing to his Kingdom advancing actions. In the life and ministry of Jesus, God is establishing the Kingdom. Jesus' words and actions were received as Good News. Provocatively, Jesus subverts some of the expectations of the elite and religious insiders by engaging the masses and reaching out especially to the outsiders (the poor, the unclean, women, collaborators with the Roman empire, and foreigners). Such persons received the Gospel with gladness, whereas the religious leaders of Jesus' day often found themselves at odds with the Good News of the Kingdom.

Jesus' presentation and embodiment of God's Kingdom is central to the Gospels. The Good News of the drawing near of God's long awaited end time rule and era of salvation stands at the heart of the Gospel. Jesus' followers exist to carry on Jesus' Kingdom work in the world and to embody the hope of the Kingdom for the watching world.

A missional reading challenges us to embody the Good News in the Gospel. The call to (re)alignment offers Good News to the world and challenges God's people to assess the extent to which its proclamation of the Gospel is an announcement of Good News to those desperate for what only God can do. This mission is central to recapturing the apostolic ethos of the early church, which proclaimed the Gospel as good news for outsiders and seekers.

Discipleship as Cross-Centered

Jesus the Messiah cannot be understood apart from his crucifixion. Jesus' death on the cross is God's answer to the disasters of Genesis 3–11. Even more, it is in Jesus' submission to death on the cross that we see the fullest glimpse of humanity as God intended and the richest demonstration of God's love for his creation (Rom 5:8). Jesus' death subverts all human claims to power and salvation. Jesus' death stands as the New Exodus event that liberates humanity for life in God's Kingdom. It casts the final word on injustice, power politics, cynicism, cruelty, disease, transgressions, and all other creation-depleting realities found in our post-Genesis 3 world. It stands as God's model for resisting the suffocating status quo of the Empire in all its forms. The four Gospels move from their various beginnings relentlessly to the death of Jesus.

The institution of the Lord's Supper creates a community shaping ritual that centers the Christ following movement on the death of Jesus (Matt 26:26–29; Mark 14:22–25; Luke 22:14–23).[1] Its links to the Passover in Israel's Scripture are obvious. The Christ following movement remembers Jesus' death through the sharing of bread and wine. The focus rests on Jesus' death as the sign of God's New Covenant (Mark 14:24 and Luke 22:20) and antidote to sin (Matt 26:28). Additionally, all the Synoptics regard the ritual as an anticipatory sign of the full consummation of God's future Kingdom. The missional implications are clear. Christ followers witness to the world of the reality of Jesus' life and work through participation as a community in the remembering of his death on the Cross. This ritual proclaims to the world that this past event holds the keys to God's future.

Furthermore, descriptions of discipleship are intimately linked with the cross. Jesus calls disciples to follow him. But all four Gospels emphasize the potential and real cost of such following by linking it with cross bearing. Matthew, Mark, and Luke all record some form of Jesus' radical invitation/warning about discipleship: *If anyone would come after me, let him deny himself, take up his cross, and continually follow me.*[2] John's Gospel ends with Jesus' restoration of Peter, which includes a statement about Peter's future death as a result of following Jesus.[3] The power of the Cross in a disciple's life is that it relentlessly calls for God's people to die up-front to our human inclination for self-preservation as the key to unlocking a true power for living. The cross of Jesus is an affront to all human mythologies of status, honor, power, and authentic living. By dying, disciples find true life. Moreover, the cross is a radical challenge to status and honor. In the ancient world, crucifixion was reserved for those of low status (slaves) or rebels against the Roman Empire. In other words, Jesus' death on the cross was more than a sacrificial death on our behalf—and I am in no way marginalizing this tectonic truth. But Jesus' death also represents a subversive challenge to the power structures of our world through Jesus' willingness to embrace a lowly status as the means to discovering an authentic power that comes through God alone.

But we must also connect Jesus' death with his resurrection on the third day. The crucifixion is a powerful reality on its own, but it is God's

---

1. John's Gospel lacks an explicit scene in which Jesus institutes the Lord's Supper but John 6 deploys Eucharistic language in its narration of Jesus' feeding of the five thousand.
2. Matt 16:24 cf. Mark 8:34; Luke 9:23
3. John 21:18–19

raising of Jesus from the grave that fully demonstrates its power and announces God's triumph over evil, death, and sin. The resurrection makes it clear that Jesus' death was no mere martyr's death, but rather the true announcement and way to God's future. A missional hermeneutic understands the cross and resurrection as the dual sided testimony of God's ultimate victory for all creation. All four Gospels reach their climax in the story of Jesus' death and resurrection. Each Gospel has its own emphases and themes, but all move relentlessly and purposively to the crucifixion and resurrection. The word is clear: Jesus cannot be fully understood apart from the cross and his vindication through the empty tomb.

What does a cross-centered discipleship ultimately mean? Through the lens of Matt 16:24 we discover that embracing the cross is the means to freeing God's people to live fully for the values and mission of the Kingdom of God. A missional reading emphasizes the moment-by-moment nature of following Jesus into the world on mission. The cross becomes the symbol of the movement. The call to self-denial and taking up the cross is more than merely embracing an ascetic mode of living. It is rather a radical and steadfast refusal to value one's own life over the mission of God. It is the opposite of Peter's actions on the night of Jesus' betrayal that permitted him to save his life at the expense of his relationship with Jesus. To take up the cross is a rich metaphor that described the last action taken by condemned persons on their way to their execution. Embracing the cross frees a person because once a person is dead to self; he or she is fully freed to follow Jesus audaciously into the darkest places on earth to announce the Good News of the Kingdom.

In sum, the backdrop of Matthew's view of discipleship is the death of Jesus on the cross. The cross is paradigmatic for the life of discipleship (Matt 10:38; 16:24). The cruciform life defines the essence of following Jesus Christ. Jesus' death on the cross is the ground of salvation. Matthew does not provide a detailed discussion of the "how" of atonement, but instead simply states its reality (e.g., Matt 1:21; 8:17 [cf Isa 53:4]; 26:28). Modern Christ followers must resist any pragmatic or theologically driven attempts to whitewash or marginalize the centrality of the cross. Jesus' call to "deny oneself and take up the cross" is counter-cultural and revolutionary. It envisions a movement of Christ followers who live as *dead (wo)men walking*—persons who have died up front to self so that they can follow Jesus into the world to bring the Gospel to those who desperately need it. Mission assumes that Jesus' life, death, and resurrection is the defining reality for our world.

Discipleship as Mission

From the beginning of the Christ following movement, mission has been central. Matthew, Mark and Luke both record Jesus calling fishermen to become fishers for women and men. The call to follow Jesus is a call to mission because Jesus' life focused on the mission of God.

All of the Gospels portray disciples as persons who carry the Good News about Jesus' life, death, and resurrection to others. As the disciples follow Jesus, he does his work of shaping them into persons who can "fish for people." The disciples' time with Jesus is not merely preparatory or academic work but real world training. Jesus molds his disciples by modeling mission. It is also worth noting that he deploys his disciples immediately into missional activity. This begins with accompanying Jesus and learning from him, but it quickly becomes deployment as a means of extending Jesus' reach. In Matt 9:35—11:1 (cf. Luke 9:1–6 and 10:1–12),[4] Jesus sends his disciples out on mission. In this text, Jesus authorizes his disciples to proclaim the Gospel in word and deed just as Jesus himself had done. This is the map for all future disciples to follow. Mission is not the work of religious professionals alone; it is the work of all followers of Jesus. Reading the Gospels missionally involves seeing them as blueprints for contemporary communities of faith to follow. The energy of mission implicit and explicit in the Gospels shapes God's people into being a missional community that reflects and embodies God's Good News for others. Of course, the Matthean and Lukan accounts end with commissions for world transforming mission (Matt 28:16–20; Luke 24:44–49; Acts 1:8).[5] But it is vital to recognize that mission is not merely a part of discipleship, but that the Gospels themselves are manuals for what a missional discipleship truly looks like. In contrast to Israel's mission of preparation for the coming

---

4. Note that the Lukan sending involves both disciples (9:1–6) and an additional seventy witnesses (10:1–12). The latter text suggests a fulfillment of the mission to the nations by corresponding to the number of nations listed in Gen 10.

5. The purpose of John's Gospel is missional (20:30–31). Mark may also be read in this manner. It is worth noting that early Church editors added endings to Mark's Gospel that add an explicit missional thrust to them. Although the so-called "Shorter" and "Longer) endings are not original to Mark, they demonstrate that the early church understood mission as the natural implication and imperative of the Gospel itself.

of Messiah, post-resurrection, the mission of God's people becomes one of actively engaging and going to the nations to live and serve as God's witnesses. An encounter with the Gospel serves as a commission for mission.

Discipleship as Movement

Jesus lives out his ministry as an itinerant teacher, preacher, and miracle worker. He does not abide in any one place for long but continually moves to the next town or city. The baseline call of Jesus to others was "Follow me." The Gospels model for the people of God the necessity of a dynamic movement. Jesus is on the move in the stories that the New Testament preserves for the Church.

In many ways Jesus' encounters with people appear random. But randomness is part of the method. As Jesus moves from place to place people come to him hoping for a miracle or to hear his authoritative teaching. Jesus embodies his own sense of "sent-ness." A missional reading highlights this ethos. Following Jesus involves walking about with eyes to see and ears to hear the needs of the world. The Gospels portray Jesus as one who is ready, willing, and able to minister to all those who come to him. Jesus' movement from city to city offers a key message to the Church. The movement of following Jesus involves embracing this same sense of sent-ness.

The itinerant nature of Jesus' public ministry invites modern Christ followers to reflect critically on present day practices that often focus on the building of buildings, the attraction of crowds, and the preservation of existing communities. There is obviously a place for such goals, but it is crucial to evaluate them in light of Jesus who dismissed crowds who gathered to hear him so that he could move to the next destination on the journey (Matt 15:32–39). Jesus embodied a willingness to leave the ninety-nine to go after the one who was lost (Matt 18:10–14).

Discipleship as Boundary Breaking

Jesus' Kingdom embodying mission tore down the barriers that divided people in his day. The model of Jesus is of a mission that embraces all humanity and one that tends to be offensive to the religiously minded.

In Matt 8:1—9:35, Matthew skillfully wove a series of Jesus' miracles into one extended narrative. In the initial segment (8:1–17) Jesus signifies the arrival and meaning of the Kingdom through a series of actions that shatter traditional religious and cultural boundaries. Jesus conducts three miraculous healings: the cleansing of a leper (8:1–4), the healing of the servant of a Roman soldier (8:5–13), and the healing of Peter's sick mother-in-law (8:14–15).

Matthew reports these initial three events together for a theological reason. Each of the three persons whom Jesus heals represents a marginalized group in the pious circles of first century Judaism. The leper was ritually unclean and forced to exist on the fringes of society as an unwanted outcast. The Roman centurion signified the power of the oppressive Roman Empire and served as a constant reminder of God's people's plight. The healing of Peter's mother-in-law demonstrates the commitment of Jesus to both women and men. It was unusual for a spiritual leader to mix with women. This miracle is one of many actions in which Jesus tore down the walls between the sexes.

Jesus acts of boundary breaking are central to defining the ethos of the Kingdom. The good news is for *all people*. In particular, Jesus shows that the Gospel moves forward by engaging *outsiders* and *seekers*. Transformed people then become *insiders* who can serve as conduits of God's grace to others. Jesus' boundary breaking created new *mission* driven people.

Thus, Jesus models a cross-cultural and boundary exploding mission for his followers. It is a Gospel that is liberating and egalitarian in outlook. It is for *everyone* including those persons marginalized ethnically, politically, or socio-economically. When God's people engage in boundary breaking ministry, they keep social justice on the front burner by modeling love for neighbor. As we seek to live as missional communities today, Jesus' example is key. How would our modern churches answer these questions:

- Where would Jesus establish new faith communities today?
- How does this compare with our contemporary practices?
- Who are the *outsiders* in our present context?

A missional reading reminds God's people that a biblical model of missional outreach will always include persons *different* from us.

Discipleship as a Critique of the Religious Status Quo

Jesus' ministry involved frequent confrontations with the religious status quo of his day. Ironically, this included friction with the traditionalist

Sadducees and the reform-minded Pharisees.[6] A missional reading of the text is interested in the ways that Jesus' engagement with religious insiders serves as a warning to modern Christ followers, lest we fall into the same traps of the insiders of Jesus' day.

Part of Jesus' critique is the implication that outsiders may be in a better position to hear God than religious insiders. If the core call of God is realignment, then there will always be a danger that *insiders* may choose not to realign with God's contemporary mission. Over time, what began as a vital movement crystallizes into a suffocating *status quo* that ends up hindering God's work in the world. New life may be added to God's people by the inclusion of outsiders, but this inclusion often comes at the cost of conflict with religious tradition, especially religion's calcified leaders.

Matthew 9:9–13 records Jesus' calling of Matthew the tax collector, along with a confrontation between Jesus and the Pharisees over Jesus' dinner with "tax collectors and sinners." Jesus' inclusion of Matthew into his band of disciples is a clear example of boundary breaking and a profound statement about mission in itself. The Pharisees, who in many ways reduced the Torah to Sabbath keeping and table rules, were incensed that Jesus would risk ritual contamination by choosing the company of persons who any decent *religious* leader would know to avoid. Jesus' rebuke is classic and cuts to the heart of his critique: "Those who are strong have no need of a doctor, but the ones who are ill do. Go and learn this: I am desiring mercy and not sacrifice. For I did not come to call righteous people but sinners" (9:12–13). Since the Gospel is for the world, God's people must be willing to move out of their own circles to interact and engage people who are desperate to learn and experience God's grace and mercy. This text is also vital for reflecting on the relationship between holiness and mission. Holiness, as Jesus models it, is a holiness that engages the world with an understanding that a true holiness can *infest* the world rather than be *infected* by the world. Holiness often comes with calls to separate *from* the world, but Jesus points the way forward to a *missional holiness* that carries light into places that the merely religious people consider to be dark and void of hope. Dining with tax collectors and sinners ran counter to the religious status quo of the Pharisees, but Jesus values the reaching of new people over the misplaced religious sensibilities of insiders.

---

6. By traditionalist, I am simply referring to the Sadducee party as the keepers of the temple and the status quo of Roman occupation. By reform-minded, I understand the Pharisees as a group committed to the sanctification of Israel through a ministry of teaching and Torah observance.

Another danger for religious insiders involves viewing the world through a self-justifying framework that finds pride in the contrast between them and us. In Luke 18:9–14, Jesus offers a parable about a Pharisee and a tax collector. Both men enter the temple to pray. The Pharisee's prayer is a profoundly self-serving one that attempts to elevate himself before God on the basis of *religious practices* in contrast to those of *outsiders* including the tax collector in his presence. The Pharisee's words demonstrate a 'scarcity' understanding of God's grace that reduces life to the mere performance of correct actions detached of any sense of mission or the values of God's Kingdom. It takes pride in one's performance in contrast to "sinners" rather than in understanding one's spiritual life in light of God. The tax collector on the other hand simply prays, "God, be merciful to me, a sinner." According to Jesus, of the two men only the tax collector went home justified before God.

Even knowledge of the Scriptures is no guarantee of hearing and discerning God. For example, in Matthew's infancy narrative, pagan astrologers from the east are contrasted sharply with Herod and all Jerusalem (including the chief priests and scribes). The astrologers have come to Jerusalem looking for the Messiah in response to their interpretation of astronomical phenomena. Herod calls on the religious leaders to provide insight and appropriately they cite the Micah 5:2 identification of Bethlehem as the place to find the Messiah. But astonishingly enough, no one travels to Bethlehem to worship the newly born Messiah except for the astrologers. Instead, Herod and all Jerusalem (including the religious establishment) are "frightened" at the prospect of the Messiah's birth and ultimately respond to the Messiah's announced birth in Bethlehem by murdering all boys under two. In contrast, the astrologers find the baby Jesus, worship him, and give gifts in symbolic surrender to this newly born King. This episode, in particular, is a warning to God's people today of taking care lest one's knowledge of Scripture actually blind one to God's desires and intentions in and for the world.

Nothing is more suffocating or potentially harmful to God's mission than a status quo religion that is more concerned with protecting its own power base, propagating tradition in anachronistic and legalistic ways, exalting itself by criticizing others, or promoting ideology over relationship than it is with declaring God's eternal "Yes" to those women and men desperate for the Good News that God has called us to share. The Gospel is for *outsiders*. God leads *outsiders* to God's people. Those religiously inclined must not be blinded to this reality lest they find themselves on the outside of God's Kingdom.

The Mission of the Church

The New Testament is the unfolding of God's mission through the decisive saving action of God through the life, death, and resurrection of Jesus the Messiah. This section offers a programmatic overview of the New Testament materials as a means of completing the story begun in Israel's Scriptures.[7]

God's sending of the Son into the world fulfills the promise and expectation of Israel's Scriptures. Jesus models the authentic human life of mission, community, and holiness. As we saw in our reading of the Old Testament, this was Israel's mission post-Genesis 3–11. To embody a missional community, he calls and shapes a band of disciples to serve as a newly constituted and restored people of God. Through his life, he embodies and fulfills all that Israel, as a nation, was to accomplish. Through his twelve disciples he reconstitutes the people of God in microcosm. But Jesus is more than merely the ultimate expression of Israel. His sacrificial death on the cross and his resurrection on the third day secured the victory of God over death, sin, and evil.

The New Testament Scriptures reflect theologically and missionally on this good news about Jesus. A missional reading of the New Testament recognizes the diversity of the biblical material, but also recognizes they center on the life of a missional community that exists to reflect and carry the Gospel to the world. According to the New Testament, the risen Jesus *sends forth* God's people (i.e., the Church) to announce the Good News of the Gospel to the nations.

The New Testament records the advance of God's mission in light of the life, death, and resurrection of Jesus the Messiah. Each of the New Testament documents seeks to shape a missional identity and ethos in the communities that originally received them. Recognizing this is the goal of a missional hermeneutic of the New Testament.

Following the death and resurrection of Jesus, the Holy Spirit is unleashed fully for God's mission. The coming of the Spirit marks the creation of the Church as the fullest expression of God's people. The decisive

---

7. This survey will not include treatment of the Johannine materials or the General Epistles. Like my treatment of the Old Testament, I am being selective given the nature of this book.

difference between the Old Testament people of God and the New Testament people of God is the universal empowering of all God's people through the coming of the Holy Spirit. In the Old Testament, God's Spirit is present as early as Gen 1:2, but it did not manifest its power in the life of the vast majority of individual members of God's Old Testament people. In the Old Testament, the Holy Spirit indwelled select individuals to empower them to accomplish God's mission. During the building of the Tabernacle, the Spirit endowed Bezalel with artistic ability and skill in design so that he could lead the team of artisans and skilled workers to build the various cultic elements for the Tabernacle. Israel's judges also received the Holy Spirit to enable them to deliver God's people from their enemies. As the Old Testament develops, part of the expectation for the future actions of God was that God would do a new work in the life of his people. This hope and vision was encapsulated in the prophet Joel's description of God's new era of salvation in terms of a universal outpouring of the Holy Spirit on all flesh.

The Holy Spirit cleanses and equips the Church to function fully as the people of God as they embody the Gospel and testify to its Good News in anticipation of the coming New Creation. It is the Spirit that drives the advance of the Gospel. It is the empowering presence of the Spirit that marks the era of the Church as a "go to" people.

The principal story of the New Testament is the full engagement of the nations with the Gospel through the power of the Spirit. If the missional ethos of the Old Testament was essentially a preparatory one of a non-engagement and "come to" model, then the New Testament represents a shift as God's people now practice a true missionary model by carrying the Good News about Jesus the crucified and risen Lord across the Mediterranean world. Within the canon, the Book of Acts functions to narrate this movement by tracing the Gospel's travels from Jerusalem to Rome.

The Book of Acts

Acts completes the story begun in the Book of Luke by narrating the spread of the Gospel from Jesus' ascension to heaven to Paul's imprisonment in Rome. The contribution of the Book of Acts to understanding the missional nature of God's people is clear. A missional reading of Acts listens to the story of the emergence of the Christ following movement in the first century Greco-Roman world as a guide to twenty-first-century mission.

The central insight of Acts is the empowering role of the Holy Spirit in the advancement of the Gospel. The Book of Acts is Spirit-driven. So much so that it is more appropriate to think of the Book of Acts as "Acts of the Spirit" rather than "Acts of the Apostles."

The Book of Acts opens with the Risen Jesus prepping his disciples for their post-resurrection mission. This is a new era for the people of God. Jesus' words are programmatic and visionary: "But you all will receive power when the Holy Spirit comes down upon you and you will be my witnesses in Jerusalem, in Judea and Samaria, and to the end of the earth" (1:8). This text is full of meaning.

Fundamentally, this text reconnects the mission of God's people explicitly with the Genesis 1–11 world. If the Gospel story from Genesis 12 until the coming of Jesus focused on the creation of a new humanity to reflect God's character in the world, the post-resurrection era of the Church shifts to a "go to" ethos in which the people of God now engage actively the nations with the Good News about God's abundant and transforming love.

Notice the language of Acts 1:8. It is a vision for world mission. It assumes that mission will continue in the area of the disciples' current geographic reality: Jerusalem and the wider land of biblical Israel. These had been the areas in which Jesus himself had served. But now there is a push beyond these regions to the rest of the earth. The Gospel came to its initial fulfillment in the land promised to Abraham and his descendants. Now post-resurrection, it is time for the good news to spread to the nations in anticipation of the New Creation. This reconnects the Biblical story line with God's universal mission to all Creation. This fulfills the original mission of humanity (Gen 1:26–31). Under the power of the Spirit, the Church re-engages this mission with the hope of reaching the nations with the Gospel.

The Spirit is the catalyst for this new movement of God's work in the world. With the resurrection and ascension of Jesus the Messiah, God sends the Holy Spirit into the world to empower his new humanity—the church—to serve as clues to the Kingdom of God. The sending and empowerment of the Spirit is the qualitative difference between the Old Testament people of God and the New Testament people of God. The Spirit guarantees the success of God's mission. God's people, the church, are people of the Spirit. The Book of Acts demonstrates this in dramatic fashion.

Acts 2 powerfully tells the story of the initial filling of Jesus followers with the Holy Spirit on the Day of Pentecost. Jews and god-fearers from all over the Roman world had gathered in Jerusalem for the feast of Pentecost. Jesus' followers had likewise gathered together. Suddenly, on the morning of Pentecost the Holy Spirit descended upon them in the form of tongues of fire. All of Jesus' followers who were present (perhaps as many as 120; cf. 1:15) were instantaneously gifted with the ability to speak one of the many native languages of those gathered in Jerusalem. They began to announce the good news about Jesus' life, death, and resurrection. This reality reversed the confusion of Babel (Gen 11:1–9) and demonstrated the *translatability* of the Gospel cross-culturally. This is a key element, as Jesus' followers could have spoken in Greek and addressed the crowd as a whole. But the mission of God is for the nations and, thus, the followers address the nations contextually in each person's native tongue. Peter addresses the crowd and announces that this miracle of speech is the fulfillment of the ancient prophecy from Joel 2:28–32. God's future age of the Spirit, as inaugurated by Jesus, has now come. Peter goes on to announce cogently the Gospel to all who gathered around him. The immediate result of the proclamation of Jesus' death and resurrection through the power of the Spirit was the addition of three thousand persons to the Christ following movement.

The Book of Acts marks the spread of the Gospel around the world by tracing the advancement of the baptism of the Spirit. Whenever the Gospel reaches a new people, the Spirit's coming signifies the creation of a new Jesus community. Unlike in the Old Testament, in the New Testament all of God's people receive the Spirit for empowerment and cleansing. Acts records the apostles performing miracles and preaching in the power of the Spirit. As the Gospel reaches a new area in fulfillment of Acts 1:8, the Spirit fills believers in each region.

In subsequent chapters, the Gospel advances through the work of the Spirit. This will be a recurring pattern. In fact, although the full name of Acts is "The Acts of the Apostles," a better title would be "Acts of the Holy Spirit." We will now trace briefly how this narrative thread plays out in the rest of the book. In Acts 3, Peter and John encountered a crippled man on their way to the temple. Peter heals the man and boldly proclaims the Gospel in Solomon's portico. This scene catches the attention of the authorities who then arrest Peter and John. In Acts 4, Peter and John appear before the religious authorities in Jerusalem. The Spirit fills Peter (4:8) and enables him to boldly proclaim the Gospel before the council.

In Acts 7–8, an intense time of persecution erupts against the earliest Christ following movement. However, human power cannot quench the

Spirit. Instead of stopping the Gospel in its tracks, the persecution has the opposite effect of helping to advance the Gospel by pushing it out of Jerusalem into surrounding regions. This is an important insight for a missional reading. The arrival of persecution does not mark the end of Christian witness, but instead it often enhances Christian witness (e.g., Philippians 1:27–30). The persecution in Jerusalem forces Jesus' followers to flee, but in the process, they are carrying the Gospel to new people and new places. The inhabitants of Samaria are the first beneficiaries. Jews and Samaritans had a shared history but also much animosity with each other. This does not stop the Gospel. Acts 8:4–25 reports the missional work of Philip among the Samaritans. They receive the Gospel. Reports of the reception of the Gospel by the Samaritans make it back to the apostolic leadership in Jerusalem. They appoint Peter and John to travel to Samaria in order to equip the new believers there. The believers in Samaria had received water baptism, but they did not yet have the baptism of the Spirit. Peter and John pray that God would send his Spirit upon the Samaritans, and they received the Holy Spirit (8:15–17). The Spirit's arrival marks the advance of the Gospel to a new place and new people.

Next the Spirit empowers the Church to bridge the cultural gap between Jew and Gentile. In Caesarea, the first Gentiles receive the Gospel (10:44–48). The book of Acts marks the acceptance of the Gospel by a new cultural group with a report of the arrival of the Holy Spirit on the believers. In due course, the Spirit baptizes Jews (Acts 2), Samaritans (Acts 7), and Gentiles (Acts 10). This continues the fulfillment of Joel's vision of the Spirit being poured out on "all flesh" (Joel 2:28). The gift of the Spirit is for everyone. The artificial boundaries of humanity dissolve: Jew and Gentile, young and old, rich and poor, slave and free, male and female.

God's Spirit is the driving force in the expansion of God's people from the day of Pentecost in Jerusalem (Acts 2) to Paul's house arrest in Rome (Acts 28). The early apostles and witnesses were open and sensitive to the Spirit's promptings. For example, in Acts 8:26–40, the Spirit leads Philip (8:29) to engage an Ethiopian eunuch in a conversation that leads to the man's conversion. The Holy Spirit fills Saul (9:17) after his Damascus road encounter with the Risen Jesus (9:1–9) and he becomes Paul. Paul's encounter transforms him. He shifts from being a persecutor of the church to being the person whom God uses to carry the Gospel to the Gentile world. His journeys ultimately bring him to Rome.

Acts 13–28 describes the forward advance of the Gospel from the regions of Jerusalem, Samaria, and Syria into Asia Minor (modern Turkey), Greece, and eventually Rome itself. Acts 13:1–4 narrates how the Spirit selected Paul and Barnabas to serve as ambassadors of the Gospel. We often think of Paul as a man with a driven personality. But Paul is not merely an ambitious and visionary missional leader; his exploits are the product of the leading of the Spirit. The Holy Spirit calls Paul (Saul) and Barnabas to preach the Gospel in these new lands. Eventually, Paul and Barnabas separate to pursue different calls (Acts 15:36–41), but Paul continues to carry the Gospel to cities that have not yet heard the name of Jesus. Under the guidance of the Spirit (16:6–10), Paul leaves Asia Minor to evangelize Macedonia and Greece. Paul continues to proclaim the Gospel until Acts ends in Acts 28 with Paul preaching about Jesus in Rome, the capital of the empire. This is significant because it represents a partial fulfillment of Acts 1:8. The Gospel has now moved from Jerusalem, the spiritual center of God's people from the time of David to Rome the center of the dominant empire of the first century.

Provocatively, Acts concludes in an open-ended fashion. Acts 28 reports that Paul arrived in Rome and lived under house arrest for two-years. During that time, he taught openly about the Kingdom of God and Jesus. Interestingly, the Book of Acts ends abruptly. The reader does not learn the outcome of Paul's stay in Rome nor of any additional advance of the Gospel. Scholars do debate the ending of acts.[8] But is is clear that the reader is left to wonder what happens next. This invites the reader to create his or her own ending. In the absence of an Acts 29, we must imagine the next chapters in the advance of the Gospel and even to see our own day as part of the ongoing story of God's people. The story of Acts 29 and beyond remains one to be written by Jesus' followers today.

The Book of Acts serves an important role in developing a missional hermeneutic through its emphasis on the work of the Spirit. God advances the Gospel through the Spirit's empowerment. Our hermeneutical reflection is vital but the Good News is that the Spirit continues its work.

---

8. The issues turns on the meaning of "ends of the earth" in Acts 1:8 and the extent to which the Gospel reaching Rome represents the fulfillment of Jesus' promise.

Acts and Incarnational Mission

The Book of Acts also models an incarnational mission as part of its global and cross-cultural vision. The model has three key elements that invite our reflection. (1) The mission of God is a cross-cultural one and Jesus bridged the divisions that exist between insiders and outsiders. (2) Gentiles did not have to become Jewish with respect to the Torah in order to follow Jesus. (3) The Holy Spirit deploys various methods of advancing the Gospel depending on the context of its audience including use of Scripture, miracles, and the utilization of Gentile cultural and religious symbols (i.e., extra-biblical ones).

First, Acts demonstrates decisively that the Gospel is transcultural and that it can be translated into different cultures. The gift of tongues at Pentecost (Acts 2) demonstrated the Good News could be delivered in languages outside of the Hebrew/Aramaic/Greek of first-century Palestine. Moreover, the reality of the Spirit falling on Samaritans and Gentiles served as a tangible demonstration of the Gospel's inclusiveness. Acts 10 narrates the remarkable story of Cornelius and Peter. Both men receive visions that prepare them for an encounter that will change both of their lives. Cornelius, who is a God-fearing Roman Centurion, receives a vision in which God tells him to send for Peter. The next day, Peter receives a vision in which he learns that God has pronounced the formerly unclean, clean. When Cornelius sends for Peter, Peter realizes that the vision was God's way of preparing him for a mission to the Gentiles. He goes to Cornelius and presents him with the Gospel, which Cornelius and his friends and relatives receive. While Peter is still speaking, the Holy Spirit fills the Gentiles and, thus, marks their entrance into the people of God (10:44–48).

Second, as Gentiles became Christ-followers, the Jewish Christian leadership faced the issue of how the Torah's laws affected these new believers. The question in its most basic form was this: Did a Gentile have to become a Jew in order to live as a follower of Jesus? In particular, there was a dispute over the question of circumcision. Did male converts to the Christ following movement need to be circumcised? Acts 15 recounts a remarkable conference involving Paul, Barnabas, and the apostles and elders in Jerusalem. Paul and Barnabas shared the fruits of the Gentile mission, including all of the signs and wonders that God was doing to advance the Gospel. James, speaking on behalf of the Jerusalem leaders, discerned that God was indeed doing a great work among the nations in fulfillment of

Amos 9:11–12. Gentiles did not need to embrace fully the Mosaic Law. In particular, they did not need to be circumcised. James wrote a pastoral letter that boiled down the Mosaic laws to avoiding idolatry and sexual immorality. This episode affirms that Gentile converts to the Christ following movement did not have to become practicing Jewish Christians. The key lesson here is that the Gospel can be contextualized into new cultures. Acts 15 also affirms that there are transcultural principles of moral conduct that establish a core ethos for Christ followers.

Last, Acts describes several modes of communicating the Gospel that push us to think beyond cookie-cutter approaches and remind us that the Holy Spirit deploys a variety of methods depending on the context. Sometimes the apostles proclaim Jesus via the exegesis of Israel's Scriptures; sometimes it is through powerful signs and wonders; sometimes it is by cross-cultural contextualization, or some mixture of these options.

The Book of Acts shows that Jesus may be proclaimed to Jews and God-fearers by means of demonstrating that Jesus is the fulfillment of Israel's Scriptures. This is the heart of Philip's encounter with the Ethiopian eunuch in 8:26–40. Philip hears him reading from Isaiah 53 and begins a conversation in which he tells the eunuch about Jesus by starting with Isaiah. This convinces the eunuch who immediately requests baptism and becomes a believer in Jesus.

The Book of Acts demonstrates that miraculous signs can serve evangelistic purposes. Acts 16:16–34 tells the story of Paul and Silas imprisonment in Philippi and the conversion of its jailer. Paul and Silas are accosted by a mob for disturbing the city. During the night while Paul and Silas are singing hymns to God, there is a violent earthquake. The quake is from God, as not only is the prison shaken but all of the doors open and the chains of the prisoners are unshackled. Fearing that all have fled, the jailer is about to fall on his sword when Paul calls out to him with the news that no one has escaped. In response to this miracle, the jailer falls before Paul and Silas and asks, "Masters, what must I do to be saved?" Paul and Silas share the word of the Lord with the jailer and his household. That very night he and his household joined the Christ following movement and were baptized.

Acts also shows the possibilities of contextualization for cross-cultural engagement. Acts 17:16–34 narrates Paul's activity in Athens, the center of Hellenistic culture and philosophy. Paul has the amazing opportunity to share the Gospel with a group of Stoic and Epicurean philosophers on the

Areopagus. Since Paul is addressing Greeks with no background in the Old Testament Scriptures or the God of Israel, he does not use Scripture to address them. Instead, he imaginatively begins by affirming the religiosity of the Athenians and starts his Gospel proclamation with reference to an altar inscribed with the phrase: "To an unknown god." Paul uses this as a beginning point to tell about the Creator God who sent Jesus. Moreover, Paul quotes from the Greek poet Aratus to support his claims that all people have their source in one Creator God. Paul ends his proclamation by referencing Jesus, not as Israel's Messiah, but rather as a *man* through whom the Creator God will judge the world in righteousness. The truth of this claim, Paul says, rests in the reality that God raised this man from the dead. It is fascinating that Paul does not state the name Jesus explicitly. Verses 32–34 record the reactions of the crowd: some scoff at the mention of resurrection; others express interest to hear more. Most profoundly, some join the Christ following movement. Paul models a contextualized Gospel presentation in which he uses cultural symbols from his target audience to proclaim the Gospel fully without watering down its content.

The implications of the various Gospel approaches in the Book of Acts are vital if a bit disconcerting to twenty-first-centry believers in the West. We tend to value systems and programs. In the Book of Acts, the Holy Spirit is the means, and the Spirit uses faithful witnesses to reach others with the Gospel depending on the needs of the audience. The Good News of the Gospel is Jesus. The witnesses in Acts always proclaim Jesus, but the means of getting to Jesus depends on the context of the audience. This does not guarantee success as in 100 percent conversion, but the Gospel spreads on its way to the next person and the next region in fulfillment of Acts 1:8.

Pauline Materials

The Pauline materials are richly complex. A missional reading of Paul looks at his corpus as a means of shaping Christ followers in the various Greco-Roman cities into Christ-centered missional communities capable of manifesting and proclaiming the Gospel cogently in their contexts. The following is in no way a comprehensive look at Paul's writings. I will touch on a few key elements in Paul that point forward for a missional hermeneutic.

General Approach to Paul

The letters of Paul[9] as well as the General Epistles represent messages written to discrete communities of faith across the Mediterranean world. A missional approach to these letters reminds us that they are concerned primarily with shaping communities of God's people into outposts for the advancement of the gospel. Doctrine and ethics are central only as they serve to enhance the mission of God in that particular city. Guder has been on the forefront of emphasizing this aspect. He writes concerning the New Testament documents:

> New Testament communities were all founded in order to continue the apostolic witness that brought them into being. Every New Testament congregation understood itself under the mandate of our Lord at his ascension: "You shall be my witnesses." . . . To that end, the New Testament documents were all, in some way, written to continue the process of formation for that kind of witness. They intended the continuing conversion of these communities to their calling—and that is how the Spirit used (and still uses!) these written testimonies.[10]

This understanding of the New Testament materials is a shift away from viewing these books as essentially raw material for creating systematic or dogmatic theologies. The Apostles were committed to carrying the Gospel to the world in obedience to Jesus' Great Commission (Matt 28:18–20; Acts 1:8) as the fulfillment of God's calling of Abraham (Gen 12:3b; cf. Exod 19:4–6). A missional reading of Scripture is interested in how each letter shapes and forms a discrete Christian community to serve as God's missional community that will embody and reflect God's character to/for/in the world.

Paul the Apostle's Missional Ethos

Paul recognized that in the life, death, and resurrection of Jesus, God has inaugurated the new age of salvation known as the Kingdom of God. In this kingdom, God fully welcomes all nations. Paul's mission was to proclaim the Gospel across the Roman world to both Jew and Gentile. Paul lived out

---

9. Meaning the full Pauline corpus and not merely the critically assured minimum of authentic Pauline letters.

10. Guder, "Missional Pastors," 4.

his calling as an apostle by opening up new regions and introducing new people to the good news about Jesus the Messiah. Paul embodied a "go-to" ethos that the post-resurrection people of God must own out right as their mission. Paul recognizes the necessity of proclaiming the good news about Jesus across the known world of the Roman empire as the fulfillment of God's creational intentions. Near the end of his letter to the Romans, Paul writes of his desire for a visit and explains his delay in coming. His reason is provocative: "Thusly I aspire to announce the gospel not where the Messiah has already been named so that I might not build on someone else's foundation, but as it has been written, 'Those who have never been told of him will see and those who have never heard will hear.' Therefore this is the reason that I have so many times been hindered from coming to you. But now I no longer have any place in these regions to preach so I desire as I have for many years to come to you as I journey to Spain" (Rom 15:20–24a).

Paul is not a glory hound or self-centered in his ambitions. He is not striving for his own status or to set himself apart from other Gospel workers. He is not making notches on his belt for each convert. In his own writings Paul often names many co-workers who served as his partners in advancing the Gospel. These persons include Timothy, Barnabas, Aquila, Priscilla, and Epaphroditus. In 1 Cor 3:5–9, Paul teaches that God is the ultimate reason for the success of the Gospel and that each Christ follower has a role to play in the mission.

Yet Paul's words in Romans 15 are bold and daring. They implore his readers to focus continually on the mission of proclaiming the good news to new people in new places. Paul served as an apostle roughly during the 40s to early 60s AD. At this time, Christ followers were merely another minority religious sect in the Roman Empire.[11] The churches of Paul's day were small house churches of perhaps a few dozen people. There are so few believers that Paul knew most of them by name, as is clear from the many personal greetings in his letters. Therefore, the missional mindset of Paul pushes the Gospel forward rather than focusing on building up existing bodies of believers. Churches exist as outposts from which to launch the next mission. God's mission is always expanding. There is no room for a maintenance mindset. Paul wanted to visit Rome but his plan was linked to a bigger mission of reaching Spain with the Gospel. A missional reading recognizes the ongoing apostolic mission by reading Paul's writings as

---

11. There may have been as few as twenty-five thousand by the end of AD 100. See the discussion in Stark, *Rise of Christianity*, 6–13.

instructions for God's people to engage their cities and regions with the Gospel.

Paul and the Power of the Spirit

The mission of God is carried out in the power of the Holy Spirit. Paul understands this. Hearing Paul's emphasis on the Spirit is critical for missional leaders. Being mission focused is crucial, but apart from a mission-focus powered by the Spirit, we are not participating in the fullness of God's post-Resurrection mission to the world because we will be merely doing the work in our own strength. As we saw in our review of the Gospels and Acts, it is the universal outpouring of the Spirit post-Resurrection that is the decisive difference between the Old and New Testaments in terms of a believers life with God. It is the Spirit that empowers and transforms the people of God from being a static, come-to community, as was the case in Israel (and one that consistently failed to live up to God's call) to a mission-centered force that exploded post-Pentecost to carry the Gospel around the world.

To understand the power of the Spirit in the writings of Paul, we must grasp the language of the Spirit's antithesis—the flesh.[12] There are two ways to live as a Christ follower according to Paul. A Christ follower may walk according to the flesh or walk according to the Spirit. Too often the flesh is mistakenly thought of as one's sinful nature. This is a misreading. Living by the flesh inevitably leads to sin, but the flesh itself is not evil. The problem with the flesh is simple—it is inadequate to power one's life as God has intended it. To walk according to the flesh is to depend upon one's own powers, talents, ability, and strength to make it through the world. In contrast, to walk according to the Spirit is to open oneself to God and depend fully on the Spirit for discernment, purification, and empowerment for living rather than reliance on self.

Romans 8 is a key text because it pulls together much of Paul's thinking about the Holy Spirit. In Romans 8, Paul describes the transforming work of the Spirit in the lives of Christ followers, the inner-witness by which the Spirit provides assurance of adoption as a son or daughter of God, its help in our prayers, and its gifting of God's people for the common good of the church and advancement of God's mission in the world.

---

12. Greek *sarx*.

First, in Rom 8:1–14, Paul describes the contrast between a life in the flesh versus a life in the Spirit. Paul exhorts Christ followers to live by the Spirit. He assumes that every Christian is filled with the Spirit. The central problem, however, is that every Christian does not rely on the Spirit. The constant temptation for a Christ follower is to depend upon his or her own gifts, talents, passions, and strengths (i.e., life according to the flesh). Paul's antidote for this problem is clear: *resist self-reliance by being fully dependent on God.*

Second, in Rom 8:15–17, Paul notes the role of the Spirit in giving Christ followers assurance of their true standing with God in Christ. It is vital for God's mission that God's people understand that they are truly children of God. As we saw in our discussion of Exod 19:3–6, God's mission requires of God's people that they serve as his witnesses. In many ways, they are called to the role of servants of the nations. Christ followers can only embrace the fullness of this calling to the extent that they understand their security and standing in Christ. Thus, the Spirit's role is providing assurance of salvation is vital for God's missional plans.

Third, in 8:26–27, Paul describes the Spirit's guidance in shaping the prayers of God's people. Paul designs his words to strengthen the intercessions of God's people. This text assures God's people that God welcomes and hears their prayers. The advance of God's mission is dependent on the power of God, but don't lose sight of the reality that it also depends on the work of God's people who live confidently as God's agents of blessing through a moment-by-moment relationship with God fueled by prayer.

Any treatment of Paul's understanding of the Spirit must also reflect on his theology of gifting. Key passages of Scriptures for this include Rom 12:3–8; 1 Cor 12–13; and Eph 4:11–13. A close reading of these texts makes it clear that Paul understands that there are varieties of gifts and presumably more exist than those listed. However, Paul attributes all of the listed gifts to the Spirit. He also assumes that God gives all gifts for the purpose of building up the Church so that it can participate fully in the mission of God in the world. Paul emphasizes that the most important manifestation of the Spirit is an other-centered love as the key marker of the work of the Spirit in the lives of Christ followers. The Spirit empowers the Church with the talents and gifts that it requires to unleash the Gospel. The people of God are a spirit-empowered body with each individual deploying her and his gifts for the benefit of the world.

(RE)ALIGNING WITH GOD

The Mission of Reconciliation

At the center of Paul's Gospel was the message of reconciliation. The Gospel tears down the walls and realities that separated humanity from God, humanity from others, and humanity from the created world.

The key event was the work of Jesus the Messiah on the cross and his resurrection from the dead. These must be held together. Paul summarized his Gospel by utilizing the early church's creedal formulation, "Messiah died for our sins according the Scriptures, he was buried, and he was raised up on the third day according to the Scriptures . . . . " (1 Cor 15:3–4). Jesus' crucifixion demonstrate God's love (Rom 5:8) and brought about reconciliation for all who believe. Paul sums this reality up in 2 Cor 5:19, "For God was in Messiah reconciling the world to himself, not reckoning to them their sins." The restoration of the divine-human relationship opens up the possibility for men and women again to live fully as God had intended. The healing of the vertical relationship between God and humanity is crucial but it is only one of the fruits of the reconciling power of the Gospel.

Throughout his writings, Paul decisively proclaims Jesus' death on the cross and God's raising of him from the grave as God's ultimate triumph for his creation. Fundamentally, the Gospel of Jesus dramatically changes the way the world is seen. It challenges God's people to reassess and shift their understanding of their existence and purpose. We've argued throughout this book that God calls his people to live as a missional community that reflects and embodies God's character. Indeed, this began with the creation of men and women in God's image in Gen 1:26–31. Now that God has worked reconciliation through Jesus the Messiah, God immediately appoints the reconciled people of God to serve as ambassadors to the nations of God's mission of reconciliation. Paul writes, "Therefore we are ambassadors on behalf of the Messiah as though God is appealing to you through us. We ask you fervently on behalf of the Messiah: Be reconciled to God" (2 Cor 5:20).

The New Testament reiterates this missional role that God's people are to play and calls them to a new self-understanding in Jesus. It is no longer about God's people apart from the nations. If the Old Testament from Genesis 12—Malachi focused narrowly on the creation and preparation of the people of God for the coming of the Messiah, Paul acts on the full implications of God's victory through Jesus for all creation and explains these through his writings. He makes it clear that the Gospel opens up membership in God's people without requiring the Gentiles to first become Jews. Paul begins his letter to the Christians in Rome memorably with a declaration of his calling as an apostle: "I am obligated to both Greeks and barbarians, both to the wise and unwise. Thusly, I am eager to proclaim the Gospel also to you in Rome. For I am not ashamed of the Gospel for it is the power of God for salvation to all who are believing, to the Jew first and then to the Greek" (Rom 1:4–16). Look at some words that may surprise you: "barbarians" and "unwise." It is not surprising that Paul reaches out to *outsiders* among the "wise" and the culturally superior "Greeks", but Paul recognizes that the Gospel is for *everyone*. Moreover, Paul sees the healing of the divisions between nations. In particular he emphasizes that the Gospel is for *Jews* and *Greeks*. In Eph 2:13–14, Paul declares the reconciliation of Jews and Gentiles, "But now in Messiah you, yourselves, who were once far away have become near by the blood of the Messiah. For he, himself, is our peace—the one who made both groups into one and has broken down in his flesh the wall of division that is the hostility between us."

In Jesus the Messiah, humanity finds its essential oneness. Jesus is the connector of all people. There is only *one* humanity. This recognition is crucial for a missional reading of the Bible. We must learn to speak of humans (rather than of Christians and non-Christians) and of the possibility of becoming truly human in Jesus the Messiah.

In like fashion, the other divisions between people: gender, class, and status disappear *in Jesus the Messiah*. The coming of Messiah ushers in a new future for all humanity. Paul articulates his thinking most succinctly in Gal 3:28, "There is no longer Jew or Greek, there is no longer slave or free person, there is no longer male or female. For all of you, regardless of ethnicity, social status, or sex, are one in Messiah Jesus." The Gospel subverts the societal and cultural norms that suffocate the potential that God has infused into all creation. Paul is not blind to the diversity in the world or even to the uniqueness of each human person. Rather, Paul is asserting that the Gospel makes it possible for a deeper unity in the Messiah that welcomes the other and creates a mosaic out of the fractured humanity of Genesis 3–11. This new mosaic offers a vision of a new humanity in Christ. Paul's vision is not a mono-cultural one that privileges any discrete expression of humanity. Paul understands the people of God as a body. Jesus is the head and each person serves the whole for the sake of God's mission. This reality is true, regardless of a person's sex, ethnicity, education, class, status, or nation of origin. Again, differences are not brushed aside. Unity is found in Messiah Jesus and his mission in the world. In our world today, this implies the importance of making tangible the potential for reconciliation between people. The Gospel says, "No" to all of our attempts to separate. To love God and neighbor implies the necessity of reconciliation on the human level. Reconciliation where animosity or even hatred existed is a potent testimony to the world of God's victory in Jesus the Messiah. Whenever reconciliation happens, God's people are announcing the fullest expression of God's kingdom and the future New Creation in advance. Revelation 5:9–10 describes this: "They sing a new song: 'You are worthy to receive the scroll and to open it seals. For you were slain and ransomed men and women for God with your blood from every tribe, language, people, and nation; you have made them for our God a kingdom and priests. They will reign on the earth.'" Notice in the language of Revelation an allusion back to the calling of God's redeemed people in Exodus at Sinai of living as a "kingdom of priests and a holy nation" (Exod 19:5–6).

God's work in Messiah Jesus also has profound implications for the healing of all creation. God appointed men and women as stewards over creation in Gen 1:26–31. This calling remains part of God's mission, but post-Genesis 3–11 God's mission is principally focused on the salvation of the pinnacle of his creative work—humanity created in his image. Jesus came to make us fully human again so that we can live as the people whom God created us to be: his hands, his feet, his mouthpieces for the world. But without a redeemed humanity there is little hope of humanity fulfilling God's original creation-focused mission. Paul also understands that God's victory in Jesus has cosmic implications. Jesus' resurrection and the gift of the Spirit announces the nearness of the full redemption of all creation (Rom 8:18–23).

Paul does not describe in detail what he specifically means by the full redemption of creation, but if we are to capture the Gospel in all of its richness we must gain a sense of Paul's cosmic vision. The future has come near in the person and work of Jesus the Messiah. This is the Good News that Paul spread across the Mediterranean world. This is the message that God's people today carry with them.

In conclusion, Paul proclaimed that the Gospel makes it possible for a full salvation that heals the disastrous effects of humanity's tragic choices sketched out in Genesis 3–11. God achieves this reconciliation through the life, death, and resurrection of Jesus the Messiah. As Paul writes in 2 Cor 5:17, "So if anyone is in Messiah, there is new creation! The old has passed away. Look the new has become reality." Once we begin to talk about new creation, we are poised to talk about the Bible's eschatological vision of the final act in the Biblical story.

New Creation

The New Testament witnesses to God's final victory over sin, injustice, and brokenness by announcing God's abundant future. Jesus' resurrection adumbrates New Creation. New Creation is nothing more and nothing less than the full consummation of God's Kingdom. It can be experienced in the present in part. This is the reason that Jesus can declare the kingdom's reality and demonstrate its power (Matt 4:17; Mark 1:13-15; Luke 4:16-21). Paul, likewise, can write, "If anyone is in Christ, there is new creation" (2 Cor 5:17). Thus, Jesus life, death, and resurrection indeed allows men and women to become clues to God's future in the present. But there is more.

The New Testament also offers a profound witness of the abundance still to come. The New Testament does not offer a detailed blow-by-blow description of how and when the end of days will arrive. A missional reading recognizes this. Instead of focusing on trying to predict the date, a missional reading listens attentively to the biblical text to hear its shaping and transforming word. When the New Testament speaks about the future, it does so as an *encouraging exhortation to faithfulness*. The life of faith is not easy. The Biblical narrative witnesses to persecutions and hardships. But the Bible's witness to New Creation serves to call God's people to a dogged commitment to faithful living in the present in the full confidence of a secure future in God's Kingdom.

The New Testament writers recognized that God's victory through the life, death, and resurrection of Jesus secured the future. The New Testament is full of visions of God's future. God's future is bright and good. It is one of abundant love and mercy. It is the full reversal of the effects of human sin and brokenness. It includes the full redemption of all creation. It marks the return of shalom and rest. It involves the climactic consummation of God's future.

A missional reading of the New Testament's eschatological vision steadfastly stands against all readings that promote a fixation on the assigning of times and dates as well as ones that call for a pullback from cultural engagement.

First, it is enough to note that if the Biblical story was truly interested in providing a detailed and specific step-by-step guide to how the future will unfold, it could have easily accomplished this. Given the absence of this as well as the humorous but ultimately tragic attempts by so many "prophesy" experts to predict Jesus' return, Christ followers will learn to live in a dynamic tension in which they recognize by faith that the future is secure while letting go of all need for details. On matters of the end, we are on a need-to-know basis and no matter how bad we might desire a roadmap to God's future, the Bible does not provide one. We follow Jesus into the world on mission. This is the same Jesus who said, "Concerning that day and hour no one knows, neither the angels of heaven nor the Son, except for the Father alone" (Matt 24:36).

Second, God's mission to bring reconciliation and redemption to humanity and all creation moves forward under God's promise of a secure future. Rather than giving Christ followers a reason to pull back from missional engagement, the New Testament church evangelized in earnest in the expectation of Jesus' imminent return and his ushering in of the Kingdom. God's future is beautiful. God's future is secure. Therefore, the mission of God's people goes forward. In the context of the New Testament, the earliest Christians were a tiny minority. They faced hardships and persecution for their allegiance to Jesus as LORD over and against the Roman world's suffocating vision for humanity. Early Christians found themselves persecuted and reviled by both Gentiles and Jews. Thus, the choice to follow Jesus was costly. The New Testament's eschatological vision, therefore, is profoundly concerned with grounding Jesus' earliest followers with a courageous hope in God's final victory so that they may function as instruments and agents of God's reconciling Gospel.

The structure of the book of Revelation epitomizes the missional undercurrent of the New Testament's eschatology. In Revelation 1–3, John reveals a message for seven discrete churches in the Mediterranean world. Depending on the needs of each faith community, John offers words of hope and rebuke. John's vision for these communities envisages them engaged in a vibrant and faithful witness for the Lordship of Jesus Christ. All of these communities are part of the Roman Empire whose oppressive and heavy-handed tactics often threatened the lives of early Christians. Also, all of these communities lived counter-culturally in urban areas that were saturated with syncretistic religious practices as well as official Emperor centric cultic expression. The temptation to slide back into their former pre-Christian spiritualties was always present. Yet, John boldly calls his churches to *faithful obedience*. John roots his call to faithfulness in an apocalyptic vision of God's final victory over sin, death, and the suffocating status quo of the kingdoms of this world (Rev 4–21).

Some Conclusions and Implications of the Big Picture:

The biblical narrative tells the story of Creation—Fall—Israel (God's New Humanity)—Jesus the Messiah—Church—New Creation.

1) *Mission is the common thread that unites the Old and New Testaments into the Christian Bible.* Seeing the Big Picture is essential for understanding the Holy Scriptures. This is not a call for a reading of Scripture that erases tensions.[13] Rather, the differing voices in Scripture point to the *missional* dimension of the Canon. Beeby argues, "Mission rarely occurs without conflict."[14] Tensions within Scripture serve as witnesses to God's call on people in various contexts to live faithfully. Different times, contexts, and cultures call for different emphases. Beeby writes:

> This biblical parliament includes wisdom books that differ greatly from the prophets. Within wisdom Job does not agree with Proverbs, and Ecclesiastes is out of tune with almost everybody. The prophets include Jeremiah and Isaiah who concur on much but differ considerably. . . . No wonder that some deny to [Scripture] any unity. But it has a unity: a unity in tension, a harmony of conflicting forces that can speak to all sorts and conditions of humanity, in all sorts and conditions of human joy and anguish. At times we must hear one voice more than others. In affluence we must hear the vocation to poverty, in strength we must be conscious of the power of weakness; severity must temper goodness and law nourish grace lest it become cheap.[15]

Think about some of the more famous tensions in Scripture: differences in created order in Gen 1:1—2:3 and 2:4–25 or the different perspectives on faith and works found in Paul's letter to Galatians and the writings of James. Does not reading these in the larger framework of God's mission place the relationship of these texts in a new light? Rather than seeing the Bible as hopelessly diverse and without any center, an

---

13. For an excellent study on the diversity within the OT see Goldingay, *Theological Diversity and the Authority of the Old Testament.*

14. Beeby, "Missional Approach," 279.

15. Ibid.

emphasis on the mission of God serves as the light that brings out the true beauty and unity of the kaleidoscope of Scripture.

The review of the Big Picture of the Old and New Testament suggests that Scripture forms a story. It is the story of the Mission of God from Creation—Fall—Israel—Jesus—Church—New Creation in which the Creating and Redeeming God invites humanity to live as the people of God for the world.

Theologian Robert Jensen observes:

"Scripture's story is not part of some larger narrative; it is itself the larger narrative of which all other true narratives are parts. And so do not when reading Scripture try to figure out how what you are reading fits into some larger story; for there is no larger story."[16]

2) *All of Creation matters to God.* God's ultimate mission is the full redemption of all creation. As we saw, the Bible begins with a creation which God himself evaluates as "very good" (Gen 1:31). This "very good" creation is undone in part by human sin (Genesis 3–11, note specifically the cursing of the earth in the aftermath of the disobedience of Adam and Eve in Gen 3:17–19; cf. Rom 8:18–23). Likewise, the New Testament ends with a testimony of a New Heavens and a New Earth, including the creation of a New Jerusalem which functions as the focal point of God's ultimate reign.

God's love for creation implies a sufficient ground for a missional theology that is worldly in at least three respects:

First, *humans remain God's stewards over creation*—creatures, plants, and inanimate material. It is contrary to Scripture to participate in the abuse of Creation. The care of God's creation is part of the missio dei.

Second, in the post-Genesis 3–11 reality in which we find ourselves, *the world remains the context in which the present mission will occur.* The tension in Scripture involves the issue of the universal love of God for the world and his particular election of Israel to serve as God's distinct people "his treasured possession" (Exod 19:4–6; Deut 7:6 cf. Titus 2:14 and 1 Pet 2:9). To some, the particular election of Israel is a theological problem around the issue of fairness. What about the rest of the world? Does God only care for Israel? The Old Testament confronts this head on by beginning the way that it does. Scripture opens up with

---

16. Jensen, "Scripture's Authority," 34.

a universal scope. Genesis 1–11 is not about Israel but about the world. The call of Abraham in Genesis 12 is a move from the universal to the particular in terms of the narrative, but not in terms of its intent. The call of Abraham is to a single family, but it is ultimately a call to servanthood as the agents through whom God will bless the nations. Genesis 12:3b reads, "... all peoples on earth will be blessed through you."

The Mosaic Torah serves to function as the authoritative core of the Old Testament witness. It fundamentally serves as a polity for the people of God. This polity includes living in harmony with God's creational intentions, which involves humanity's mission to share God's blessings with all creation. As Christians, we may find the word "sacrament" to be helpful here. God's desire for the people of God is for them to serve as a sacrament, a means of grace, to the world. Paul seems aware of this necessity in his great chapter on reconciliation in 2 Corinthians 5. After writing, "Therefore if anyone is in Christ, there is a New Creation; the old has gone, the new has come!" (v. 17), he immediately turns to role that the "new creation" has for the rest of creation—"All this is from God who reconciled us to himself through Christ and gave us the ministry of reconciliation" (v. 18). In other words, God's response to Fall has been to call a people to serve the world (especially other humans) on behalf of the Creator. This is a *worldly* vocation.

Last, *mission began at creation*, and not merely after the Fall. Even before human sin entered the world, there was mission. God's creative acts in Genesis 1 serve as a model of this. God's actions are purposeful. He creates the "very good" ordered world out of the raw material described in Hebrew as *tohu wabohu* "a formless void" (Gen 1:2). Even humanity is given a missional function at creation. Humanity, forged in the image of God, is to reflect God's character in its vocation of care over Creation and in its filling of Creation (Gen 1:26–31).

3) Rather than talking about a "biblical basis for missions" we should affirm, as Chris Wright suggests a "missional basis for the Bible."[17] Scriptures through the power of the Holy Spirit continues to call the Church today to participate in God's mission. Mission is the reason for which the Church continues to exist. It is the role of each individual church and each individual Christian to find his or her vocation in light of this reality. Ostensibly, mission will continue on even in the New Heavens

---

17. Wright, *Mission of God*, 22.

(RE)Aligning with God

and the New Earth as humanity empowered by the Holy Spirit fulfills God's original creational intentions.

4) We need to learn a new way of reading the Bible that reemphasizes the *missional center* of Scripture. It can no longer function primarily as a source of private piety. We need to relearn to read Scripture through a missional lens in which those who already follow Jesus are shaped into missionary witnesses and those who are not following Jesus are invited to full participation in the only community that truly exists for the benefit of the world.

PART TWO

Learning to Speak Human:
Reading the Bible for All People

5

Learning to Speak Human: Methodology and Missional Hermeneutics

"The difference between the right word and the almost right word is the difference between lightning and a lightning bug."
—MARK TWAIN

"Think like a wise man but communicate in the language of the people."
—WILLIAM BUTLER YEATS

It is vital to understand the grand story narrated in the Christian Scriptures. This is the b*eginning* of realigning with God, but we have to go deeper. As Christ followers it is vital that we understand the big picture. The next challenge is to begin working through individual passages and books to study them in-depth. The true Biblicist is able to alternate between an eagle's eye view of the broad shape of the Scriptures and the ground level investigation of its smallest pieces. Both are essential.[1] Without the big picture, we run the danger of atomizing the biblical text into isolated, unrelated fragments. Without the ground-level view we risk missing the discrete witness

---

1. Ironically, both historical criticism and some recent evangelical approaches may be critiqued for fragmenting the text. Historical-critical methods atomize the final form of the text into smaller units of tradition. Likewise the average Christ follower in a Bible church often hears only a tiny portion of Scripture during the weekly sermon and the text is rarely read within its context.

of individual texts and proclaiming an ideological or theological system instead of the full counsel of God's Word.

The goal of the Bible is the conversion of its readers and hearers. The Scriptures call for a (re)alignment with God's creational intentions in light of the life, death, and resurrection of Jesus as the climactic moment of the biblical narrative. This realignment is a conversion to our true humanity as a missional community that reflects God's character in Creation, for Creation, and to Creation. All of this is for the glory and adoration of God.

Biblical interpretation must take seriously the overarching missional framework of the Scriptures. This framework does not dictate the meaning of any individual passage, but it is vital for understanding the function of an individual text within the Bible as a whole.

As we move now to reflect on a method for reading the Scriptures wisely[2], we need to remind ourselves of the contours of the Scriptures. The Bible tells God's story and invites humanity into a dynamic and saving relationship with the God of the Scriptures. It is a saving relationship between God and humanity. As our review of the Scriptural story demonstrated, humanity is lost apart from the mission of God to deliver women and men to wholeness and reconciliation. Jesus' life, death, and resurrection is the culmination of God's work. But our reconciliation with God is merely the doorway to God's vision for life. We are saved *from* sin and brokenness, but profoundly we are saved *for* God. Before sin entered the world, humanity lived as the *imago dei* for the sake of Creation. The saving work of Jesus recreates this reality. Our salvation in Jesus Christ ushers us into a new dynamic life in the power of the Holy Spirit.

This new life may be understood in light of our GPS rubric:

Global/Local Mission

God's people exist for God's mission of extending blessing to the nations and justice/righteousness to Creation. In fulfillment of God's creational intentions for a humanity that fills the earth as witnesses of God's glory and embodiments of God's grace and peace, Christ followers realign themselves for full participation in God's mission.

---

2. For reflection on reading wisely, see Briggs, *Reading the Bible Wisely*.

People in Community

God's people are a *community*. There is no biblical understanding of the solitary Christ follower. We are made for one another. The Old and New Testament narrate the story of a people called to serve in God's mission. The community is marked by its vocation as a missional community. It exists as God's people for the sake of the nations.

Spiritually Transformed

God's people are to reflect the character and ethos of the Triune God. Persons in relationship with God are to serve as "little Jesus's."[3] Christ followers are now cleansed and empowered by the Spirit to live as the people whom God created them to be. This is the epitome of the biblical narrative's consistent and persistent call to holiness of heart and life.

In short, God's people serve as a *missional community that embodies and reflects God's character to/for/in the nations*. The Christian life cannot be compartmentalized. GPS reminds us that mission, community, and character must be held together in an interdependent balance. God's global mission may be thwarted by a lack of community or character. In fact, if God's people on mission do not adequately reflect God's character, we must question whether or not they are on God's mission. Likewise, any conception of holiness that is solitary in its practice and unengaged from the work of witness in the world is inadequate. God's people are holy precisely so that they can create authentic community and serve as God's witnesses in the most ungodly places on earth. Our conception of community must be intricately bound to mission and holiness.

When we read Scripture carefully in its contexts and ponder its role in God's larger story of salvation, the Bible will confront us continually with God's call to (re)align with God's mission through the GPS. Moreover, this is not merely a message for those who are already insiders to the Gospel message. Scripture must also be read for those whom God desires to reach with his grace and mercy. The Scriptures issue an invitation to those on the outside so that they may become part of the people of God. In the following pages, I will unpack a rubric for interpreting the Scriptures for the Church and the World.

---

3. Frost and Hirsch, *Rejesus*, 6.

(RE)ALIGNING WITH GOD

Reading from a New Location

Scholarship has demonstrated the powerful influence of a reader's social location. Social location or the context in which one reads the text plays a key factor in how one hears the message of a text. The danger is turning a text into a mirror in which we see ourselves rather than experience Scripture's drive to shape us and invite us to receive its Lord and embody his ethos.

What do I mean by this? As readers we bring our gender, our theological commitments, our political beliefs, our socio-economic status, our geographical location, our age, our education, and all of our varying experiences with life, culture, and world to the text. Postmodern approaches to the Scripture have argued against the possibility of a neutral or unbiased social location.

A missional approach to the Scriptures is acutely aware of the complexity of the interpretive process and the subtle danger of the reader's situatedness in reading the Bible. But instead of despairing, a missional approach advocates a two-fold response.

First, it is vital for readers to be aware of their blind spots and presuppositions. What are blind spots? These are the unstated assumptions about life, God, and the world that we as interpreters bring to the table. Here are some of the categories that can influence us: age, ethnicity, sex, socioeconomic level, political persuasion, theology, and geographic location.

For example, when I teach a course on the book of Exodus, there is always intensive conversation around the issue of Pharaoh's hard heart. The backdrop to this conversation is the on-going theological debate over individual predestination. Most of my students are Arminian so they have a tendency to view Pharaoh as the cause of his own hard-heartedness. I can imagine students at a Reformed seminary reading the text as the story of a sovereign God electing Pharaoh to live in a state of rebellion/intransigence to God. Either of these options are possible interpretations, but as more recent interpreters have demonstrated, the issue is more nuanced and complex than the theological category of personal predestination.[4]

We must become self-aware of our blinders by reading widely (including positions that challenge our beliefs) and establishing a broad based network of friends and acquaintances. Our networks must include both Christ-followers and non-Christ-followers. Ideally it will include ethnic diversity and some balance between the genders.

---

4. For example, see Fretheim, *Exodus*, 96–103; and Ford, *God, Pharaoh, and Moses*.

Second, a missional approach to the Scriptures requires that the readers find common ground with the ancient text by adopting and locating themselves in God's mission.[5] In Part I, we argued that humanity's role in God's mission is to serve as a missional community that exists to reflect God's character to/for/in Creation. In the post-Genesis 3 reality, this involves the on-going witness to Creation but also specifically the need to extend God's blessing and message of reconciliation to the nations. The biblical narrative in the Old Testament details the potential and pitfalls of living as God's people for the world. With the life, death, and resurrection of Jesus the Messiah, the full engagement of the nations begins. The Gospels and Acts detail the missional movement of Jesus and the Apostles to carry the Gospel to those who have not yet heard. Each book of the New Testament was written to a community to instruct those fledging Gospel outposts to live faithfully as God's people for the world.[6]

The clear implication is this: if we are to read the Scriptures for all they seek to accomplish in and through our lives, we must consciously and physically locate ourselves in God's mission. Michael Frost and Alan Hirsch in their seminal book *The Shaping of Things to Come: Innovation and Mission for the 21st-Century Church* created two helpful diagrams that capture the needed shift in our reading and ministry location. In the first figure, they illustrate the Christendom model for understanding the relationship between God, Church, and World.[7] In this figure, the World is understood as a dangerous place, lost and apart from God. The Church only engages the World out of necessity. Christ followers live and work in the World, but their focus is on encountering God in the Church. Only well-trained professionals or persons with evangelism gifts engage the world with the Gospel. The intersection of the Church and God is the safe place where Christ followers seek refuge from the world through encountering and worshipping God. This is a dualistic understanding of the relationship between God, Church, and World. Reading the Scripture in such a context emphasizes biblical knowledge apart from God's mission to reach the world. The Bible may be studied and revered, but it is rarely unleashed among God's people to call them to realign with God's work. Moreover, the reading of Scripture in a place detached from the world runs the risk of irrelevancy. Our world desperately needs to hear the Gospel. Yet, when opportunities come to

---

5. Barram, "Bible, Mission, and Social Location," 42–58.
6. Guder, "Missional Pastors," 4.
7. Frost and Hirsch, *Shaping of Things to Come*, 157.

communicate, if we have cloistered ourselves too much, we may find that we lack the capacity to speak clearly in ways that connect the power of the Word with the world.

Given the realities of our changing world, it is vital for followers of Christ to reflect deeply on what it means to read Scripture in light of God's mission. Again, Frost and Hirsch can help us. In a second figure, they move to a biblical and more dynamic model for understanding the relationship between God, Church, and World.[8]

They argue for a location in the intersection of God, the Church, and World. It is at this nexus point that biblical interpreters must station themselves to stand in continuity with the social location of the biblical authors. We may call this area the borderlands.[9] As interpreters, we must learn to situate ourselves in this borderland where the God of mission is already present and read the Scriptures for both the Church and World. The borderlands is the place where outsider and insider stand on equal footing.

To read the Scriptures in the borderlands requires a paradigm shift on the part of interpreters. We are used to reading the Bible devotionally for our own personal development and edification. We are skilled at studying the Bible for use in the Church among persons who already share our commitments or who are at least too polite to challenge traditional Christian readings. We are masters of bringing safe questions to the text. But a move to the borderlands forces readers of the Bible to confront the challenge of communicating the Gospel in a contested area. How do the Scriptures speak to the homeless teen? How do you communicate the Gospel to the thirty-year old Muslim woman that you encounter? How do we teach our children to read and talk about Scripture in the increasingly multi-cultural contexts in which they find themselves? It is vital for leaders who desire to lead their communities of faith to make an impact on the surrounding culture to begin to listen to Scripture with new eyes and ears shaped by questions that *outsiders* raise.

Following the suggestion of a colleague, Walter Brueggemann believes that seminarians need to learn how to preach by engaging in street

---

8. Ibid., 158.

9. I first heard the term "borderlands" as a metaphor for missional engagement from Carlos F. Cardoza-Orlandi several years ago in a faculty retreat for the Florida faculty of Asbury Theological Seminary. He hints at this metaphor in his essay "Lampara es a mis pies tu palabra," 27–35. For another text on reading Scripture in the borderlands, see Ekblad, *Reading the Bible with the Damned*.

preaching.[10] Brueggemann gives two reasons for this proposal. First, in street preaching one's claims are *contested* in ways that normally do not occur within the "safe" environment of the Church. There will be no "preaching to the choir." On the street the crowd may heckle the speaker. The possibility of *contested* speech necessitates a *missional* reading that attempts to communicate directly with the world rather than merely edifying those already comfortable with the claims of the Church. Second, in street preaching one will face the "So what?" question. What does it matter if Jesus died on the cross? How does this make my life different in the twenty-first century? So what that the Bible is a Holy Book? How is it different from other inspired writings and holy books? Why should I believe the claims of the Gospel?

I moved to Central Florida in 2000 so that I might serve on the faculty of Asbury Theological Seminary's Orlando campus. When I arrived in mid-July, I found our new home's lawn in desperate need for a cutting. The grass was over a foot high, and I did not even own a mower. My first day in Florida was spent driving to Sears to purchase one. I went to buy a lawn mower and instead gained a powerful experience about the borderlands. I entered the Sear's store on a Saturday morning and navigated my way to the tool section. As I pulled a card and prepared to place an order, I suddenly realized that I was unable to understand a single word being spoken by the sales staff and the other customers. They were all conversing in Spanish. For the first time in my life I was able to identify for a few moments what it feels like to be part of a minority culture. I was no longer with the center of culture but on the margins. As we, in the Church, seek to engage our culture with the Gospel we need to recognize fully that we are no longer in a position of privilege in the world. The hegemony of Christendom is over. The Gospel was never intended to be contained only within the sphere of the Church. It is time now for us as readers of the Bible to locate ourselves outside of our privileged places of refuge in our sanctuaries, studies, and homes and spend time reading the Bible in the borderlands where God, the World, and the Church intersect. This may be initially disconcerting or even jarring, but it will result in a fresh reading of the Bible that will place us closer to the location of the initial readers of Scripture. We will begin to learn to read the Scriptures for both insiders and outsiders. This will lead to new questions, new readings, and a (re)conversion to the world described in the Scriptures.

10. Brueggemann, "First Retrospect," 346.

(re)Learning to Read

There is no substitute for a careful and deliberate engagement with the biblical text. The Scriptures may be likened to the earth's vast oceans. There are multiple levels and depths of meaning. If one only studies the seas from a single shoreline, one may observe and record accurate observations but much will be missed. It is vital for interpreters to go as deeply as possible into the text and to read it carefully from a variety of angles in order to engage it in its fullness. This book focuses on a missional approach to the Bible, but such an approach *assumes* a deep engagement with the text. I will turn now to a brief introduction, or perhaps refresher, on good reading practices.

The primary determinant for the meaning of a text is its context. Lawson Stone, my first Old Testament teacher, used to say coyly, "Any interpretation must be able to survive at least one close reading of the text." It is vital to read the Bible in large chunks rather than in isolated verses. Reading Scripture is an intimate dance between the reader and the text. The wise reader must be acutely aware simultaneously of the broad movements of the wider Scriptures *and* the specific details of the portion of text being interpreted. To focus only on the big picture risks missing the nuances of the Bible, which fill out and unpack its larger truths in the lived lives of its original audience. The temptation is to flatten out the Bible by making its individual sections conform to our assumptions about the big picture. To focus only on the specific details runs the danger of missing the message of the whole. It is like having a closet without hangers or shelves. All of our clothing is scattered randomly without any discernible organizing principles.

Reading Wisely and Well

Steps to achieving a close reading of a passage in its Scriptural context[11]:

1) Pray for the illumination of the Holy Spirit. Prayer is vital for engaging the Scriptures. My working assumption is that the Bible is inspired by God, preserved by God, and illuminated by God. Thus, we must pray for

---

11. I present what follows as a primer on biblical interpretation. It is by no means exhaustive. For those wanting a more comprehensive introduction to exegesis, see Klein et al., *Introduction to Biblical Interpretation*; or Gorman, *Elements of Biblical Exegesis*.

God's guidance. Moreover, let us pray that God may astonish us anew with the riches of the text.

2) Assume the posture of a servant before the text. Do not read the text with the goal of mastering it. Read the text in the hope that it will master you.

3) Read slowly. Take your time. This is particularly true for familiar passages. One of the causes of poor interpretation is the assumption that the reader already *knows* the meaning of the biblical text. Reflect on the genre of the passage. Is the text a narrative, a genealogy, prophesy, poetry, a parable, or discursive literature? If you have the ability to study the text in the original languages, do it. Reading the text in Greek or Hebrew forces the reader to slow down naturally. Regardless, ponder the words and phrases used by the author. In the popular imagination and practice, interpreting Scripture is a matter of flipping back and forth to other parts of the Bible in order to understand what a given text is saying.[12] Resist this. Stay put within the confines of the text you are studying. Describe it. Dissect it. Notice how the individual words are connected together into a tapestry. Paraphrase it. Analyze it. Observe recurring words, phrases, ideas, and themes. Break it into its logical or thematic units. Reflect on how the narrative or author's thinking progresses. Don't give up. Commit yourself to being like Jacob who refused to let go of God until he received a blessing. Biblical interpretation does not really begin until you have engaged the text in a process of careful and sustained reading and reflection. The process will be generative in terms of insights and the framing of new questions. The wise interpreter continually captures insights and observations through careful note-taking.

4) Ask questions of the text. Engaged reading involves much more than note-taking. Over time I have discovered that the best interpreters of the Scripture were those men and women who asked the most penetrating questions. The process of reading the text carefully and recording a series of observations and questions is the secret to engaging the Bible

---

12. This is a profound misappropriation and misunderstanding of the dictum: "Scripture interprets Scripture." Of course this is true. But the principal assumes that one has already carefully studied a text within its original context and found its meaning elusive. Only then does the interpreter turn to other passages where the meaning may be clearer and instructive for understanding our first text.

at a deep level.[13] In many ways, biblical interpretation is nothing more and nothing less than the answering of interpretive questions that the reader asks about the text. Observations lead to questions, and questions guide the interpreter to new insights. Ask questions that engage the text at three levels: Definition, Function, and Implications. Definitional questions attempt to gain a full description of the content of the text ("What's here?" "What is the precise and specific meaning of each element that is present?"). Functional questions focus on the "So what?" of the issue. Implicational questions attempt to probe beneath the surface to ferret out the deep meaning. Let me offer an example. If we are studying Exod 19:4–6, we will encounter a phrase that is unique in the Old Testament. In verse 6, we find, ". . . you will be a kingdom of priests and a holy nation." The twin noun phrases "kingdom of priests" and "a holy nation" are critical for the interpretation of this text. Regarding the phrases, we may ask the following *definitional questions:* What is the precise and specific meaning of the phrases "kingdom of priests" and "a holy nation"? What is the relationship between these two phrases? Definitional questions are followed by *functional* ones: Why are these particular phrases being used here? What is their significance? Finally we end with *implicational* questions: What are the full implications of our findings for understanding the theology and assumptions of Exod 19:4–6? What does Exod 19:4–6 assume to be true?

5) Read multiple translations. I recommend that interpreters use at least three different translations during the process of close reading. Make sure that you choose translations from different translational families. For example, little is gained by comparing the KJV with the NKJV. Avoid paraphrases. At minimum, the deployment of multiple translations will serve as a guard against a simple misunderstanding of the English. But more importantly, comparing translations will guide you to the seams that exist between translations. By seams, I mean those places where the exegetical difficulties present in the original show up in the form of tensions between translations that otherwise remain hidden underneath the uniformity of a given English translation. Look specifically for *substantive differences* between translations. Make sure that you

---

13. I have been formed immeasurably through Inductive Bible Study as taught at Asbury Theological Seminary. Seminal texts include: Robert Traina, *Methodical Bible Study*; David L. Thompson, *Bible Study that Works*; and Traina and Bauer, *Inductive Bible Study*.

understand the interpretive options presented by the different translations. Ask: How do the differences in translation change the meaning of the passage? For example, Gen 1:1 reads classically in the KJV, "In the beginning God created the heavens and the earth." In some modern translations, v. 1 is understood as a clause dependent on the verse or verses that follow. The NRSV is representative of newer translational approaches, "In the beginning, when God created the heavens and the earth, . . ."[14] At stake here are questions of the biblical understanding of cosmology and its relationship to its ancient near eastern context.[15] Reflect on the ways that the differences in translation seem to resolve interpretive issues.

6) Reflect on the meaning of individual words. A couple of warnings: a) Don't assume that you understand the meaning of words. When in doubt, always spend the time in word study. b) Don't abuse the principal of "Scripture interprets Scripture" in defining words. It is folly to cite the meaning of a term used by one author when we are studying the writing of another. A classic example is the definition of *faith*. The writer of the Hebrews explicitly describes *faith* (Grk: *pistis*) in this manner: "Now faith is being sure of what we hope for and certain of what we do not see" (Heb 11:1). Without a doubt, this is one of the clearest definitions of *pistis* in the Bible, but it is methodologically problematic to accept this as *the* definition of *pistis* in every other context. Words have meanings in relationship to the other words around them. Moreover, each biblical author may emphasize a different nuance of a word's meaning. c) Don't mistake common English definitions for a word for the meaning of a Greek or Hebrew term. For example, the Great Commandment or Shema contains a number of words that can be misinterpreted in translation. Deuteronomy 6:5, which reads in English translation, "Love the LORD your God with all your heart and with all your soul and with all your strength." Popular interpretations read these common English terms through a matrix more in line with Greek psychology and modern romantic sentiment than with Deuteronomy's own ancient context. Study of the Hebrew (and cognate) usage suggests that "love" is in fact

---

14. The NRSV lists two additional alternatives in footnotes: "When God began to create . . ." and "In the beginning God created . . ."

15. For discussion of the four principal ways on construing Gen 1:1–3, see Fretheim, *God and the World*, 35.

a covenant term exhorting committed obedience. "Heart" focuses on the center of human volition and rationality and not on the center of emotions. "Soul" is not the spiritual aspect or the "authentic" core of a human person, but instead Hebrew *nephesh* is descriptive of the totality of a person including the physical body. "Strength" is really better translated "everything else" or even "and then some" as it functions to intensify the seriousness and totality of the call to love God. Moreover, rather than suggesting three parallel spheres or attributes of loving God, "heart," "soul," and "strength" form a concentric structure that emphasizes to a superlative degree the whole-person commitment involved in "loving the LORD."[16]

7) Read each passage in its broader book context. We have used two metaphors for talking about reading the Scripture at different levels. We've emphasized the necessity of both an eagle's eye view of the Scriptures and a ground level analysis of individual passages. Individual books serve as the middle ground.[17] This involves more work for the interpreter, but the payoff is immense. First, look for connections. Take time to look for other places in the same book where the author deploys the same words and phrases (or close synonyms). Such repetitions or recurrences are often purposeful and can lead to substantive insights. For example, in Phil 3:1–16 Paul offers his own life as an example for the Philippian believers to emulate (3:17). When he is describing the zeal of his pre-Christ following life in 3:6, he boasts that he was a "persecutor of the church."[18] In Phil 3:7–11 Paul recounts the dramatic transformation that he experienced through knowing Christ. This transformation moved Paul from a person rooted and secure in a righteousness derived from his own credentials and accomplishments to a person rooted in a righteousness through Jesus the Messiah. In 3:14 Paul articulates a

---

16. See the masterful exegetical study of the manifold issues present in the text by McBride, "Yoke of the Kingdom," 273–306.

17. There is another intermediate level as well: corpus context. Books written by the same authors or redacted by the same community function in a way similar to book context in terms of helping to understand smaller passages and themes. For example, a passage in Galatians serves a role in the book of Galatians, but it also contributes to our understanding of Paul's other letters. The same would be true of passages in Luke-Acts, John and John's Letters, Ezra-Nehemiah, the Pentateuch, and the Deuteronomistic History.

18. Grk *dioko*

moment-by-moment orientation to life through Jesus by writing, "I am pressing on continually toward the goal to win the prize of the upward calling of God in Messiah Jesus." The phrase "pressing on" is the same Greek word typically translated "persecute" in 3:6. Observing this connection offers a real insight into the transformation of Paul. Paul, as a Christ follower is no less zealous in his faith than he was as a Pharisee. But Paul has undergone a radical reorientation. His compass point has shifted to the Risen Jesus. Paul surrendered his pre-Christian rubric of a righteousness rooted in his own abilities and accomplishments for the ultimate prize—knowing Messiah Jesus. When knowing Jesus became Paul's primary focus, Paul's gifts and graces became a means of glorifying and honoring Jesus rather than a means of boasting of himself to others. Second, it is vital to make sure that we understand a discrete text's function within the broader book. What contribution does our text play in the wider contours of the book? What would be lost or gained without it? How does it relate to the passages that precede and follow it? For example, Matt 4:17 begins a major section of Matthew's Gospel.[19] Jesus begins his public ministry by announcing the in-breaking new age of God's saving reign, and by exhorting his hearers to realign themselves continually in light of the Kingdom. This verse serves as a general programmatic statement for understanding 4:17—16:20. To understand fully every discrete section requires that the reader reflect on how it informs a way of life in line with the Kingdom of heaven and that one realign one's life in conformity to the vision of the text. In 8:1–17 Jesus models boundary-breaking acts of ministry with outsiders. This is no mere report of Jesus' historical acts. It serves as a paradigm for shaping present and future followers of Jesus to live out the ethos of the kingdom of heaven.

8) Read each passage within its broader canonical context. Texts do not exist in isolation from other texts. There are often multiple conversations taking place within the Bible between texts. In particular, it is vital to recognize and explore the ways in which the texts that we are studying stand in dialogue with other texts written before or after. For example, in its majestic praise of God, Psalm 8 looks back on the creation of humanity and God's granting of dominion in Gen 1:26–31 as a profound basis for worshipping God. As we interpret Psalm 8 it is vital to catch

---

19. Bauer, *Structure of Matthew's Gospel*.

its connection back to Genesis and reflect on the way that Genesis informs our understanding of Psalm 8 (and vice versa). But there is more to Psalm 8. The writer to the Hebrews in chapter 2 verses 5–9 quotes Ps 8:4–6 in part of his proclamation of the person and work of Jesus the Messiah. Thus, in understanding the meaning of Psalm 8 within its canonical context it is important to read it in conversation with both Genesis 1 and Hebrews 2. Likewise, this is also the case with a reading of Genesis 1 or Hebrews 2. However, not every biblical text will have explicit links to other passages as is the case with Psalm 8.

9) Establish a research agenda to engage secondary resources. Thus far, we have described the process of engaging a biblical text first hand through the practice of close reading. The best close readings do not provide the final word on a text. As suggested, many of our best observations raise additional questions. Some questions can be answered through the close reading process, but others will require the use of the fruits of biblical scholarship. After you have pondered over the text using your own observation skills, ask yourself: What are the key questions that remain unanswered that I need to resolve in order to understand this passage of Scripture? At this point, the wise interpreter will turn to resources such as Bible dictionaries, atlases, theological word books, grammar and syntax texts, journal articles, and commentaries.

10) Use the best resources at your disposal. In the age of information, Internet search engines can quickly inundate an interpreter with more data than one could process in a lifetime. Biblical interpreters must learn to read all reference material *critically*. We must also eschew the *tyranny of the available* and commit ourselves to using the finest resources so that we are engaging the best exegetical minds and not merely dialoging with those resources that make it onto the first screen pages of web searches. In general, such a commitment involves resisting popular authors and the latest fads for the commentaries and articles written by biblical scholars and for works by the classic interpreters of the past (early Church Fathers, the Reformers, John Wesley among others). It is critically important to use up-to-date Bible dictionaries and atlases so that one has access to the most recent discoveries as our understanding of the socio-historical background of the world of the Bible grows annually. Given the missional reality in which we find ourselves, we need

to deploy the best and most penetrating resources in order to engage the text at the level that we need in our day.

Key Questions to Ponder:

1) Have I prayed for the Spirit's guidance and direction?

2) Do I understand the geographical and/or cultural references in this passage?

3) How does our text function within the wider argument in the book?

4) What are the key words and phrases in the text? How are these words and phrases used elsewhere by our author?

5) If I am working on a New Testament text: What Old Testament texts are alluded to or quoted? How does the OT passage illuminate the meaning of the text I am interpreting? For OT texts: Are there quotations or allusions to other texts in the OT? If so, how do the texts illuminate one another? Is there a NT appropriation of my text? How does the NT author understand the OT text?

6) How is my passage structured? How does the structure of the passage contribute to its meaning? Does the passage flow logically? How does the story flow spacially? How do the characters function within the story?

7) For those with facility in Hebrew, Aramaic, and Greek: What nuances are present in the syntax and the word order of the original language that are ambiguous or not explicit in the modern translations? Pay particular attention to verbal aspect and force of prepositions.

8) What are the major interpretive issues present in this text? How are these resolved in the major English translations?

9) What are the possible ways that we may *misread* the text based on the English text?

10) What is the genre of my text (narrative, parable, discursive, prophetic, apocalyptic)? How does the genre affect my understanding of the passage?

11) What does this text assume to be true? How do these assumptions affect our reading of the text?

12) What elements in the text *may be offensive* in our contemporary context? What issues raised will be difficult for *insiders*? What issues in the text will be difficult for *outsiders*? What are the obvious objections that one could raise to the claims of the text? In what ways does the text answer these objections?

Remembering the Audience

The imago dei is the starting point for the communication of the Gospel. Since all persons bear the image of God we are never without a basis for sharing the Scriptural story. God created humanity to serve as a missional community that exists to reflect and embody God's character to/for/in Creation. The Gospel calls all its hearers to realign themselves continually in light of the Scriptural story. In other words, realignment involves moving toward life as God intended. As we suggested in Part One, conversion may be understood as the process of becoming human again.

Since God is calling us to return to the essence of our humanity in the Scriptures, our GPS rubric will keep us on target. The GPS gives us a starting point for engaging human beings with the message of the Scriptures rather than thinking of our audience in the competing camps of Christian and non-Christian (or insider/outsider).

But the wise interpreter must also be aware of potential roadblocks as well as minefields that complicate the communication process. We have already stressed the importance of reading the text from the context of the borderland where God, church, and world overlap. Now that we have focused on a careful and close reading of the biblical text we can return to the challenges of communicating the Scriptural truth in our day. The dual context of Church and World offer their own challenges as we read the Scriptures.

Learning to Speak Human

Challenges for Reading for the Church

The assumption of over-familiarity with the text: There is a danger whenever a familiar text is preached or taught that some in the audience will disconnect because they've already heard it all before. This temptation lurks in the heart of the interpreter as well. Sometimes the key to reading a text is simply to ponder a familiar text more carefully. Allow the text to *astonish* you anew. To refocus on a text with which you are well-acquainted, try asking this question: *If this were the only passage of Scripture that I had, what would I know?* This sort of question channels our attention toward the details of the text. We may be surprised by what we find.

Ignorance of the biblical text is the opposite but equally real issue in the Church. The loss of Scriptural memory within the Church is well known. This is true for both evangelical and mainline congregations. Twenty-first-century missional leaders have the task in many congregations of (re)teaching the Scriptures to persons who have never been fed a steady diet of Scripture. There will always be a tension between those who know the Bible and those who don't. The wise interpreter remains committed to reading Scripture for the purpose of communicating its truths clearly and cogently. Being sensitive to those who do not understand or know much about the Bible is not a move toward "dumbing down" messages. But it is a move to taking seriously the *audience* of our teaching and preaching. As a seminary professor, I often warn my students of the dangers of forgetting the audience. I have routinely heard seminarians and seminary-trained pastors use their teaching/preaching time as an opportunity to display their sophisticated theological vocabulary. One of my favorite questions for my students is this: To whom was your message addressed? I routinely hear pastors referring to texts without explanation by scholarly or traditional names such as Carmen Christi, or Christ Hymn for Phil 2:5–11, or the Song of the Sea for Exod 15:1–21, or the Yahwist's Creation story for Gen 2:4–25. My rule of thumb is this: Don't use technical terms *unless* they are absolutely necessary and on the condition that you carefully explain or define them for your audience. I would rather be understood than for people to be impressed merely by my erudition. Again this is not a call to dumb-down messages; it is begging for exegetes and communicators of the Gospel to speak *human* rather than deploying language that is foreign to the audience. The goal of a missional reading is not to water down Scripture, but to help women and men to hear clearly and powerfully the message of the Bible.

(RE)ALIGNING WITH GOD

Unleashing the Scriptures in our churches may also be hindered by a fear of controversy or of sounding heretical. The Scriptural call to *conversion* and *(re)alignment* is a serious one. It calls for life transformation, courageous living, and counter-cultural stances. The missional leader who begins to preach and teach the full story of the Bible in bold and daring ways, may find himself or herself accused of causing undue controversy within the community of faith or even of proclaiming heretical ideas. The biblical call to mission, holiness, and community will often sound *new* and *radical* in communities who have embraced or grown use to hearing a *status quo* Christianity, a middle-class Gospel, a politicized message (left or right wing), a feel good easy-believe-ism talk, or any other form of the Gospel that does not seek to (re)align its hearers continuously into a missional community that reflects God's character to, for, and in the world. The call to *mission* will often sound radical, but it is profoundly biblical to the core.

Reading the Bible in the Church creates a tendency to play it safe with the Bible. When a preacher or teacher typically only addresses insiders, it is easy to fall into stale patterns and preach the same basic message over and over again. The audience knows what to expect from the speaker. The pastor is often faced with the issues of offending Church members. This may result in messages that may be Gospel-oriented and even biblically centered, but they fail to push the community of faith to (re)align fully with the mission that God has for his people. The issue is often text selection. *What texts are selected for teaching and preaching? Who decides on the texts? What is the basis of the selection? Do God's people hear the overarching story of the Scripture regularly? Are both the Old and New Testaments used within the community? What parts of the Bible are being neglected? Why?*

Our theological traditions such as predestination, freewill, and the belief that there are no actual tensions between texts are examples of theological presuppositions that we may bring to the text. All of these may be true from our tradition, but they may obscure elements in the text if we privilege our theological commitments over a close reading of the text. Timothy Tennent, observed that Christians in the global church have not encountered the theological issues raised by the Protestant Reformation.[20] This is a reminder that our particular readings of the Scripture may not necessarily connect with persons who live outside of our contexts. This demonstrates the potential blind spots we can have as we attempt to navigate Scripture. Our denominational and ecclesial commitments can make it difficult to

---

20. Tennent, *Theology in the Context of World Christianity*.

work through certain texts. Methodists have trouble dealing with texts that sound as though they affirm *unconditional election*. Reformed communities are challenged by texts that sound as though they advocate more synergistic ways of understanding the human response to God's offer of grace. Interpreters may find it helpful to ask questions such as these: *What in this text challenges my own theological assumptions? What do I wish this text didn't affirm?*

Emphasis on discipleship as the attainment of knowledge is an obstacle. In many circles great Bible teaching can simply mean verse-by-verse exposition of texts apart from any penetrating life application. There has been an overemphasis on the knowledge of the details of the Bible without reflecting adequately on the function of these details or the demand of a given text on the life of its readers. This is one of the challenges of learning to preach and teach missionally. The temptation is to reduce teaching or preaching to pointing out interesting things in a biblical text. Many listeners gravitate to this type of teaching. It tickles the ears of the pious. It provides hearers with a Bible-fix. It may even spur feelings of religiosity. But, if the end of biblical interpretation is conversion, a focus on teaching/preaching of biblical facts apart from serious and sometimes pointed life-application will not carry the day. The biblical call for humanity to serve as a missional community that reflects God's character in all of life and to all Creation necessitates a radical shift on our understanding of discipleship. Erwin McManus has observed:

> Biblical interpretation must be missiological, not theological. A theological construct for interpretation finds success in the attainment of knowledge. The more you know, the more mature a Christian you are thought to be. And yet, knowledge of the Bible does not guarantee application of the Bible. To know is not necessarily to do. When the construct applied to the Bible is missiological, you engage the Bible to discover the response required of your life. It is significant that the history of the first-century church is called the book of Acts, not the book of Truths.[21]

Reading for the World

This leads us to the second audience for biblical interpretation. A missional hermeneutic is acutely interested in calling *insiders* to realign with God's

---

21. McManus, *Unstoppable Force*, 72.

mission. But this is only part of the goal. The Bible must also be read for the world where the *outsiders* reside. The Bible must be read for the world not merely for the sake of *outsiders* but because the God of mission is at work in the world and desires that *outsiders* become *insiders* for the sake of God's purposes for all Creation. Part of this involves the active engagement of the world with the message of Scripture. We listen to the critiques and criticisms of men and women not defensively or argumentatively but as an avenue for bringing the Scriptures into conversation with lost persons. We assume a "faith seeking understanding" stance of humility. This is not a denial of the trustworthiness of Scripture, but instead a profound confidence in God's word.

Religious/cultural pluralism grows with the loss of Christian memory in the post-Christian West. The problem is not that atheism has replaced Christianity. Instead, the Western world is thriving with religions. The hegemony of Christendom has ended. Now every world religion, syncretistic amalgamation, and cult stands on equal footing. This is a new given. There are more Muslims attending mosques in Europe today than Christians gathering for worship regularly in churches. All across the United States Christ followers are now coming into regular contact with adherents of all of the world's religions as well as secularized Westerners. Culturally, a generation has emerged in the United States that knows a little about religion and lacks a strong commitment to any particular creed. In his book, *Uniqueness of Jesus*, Chris Wright offers the analogy of a trip to the supermarket cereal aisle as an insight into the popular conception of the question of the world religions.[22] If one goes looking for a new cereal, the number of choices available is almost bewildering. Cereals today come in all shapes, colors, and sizes. Yet, at their core, a cereal is a cereal. Each one has been vitamin fortified and most will provide a person a certain percentage of key vitamins and minerals. Wright argues that most people view religion in this way: all religions are essentially the same. Individuals then choose the one that best fits their personal and cultural preferences. Reading the Scriptures for the world invites the interpreter into this context of *pluralism*. The wise reader of the Bible must now be aware of other Scriptural traditions and forms of piety found in other faiths. The audience for missional interpretation will no longer merely be women and men familiar with the Gospel, but not personally connected to it. Increasingly, we will be communicating the Gospel to persons who are more acquainted with other religions or with no

---

22. Wright, *Uniqueness of Jesus*, 9–14.

religion. The starting point and assumptions that a communicator will need to make in the emerging twenty-first-century Western context are vastly different than they were only a generation ago. Revivals among previous generations of Westerners involved calling people back to their roots in Christianity. Today we face generations whose roots are increasingly in a nihilistic secularism, an undefined spirituality, or in the religions of the world. Thus, it is vital for interpreters to study and reflect on the religious and philosophical assumptions of their audience.[23]

Contested truth claims—avoid straw men. When we only preach to insiders it is easy to paint the world in broad, brush strokes. We can make claims and blanket statements that may appeal to and be acceptable to insiders, but which will befuddle if not completely close down the communication of the Gospel to those who do not share the worldview and assumptions of insiders. It is always a temptation to oversimplify complex issues and problems. This does not mean that the biblical interpreter must somehow sanitize the Gospel. Scripture is clear, "The message of the cross is foolishness to those who are perishing. . . ." (1 Cor 1:18). The issue is not a watering down of the Gospel; the issue is the needless offense of listeners with careless statements that are peripheral to the Gospel. A missional hermeneutic is all about presenting clearly and compellingly the biblical call to conversion. If the audience is to be offended it must be the Gospel that does the offending, not the carelessness of the communicator.

Ignorance of the biblical message. Communicators must constantly strive to explain the biblical text clearly and cogently. This is an area in which we find a real overlap with reading the Bible for the Church. The biblical story is becoming lost in the Western world. Ours is a generation in which Christ followers have an opportunity to (re)introduce the Gospel.

Political correctness/sensitivity. The Western world of the twenty-first century is acutely aware of the abuses of past generations. Westerners have learned to be more sensitive about issues of social justice as related, for example, to race, culture, gender, and age. The Old Testament is the product of the Iron Age. The New Testament arose during the first century AD in the Roman Empire. Certain parts of the Bible sound barbaric in

---

23. Wright offers a series of questions to help Christians understand other religious beliefs: 1) *Who are we?* What does it mean to be a human being? 2) *Where are we?* What is the origin and nature of the world in which we live? 3) *What has gone wrong?* What is the fundamental problem in human existence and/or the world? 4) *What is the solution?* How is the problem resolved? What is the nature and process of salvation?

comparison to twenty-first-century sensibilities.[24] In the world of the Bible slavery is commonplace. Capital punishment exists for a plethora of crimes. Women do not share equal rights with men. Animals are used for sacrifice. *Outsiders* may raise legitimate concerns about these elements. For an extreme example of a reading highly skeptical of Scripture and the God that it presents, consider the words of scientist and committed atheist Richard Dawkins:

> The God of the Old Testament is arguably the most unpleasant character in all fiction: jealous and proud of it; a petty, unjust, unforgiving control-freak; a vindictive, bloodthirsty, ethnic cleanser; a misogynistic, homophobic, racist, infanticidal, genocidal, filicidal, pestilential, megalomanical, sadmasochistic, capriciously malevolent bully.[25]

Dawkins is guilty of anachronism and a deconstructionist reading against the grain and trajectory of the biblical story, but he does illustrate how an *outsider* may hear or read the text. In fact, many of these concerns are bubbling just under the surface of our communities anyway. I can remember how my own daughter cried the first time that she heard the story of Noah's Ark. She did not hear it as good news at all. She could not understand why God would kill innocent animals.

Elephants in the room. Outsiders don't know the rules. Outsiders aren't afraid to ask tough questions. Outsiders are seeking honest answers. This means that interpreters can't skirt around controversial texts or gloss over difficult words or phrases. This is a positive development. In our twenty-first-century missional reality the clear communication of Scriptural truth is a necessity. It places certain demands and expectations on the interpreter. If the Scripture is read in public its content must be engaged. When outsiders hear a controversial text read and have a question they will raise it. Thus, we as interpreters must learn to read the text through the lens of an outsider. Erwin McManus of Mosaic in Los Angeles calls this "reading the text in 360 degrees."[26] He argues that too often believers have a tendency to read the Bible only through the eyes of the faithful protagonists

---

24. Ironically, it is the influence of the Bible on Western culture that in many ways is responsible for the current climate of freedom and justice. In other words, we may not be as sensitive about these topics if in fact our culture had not been so thoroughly shaped by Christianity.

25. Dawkins, *God Delusion*, 31.

26. McManus "Talk Back."

in the story. We are always David and Israel rather than Goliath and the Philistines. However, if you are on the peripheries of the community you may sympathize with the antagonists in the biblical narratives more than the heroes. The sensitive interpreter needs to be aware of these counter-intuitive (from the *insider* perspective) ways of reading and recognize that many in our audience will be raising questions in their minds that need to be addressed. This means that interpreters must address any difficult or potentially controversial element in our texts rather than merely skirting around them. Ask questions such as these: *What in this text is potentially offensive? What part of the passage do I wish was not present?*

Reflection on Realities of Taking the Audience Seriously

The interpreter must: 1) address the obvious issues, especially those that are controversial or easy to misunderstand, 2) anticipate and answer objections to the message of the text, 3) not assume that the audience understands the contours of the Gospel, 4) make sense of the text within its Scriptural context, 5) be sensitive to the realities and personal experiences of audience members, and 6) trust the Holy Spirit is working in the midst of the community.

Toward Reading the Bible for Humans

It is important to remember the dual context of insider/outsider or reading for the Church/reading for the world. However, ultimately a missional hermeneutic calls us to proclaim the Gospel to humans. The GPS rubric assumes that the Bible seeks to convert all people to their true selves as God intended for them to live and be. As we argued in Part One, humanity was created to be a missional community that reflects and embodies God's character to, for, and in the nations. All people were created to participate in God's global mission as people in community that are transformed by the Spirit.

The reality of the *imago dei* leaves us with a starting point for communicating with women and men. GPS suggests that there are three intrinsic or deep longings in every person to whom we will ever communicate. First, since God created humanity for mission, mission is part of our DNA. This means that every person who has ever lived longs to live a life of purpose. No one wants to get to the end of his or her life and be filled with the regret

(re)Aligning with God

of an unfulfilled life. The truly purpose-filled life is one committed to God's mission in the world. Second, every single person desires to be loved authentically by others. This is a desire for a genuine community. Last, every man or woman hopes to become a better person. There is a nagging sense that we are not all that we should be. This longing is the result of our fallenness. It can only be realized through the transformation of the Holy Spirit and growth in holiness.

So what does the *imago dei* and GPS have to do with reading the Scripture for humans? It is about helping our audience to hear the Scriptures as a call to becoming the persons whom God created us to be. This includes an invitation to mission, community, and holiness. For the *insider* this will come as an exhortation to realign with God's mission; for the *outsider* it will be an invitation to align with God's work in the world. But in both cases it will be heard as a call for conversion.

In the Church we tend to save the harshest words for those outside of the community. Yet, Scripture consistently points the finger most pointedly at the faith community. The biblical message is clear about the *lostness* of all people. A missional reading of the Scripture is a relentless call for (re)alignment. People of faith are called continually to realign with the values and ethos of God's kingdom; people who are not yet following Jesus are invited to align with God's purposes.

Asking New Questions

Reading the Scripture is not a mere exercise in past-historical meaning or in affirming the biases of contemporary readers. The Scripture desires our conversion. Biblical interpretation is incomplete until its readers deal with the conversion issue. How can teachers and preachers use the GPS rubric to call hearers of a biblical text to (re)alignment?

As we move from interpretation of the text to intentional reflection on its call to (re)alignment, we focus on how a text may be applied or appropriated into our lives as individuals and as part of the community of faith. A text cannot be applied or appropriated into our contemporary setting apart from substantive engagement with it through the sort of close reading suggested above. But any reading apart from application serves merely antiquarian interests. We must press on in our interpretive work to hear Scripture's call in our day. How do we do this?

Missional Appropriation

1) Focused attention must be given to discerning the original application present in the text under consideration. This step serves as a guide to thinking through the application of the text in contemporary communities of faith. The assumption here is that understanding the purpose of the text for its initial audience is the best starting point for hearing the text in our world today.

   Here are some key questions to consider:
   - To whom was the message of the text directed? The faith community, individuals or groups outside of the community, all of the above?
   - What assumptions does this text make about its audience?
   - What kind of world does this text imagine to be true for its audience?
   - What effect did this text intend to have on its audience?
   - Is there any evidence in the text that would limit its application in any way?

2) Reflect critically on the message of the text in light of the biblical canon. Every text in Scripture sounds a note that is included in the symphony of the whole. To hear any text clearly involves assessing its role within the biblical materials as a whole. This is not a move to mute an individual text or to flatten the meaning of distinct voices so as to mesh it with the whole. It is a desire to reflect theologically on the contribution of any text to the overall message of the Scripture. It recognizes the Canon of Scripture as the final authority for faith and practice.
   - How does our text fit into the overarching narrative of the Bible (Creation—Fall—Israel—Jesus the Messiah—Church—New Creation)?
   - How does it contribute to our understanding of the big picture?
   - How does it contribute to the theological voices of the Bible?
   - How does the message of the text stand in continuity or tension with other voices in the Scripture?

3) Synthesize the key message(s) of our text in light of reflection on its original application and its fit within the Canon. What is the distinct

contribution of this text to the message of the Bible? If this were the only biblical text in our possession what would we know?

4) Deploy GPS to appropriate the text for a twenty-first-century audience.

As we have argued, the goal of the Gospel is conversion. The text calls all its hearers to align or realign themselves with the mission of God in the World. It speaks to both insiders (Christ-followers) and outsiders (non-Christ followers). As we move to make specific applications and appropriations of the biblical message, we must keep this dual audience in mind. A missional hermeneutic listens to Scripture as a means of calling all people to live as the women and men whom God created them to be—a missional community that reflects and embodies God's character to/for/in the world. Mission, transformed character, and community are the key elements of what it means to be human. These are the broad contours that capture the distinct call to (re)align with God. These themes are captured succinctly in our GPS rubric.

Here are some key application questions to shape the description of the Realignment to which our text is calling both insiders and outsiders:

a) Global mission:
   Insider: How does this text envision God's work in the world? Where do God's people fit into this mission? How do God's people need to change to participate more effectively with God's work?
   Outsider: What sort of world is this text inviting me to spend my life working to create? What would my life look like if I joined this mission?

b) Persons in Community:
   Insider: How does this text envision the corporate life of God's people? How do God's people need to change in order to embody the portrait of community assumed by this text?
   Outsider: What type of community is this text inviting me to explore? How is this text inviting me to participate in a community that exists for something greater than my own wants and desires?

c) Spiritually transformed:
   Insider: What does this text tell us about the character or ethos of God's people? What are God's people supposed to become?

How do God's people need to change in order to more profoundly reflect the character of God? What sort of person do I need to become in order to live out this text?

Outsider: What type of lifestyle/character is this text inviting me to embody? How would my life be enriched by aligning my character with the vision of this text? How would my life be different by following Jesus Christ?

Three Cautions:

1) I am not suggesting that every biblical text will speak to each theme. Some texts will yield fruit through all three lenses; others may only relate to one or two of the broad themes. GPS is a rubric that will help to move interpreters from text to addressing its modern hearers. The text itself is the guide to its meaning. Our interpretations must be congruent with a close reading of the text.

2) It is vital for interpreters to think clearly about their audience at all times. The dual focus on *insiders* and *outsiders* unleashes the Scripture to speak to the whole audience.

3) Make sure that the interpreter is the first "convert." A missional hermeneutic preaches to the borderlands where church, God, and the world intersect. It involves the preacher/teacher following Jesus' movement into the world. If we are to invite the world to become part of God's work and to call the community of faith to a (re)alignment, then we ourselves must be continually converted to the reality that the text is prescribing.

Deploying New Language

Biblical interpretation does not end until it is communicated clearly to others. The goal is the conversion of its hearers. This begins with the interpreter, but the Scriptures are meant for public consumption. The final piece in learning to speak human involves connecting the Scriptural truths with the context of your audience. At some level, if we have been attentive to the missional context and actively engaged in God's work in the world, it should not be difficult to speak clearly and cogently.

It is profoundly incarnational to deploy language from the target culture and by pouring Gospel content into its words. Paul's dictum in 1 Cor 9:23 is crucial: *I become all things, to all people so that by all possible I may save some.* The force of this language is crucial in our contemporary missional context. Given the realities of the loss of the Christendom paradigm, we find ourselves facing many of the challenges of Israel in the midst of the nations during the Iron Age, the early centuries of the Christ following movement as well as those faced by our brothers and sisters in the global Church. We must maintain a true biblical faith and orthodoxy while at the same time engaging the surrounding culture and people with the Gospel in a manner that is understandable. But we also face the necessity of (re)converting God's people for mission. In the earliest centuries of the Christian era Christ followers understood the centrality of mission. This is not true for much of the Church in the West. The Church must be awakened to its calling to extend God's blessing to all persons and nations as a *missional community that reflects God's character to/for/in the World.*

The challenge confronting the interpreter is this: the biblical interpreter must continually assume a dual audience of insiders and outsiders while simultaneously calling both to (re)align themselves with God's mission. How do we accomplish this? How do we navigate the challenge of a diverse audience?

The key is to read the Scriptures for human beings rather than for *insiders* and *outsiders*. This is not a cute semantic shift. Learning to speak human is rooted in our GPS metaphor. When we read the Scriptures through the triad of mission, holiness, and community, we are engaging the text not merely as Christians or non-Christians, but as human beings created in God's image who will remain restless and less than satisfied until we are reconciled with God and shaped into the persons whom we were created to be. The Scriptures testify to God's acts and purposes in Creation and seek to convert its readers to its viewpoint and world.

The key to developing this new language for proclaiming the Gospel is learning to listen to the culture for metaphors that may be adopted and adapted for use in communicating the good news. It is not about our *creativity* as communicators but about our capacity to listen to and study attentively the culture. Our assumption is that our missional God in the person of the Risen Christ is leading his people into the world on mission. Jesus goes before us. It is our task to be attentive to the Spirit's leading so that we may build upon what God is already doing. In other words, the new language already exists. It is up to us to find it, refit it with Gospel content, and deploy it. Think of Paul on Mars Hill in Acts 17. It is about committing to using the language of the street and the marketplace rather than only the language of the church. When we read the Scriptures within their ancient contexts we will discover that the biblical authors in both testaments have drawn deeply from the prevailing culture in deploying the metaphors and symbols of the day as vehicles for telling God's story.

Let me offer examples from the Bible:

The creation stories in Genesis (Gen 1:1—2:3 and 2:4–25) are profound in the setting of the stage for the remainder of the Scriptural story. But they are also part of the broader Ancient Near Eastern culture that produced other Creation stories. This is not the place to debate the origin of Israel's creation stories vis-à-vis those of her neighbors, but a close study reveals a common vocabulary that is deployed distinctly to highlight Israel's understanding of Creation in light of and against the Ancient Near East. Profoundly, these stories declare the existence of a Creator God who is able to act unilaterally by his word apart from any context of conflict with the "gods" to bring into being and shape the Creation. Moreover, elements that were worshipped by Israel's neighbors (e.g., the sun, moon, and stars of Day 4) are merely reckoned as parts of God's creative work. Most importantly, these texts emphasize the profound role that humanity, both women and men, were to play in God's creational intentions. It is humanity alone that bears the divine image (Gen 1:26–27). Humanity stands at the pinnacle of God's creative work in the Six days of God's acts (Gen 1:1–31) and at the center of the narrative developed in 2:4–25. These elements served a profound role in their Near Eastern context.

The Song of Moses and the Israelites (Exod 15:1b–18) is a powerful hymn that celebrates God's victory over Egypt at the Sea and God's future victories on behalf of his people. Yet, a careful study demonstrates that it is presented using language and motifs drawn from the Baal Epic known within the wider regions of Syria-Palestine.[27] The Song of Moses and the Israelites deploys the mythic themes of conflict, order, kingship, and palace (or temple) building in order to emphasize the transcendent meaning of the Lord's vanquishing of the forces of Egypt as a demonstration of his sovereign power to reign. Moreover, by drawing from Canaanite mythic patterns, the Song of Moses and the Israelites serves to subvert the status

---

27. Russell, *Song of the Sea*, 79–86. Cf. Cross, *Canaanite Myth*, 112–44 and Craigie, "Poetry of Ugarit and Israel," 3–31.

quo religions of Canaan by boldly proclaiming Israel's Gospel of a God, the LORD, who enters the human historical plane on the side of an oppressed people against the power of Egypt, and, who, after the defeat of Egypt, simultaneously causes dread and terror in God's people's future enemies and brings God's people to his holy mountain. Such actions are astonishing within their Ancient Near Eastern context. Gods typically sided with the powerful, and gods do not invite mere mortals to their cosmic mountains. Yet, this is precisely how Israel experienced its salvation from the forces of Egypt. The Exodus story is profound and powerful regardless, but seeing how it spoke directly to its Near Eastern context raises the communicated truth to a new level and serves as a model for gaining the Gospel a hearing in our day.

Paul's exhortation to the Philippian Christians in 1:27a draws on the motif of "citizenship" to articulate Paul's vision for a missional ethos in Philippi. Many of the Philippian Christians enjoyed the status of being Roman citizens. This gave them privileges and rights that very few within the empire enjoyed. At the core of this exhortation is a verb that most English translations struggle to translate. *Politeuomai* has at its root the idea of serving as a good citizen. Most English translations incorrectly mute the force of the verb by choosing phrasings such as "conduct yourselves" or "live your life." In Paul's other writings he uses the Greek word *peripateo* meaning "walk/live" (1 Thes 2:12; Col 1:10; Eph 4:1) in similar expressions. But these miss the allusion to citizenship that would have been unambiguous to the Philippian Christians. If Paul merely wanted to say "conduct yourself" or "live your life" he could have used *peripateo*. But he doesn't. Moreover, it makes it difficult for the English reader to see that the main argument of Phil 1:27—4:1 is framed by references to citizenship (1:27 and 3:20). Paul consciously chooses *politeuomai* because he is using the Philippians' context to help them understand what it means to be a Christ follower in Philippi. They are no longer to live merely as *Roman citizens*. Their lives are now to be shaped by the values and ethos of the Kingdom of heaven.

Implications: Be creative in engaging contemporary culture. Be committed to finding the best words. The Gospel is translatable into new cultures and languages. This is the beauty and the power of the Gospel. The Scriptures are filled with examples of this. The simple observation that New Testament was written in Greek rather than the original Aramaic tongue of

Jesus inculcates into the Christ following movement the practice of intercultural translation.[28]

Necessity of translation: Paul rooted his missiological practice in contextualization. Learning to speak human assumes that all persons are created in God's image. All persons will be most satisfied by a life in which they are fully aligned with God. Here are some examples of the shifts that I have made language-wise:

- Repentance = realignment
- Sanctification = becoming the person whom God created you to be
- Spirit empowered = unleashed fully by God

Some of the topics in this chapter may have seemed daunting. Interpreting God's Word is serious business. Let me end with a few words of encouragement.

1) Reading the Scriptures for the Church and World is deeply satisfying personally. The missional center of the Scripture as encompassing mission, community, and holiness resonates with people. When we learn to communicate the Gospel through the rubric of GPS, we will find that we are actually calling people to the true essence of their humanity.

2) We must recognize that a missional hermeneutic does not remove the offense and scandal of the Gospel. It remains "foolishness to those who are perishing . . . a stumbling block to Jews and foolishness to the Greeks." A commitment to missional reading embodies Paul's dictum: "I become all things to all people so that by all possible means I may save some." This is done in the recognition of the word *some*. Our work of interpretation is done in the hope of the conversion of the *some* by presenting the Gospel clearly and cogently to *all*.

3) When in doubt, leave your study and spend time in the community with persons who are not yet following Jesus. Build deep and authentic friendships. These relationships will provide natural forums to gain confidence and fluidity with language that communicates the Gospel clearly and cogently.

---

28. Over against the insistence of some Muslims of the necessity of reading the Quran in Arabic.

4) God is with us. Read the Scriptures prayerfully, live faithfully, and trust that God is working in the people with whom we are communicating. Conversion is the goal of the Scriptures, but our own gifts, effort, and insights are not the sole means or even the decisive means. It is the Spirit of God who goes before the proclamation and teaching of the Word. It is the work of God to bear fruit through the teaching and preaching of Scripture. We are merely servants who sow the Word.

So what does it look like to read the Scriptures through lens of GPS? In the next chapter we will turn to examples of missional reading from both the Old and New Testaments.

6

Reading the Old and New Testament Missionally: Jonah and Philippians

We've presented a broad overview of God's missional story. We've reflected methodologically on applying a missional hermeneutic. Now its time to present an extended application of a missional hermeneutic to two entire books: Jonah in the Old Testament and Paul's Letter to the Philippians in the New Testament.

I've selected these two books for a few reasons. First, both are relatively short at four chapters each while still being rich in content. Second, Jonah serves to illustrate well the dynamic of *insider* and *outsider* that is critical in a missional hermeneutic. Third, in Philippians, Paul models a contextual and incarnational approach to presenting his Gospel. Fourth, Jonah and Philippians are representative of the most common genres in the Bible (Jonah: Narrative and poetry [chapter 2]; Philippians: epistolary/didactic). Last, Jonah and Philippians offer an example from each Testament.

Jonah

The basic story line of Jonah is well known, but its deeper message is often obscured by the memorable episode in which Jonah is swallowed by a large fish. When we allow our eyes to pull back from focusing on the fish, we will discover a message of good news for the nations and a challenge for God's people. The book of Jonah also paints a compelling picture of the heart of God for his creation.

(re)Aligning with God

The book of Jonah offers a powerful word for both insiders and outsiders. Jonah is one of the few moments in the Old Testament where there is an explicit and intentional focus on reaching outsiders with the good news about God. God calls Jonah to leave the safe confines of Israel and journey northeast to the city of Nineveh, the power center of the mighty and much-feared Assyrian empire. The Assyrians were the dominant political and military force from approximately 900–612 BC. This time spans roughly the era following the united monarchy down to the eve of the final destruction of Judah at the hands of the Babylonians. During this time period, Assyria slowly intimidated and gained control over most of the Near East. They wiped out the northern Kingdom in 722 BC and devastated the Judean countryside during the reign of Hezekiah (ca. 701 BC). The threat of the Assyrian military serves as a key part of the backstory to the history of Israel and Judah. So the call of Jonah to Assyria is not a romantic calling to extend God's love to an unreached population; it is God sending Jonah to a cruel and menacing nation that practiced violence and injustice to all who opposed its desire for world domination.

The book of Jonah opens with God's initial call for Jonah to travel to Nineveh and cry out against it. Jonah strongly resisted God's commission and fled in the opposite direction to Joppa, a port city on the Mediterranean. The narrator does not reveal to the readers the reason for Jonah's resistance. The reader is left to his or her own imagination. On the one hand, most of God's people would rejoice at the thought of God sending a prophet to condemn a hated enemy. But on the other hand, it is understandable why Jonah would not want to accept this commissioning. Preaching against the world's leading superpower in its own city would certainly not be the wisest action if one valued his or her life. Jonah's refusal to receive this calling sets in motion a remarkable story that offers a strong word to God's people about the centrality of mission and the expansiveness of God's grace and mercy. This is a book that is as much about insiders (represented by Jonah) as it is about outsiders (the Ninevites but also the sailors whom Jonah encounters at Joppa). As we reflect on the missional implications of the book of Jonah, we will observe how these characters respond to God.

First, Jonah flees from God by heading to Joppa and securing passage on a ship. God responds by sending a massive storm that threatens to crush the ship. The sailors are terrified. They cry out in horror to their various gods for help. They begin the desperate measures of throwing off the boat any excess weight. Remarkably, Jonah retreats from the deck and is fast asleep in the hold of the ship. The captain finds Jonah and implores him to call on his god. His words are telling, "Perhaps the god will be kind to us and we will not perish" (1:6). The religiosity of the captain and crew is revealing. They are not rigid religionists. Their spirituality is acutely practical. They are willing to pray to any god who may help them. They are open to the possibility of salvation at the hands of any god. Polytheism is the religious milieu. Note the connections with the modern world. As Christianity recedes in the Western world, we find ourselves again in a time in which people remain believers in the spiritual, but not committed to any particular sect. Yet, there remains an interest and openness to spirituality.

Our text, however, records no prayer from Jonah at this point. This is telling. Pagan sailors pray, but Israel's prophet does not. When the frightened sailors cast lots in an attempt to discover the person responsible for their predicament, the lot falls on Jonah. They pry from Jonah the details of his story and Jonah opens with a bold theological statement: "I am a Hebrew and I fear the LORD the God of Heaven who made both the sea and dry land" (1:9). This will be the first of three bold theological statements that Jonah makes (see also 2:9 and 4:2). In all cases, Jonah gets his theology correct but is oblivious to its fuller implications. In this scene Jonah confesses his belief in the LORD who created the sea and dry land and purports to "fear the LORD." Yet, he reports to the sailors that he is attempting to flee from such a god. The sailors immediately recognize the futility of this and become even more terrified. Jonah counsels them to throw him overboard, but the sailors demonstrate compassion and care by attempting to row out of the storm. The pagan sailors who do not know the LORD thus demonstrate more humanity and god-like compassion than Jonah will at any point in the story.

The sailors only acquiesce to Jonah's wish when they recognize that the sea is getting worse by the minute. Amazingly, they offer a prayer to the LORD as they reluctantly toss Jonah overboard, "Oh Lord please do not let us perish on account of this man's life. Do not hold us guilty of innocent blood for you have acted as it has pleased you." As soon as they finish praying, they throw Jonah into the sea and the storm immediately stops. The sailors' response dwarfs Jonah's behavior thus far in the book. Jonah 1:16 reports, "The men feared the LORD *greatly* so they offered a sacrifice to the LORD and made vows." The book of Jonah is mainly about the characters of the LORD and Jonah, so its does not again mention the sailors, but it is arguable that we should read 1:16 as a report of their alignment with the

(RE)ALIGNING WITH GOD

LORD. We don't have to press this to recognize the implications of their actions. In contrast to Jonah, who allegedly knows and fears the LORD and yet runs away from him and does nothing other than mouth words about his relationship (albeit good theology), the sailors respond positively to the revelation that they receive, show compassion for Jonah, and take actions that indicate a worship of the LORD.

Notice how the opening chapter of Jonah portrays outsiders. They are open to religious expressions different than their own. They value human life and attempt to save Jonah. They are capable of theological reflection and, unlike Jonah, the sailors actually demonstrate an awareness of the theological implications of Jonah's identification of the LORD as the Creator God. The sailors pray directly to the LORD and offer a sacrifice and make vows in response to the LORD's ceasing of the storm once Jonah hits the water. What is the missional function of these elements? It is a reminder to God's people that *outsiders* are open to the gospel. Outsiders will likely be practicing other religions or even some odd mixture of religious commitments. Our text does not condemn the sailors for their prayers to other deities. Rather it focuses on their response to revelation about the LORD when it comes their way. The lesson for *insiders* here is a poignant one: don't be offended by the religious practices of *outsiders*. At some level their interest in religious practices represents an openness to receiving an invitation to a relationship with the Creator God of Scripture who sent Jesus into the world to model an authentic human life lived out in love and to achieve God's final victory over sin, injustice, and evil in all its forms.

In the second chapter of Jonah, we encounter the great fish. It is crucial for understanding the book to see the fish not as a punishment for Jonah but as an agent of God's grace and mercy. This will be the first of two times in the book of Jonah in which God uses a part of his creation for the benefit of Jonah.[1] The LORD acts to save Jonah despite Jonah's disobedience. This is a powerful portrait of God's love. God does not allow Jonah to drown but rather he delivers him from death in the sea. God does not reject Jonah despite Jonah's rejection of God's call. This is a powerful word for insiders of God's compassion and capacity to remain faithful even in the absence of faithfulness on the part of his people. Jonah responds memorably to the LORD with a prayer of thanksgiving for God's salvation. This is Jonah's first

---

1. The second occurrence will be the plant that grows and provides shade for Jonah's head (4:6). There are of course two examples of nature serving to teach Jonah lessons by offering a threat to his personal peace: the stormy sea (1:4) and the worm (4:7).

positive action in the book. It is worth noting that in 2:9 Jonah promises sacrifices and faithfulness to complete his vow. These actions mirror the response of the sailors in the first chapter. Jonah is grateful for the kindness that God shows to him despite his failure to go to Nineveh.

The last line of 2:9 contains the second of Jonah's theological affirmation. In response to God's actions in sending the fish to save him from drowning, Jonah ends his thanksgiving by saying, "Salvation belongs to the LORD." Thus far he has recognized that God is the creator of all (1:9) and now he declares that the LORD is the source of salvation.

As we will soon learn, Jonah is happy to receive God's blessings and kindness, but he will not be so pleased when God extends his favor to a group of *outsiders* whom Jonah does not like. But we are getting ahead of the story a bit. After Jonah finishes his prayer, God speaks to the fish and it spits Jonah out onto dry ground (2:10).

Jonah 3:1 opens up in identical fashion as 1:1. God renews his call for Jonah to travel to Nineveh and proclaim God's message. This time Jonah rises up and travels to Nineveh. Nineveh is described as an exceedingly great city that is as wide as a three days walk. This emphasizes the missional need of Nineveh. In 1:2, Nineveh's wickedness was noted. Here its vastness takes center stage. This is a key word for *insiders*. Sometimes there is a tendency to focus on the evil present in the world rather than seeing the opportunity that is there.

Jonah travels through the city and announces the impending destruction of Nineveh in forty days. Jonah's preaching creates an immediate response. The Ninevites from the great to the small repent and turn to the LORD by putting on sackcloth and sitting in ashes. Even the mighty king of Nineveh steps in. He orders a fast, a time of prayer to God, and a turning away from all evil ways. The extent of this corporate time of repentance is demonstrated in the king ordering that even the animals of Nineveh are to be covered in sackcloth. This scene is remarkable. Jonah witnesses nothing more and nothing less than the full repentance of Nineveh. Like the sailors, the Ninevites show themselves to be open to revelation about God. In contrast to Jonah, they respond fully and whole-heartedly to word of God. This is a word for *insiders* about *outsiders*. Don't ever underestimate the power of the word of God to change lives. Even those whom we may consider beyond the reach of God's grace may respond positively to the good news about God. God asks his people for faithfulness. As Jesus will exhort his disciples in the Gospels, God's people are to sow seed faithfully in expectation of a harvest (Matt 13:1–9).

The readers of Jonah would be stunned at this point. The hated and feared Ninevites, including the dreaded and powerful king of Nineveh, have repented fully and thrown themselves unabashedly into the mercy of God. Jonah had announced the destruction of Nineveh for its many sins. How would God respond? In Jonah 3:10, the reader learns that God sees the repentance of the Ninevites. The God of the Scripture does not merely watch over God's people. God is aware of all parts of his creation. In response to the repentance of Nineveh God relents from the judgment that he planned to bring against Nineveh. He does not destroy Nineveh as he had announced through Jonah. Just as God had turned away from destroying Israel in the shadow of Sinai at the intercession of Moses (Exod 32:7–14), so God now relents from his planned judgment on Nineveh. This is exceedingly good news for Nineveh, but also for all *outsiders*. God is gracious to more than merely his own people. This is a crucial reminder of the biblical narrative. God's people exist for the sake of the lost world of Genesis 3–11. The extent of God's love for the world will be fully revealed in the life, death, and resurrection of Jesus, but it is already adumbrated here. The implications are immense. If God can relent of his judgment on the wicked Ninevites, is anyone beyond the reach of God's love? Is there anyone in our twenty-first-century context who is beyond the reach of God's grace and compassion?

This may be really good news for Nineveh and by implication all *outsiders*. But it is not good news for Jonah. He is greatly displeased. In Jonah 4, the reader gets the opportunity to watch and overhear a remarkable conversation and encounter between Jonah and the LORD. In 4:2, the narrator pulls the curtain back and we learn for the first time the actual reason that Jonah had fled from the LORD. He was not afraid of the Ninevites at all. Instead, we learn that Jonah fled from his mission because he feared that God might in fact be open to showing compassion to the Ninevites. Of course, this is precisely what occurred! In 4:2 Jonah makes the third of his theological affirmations. He quotes from the most sublime revelation of Yahweh's internal character in the Old Testament (Exod 34:6–7a). On Sinai, at precisely the moment that Israel looked lost in the aftermath of the Golden Calf debacle, God showed himself to be a God of limitless love and compassion. Jonah understood this, but it caused him to cringe. Of course, as we've seen, Jonah was happy that God extended his limitless love and compassion to him in spite of his actions, but he did not like it that God might actually love his enemies with this same compassion. Jonah could affirm that salvation may be found in the LORD, but he did not want this to be true for others. For the second time in the book, Jonah's life does not match his theology. This is the danger for *insiders*. We forget that God loves our enemies. In fact, we forget that the reason for our existence as God's people is so that *outsiders* can have the opportunity to become insiders. Jonah almost functions as a caricature here. He is so displeased with God's mercy to the Ninevites that he asks God to take his life rather than having to witness the sparing of Nineveh from the wrath of God. God then asks Jonah a poignant question: "Is it proper for you to be angry?" The obvious answer is "No" but in the book of Jonah, insight does not come easily for Jonah.

By asking this question, God demonstrates that he is not giving up on Jonah. This is profoundly good news for God's people as we struggle to realign ourselves continually with God's missional purposes in the world.

Jonah remains obtuse and verse 4:5 reports that Jonah retires out of the city. He builds a shelter for himself. Our text informs us that Jonah sat in its shade "waiting to see what would happen to the city." The reader is left to interpret Jonah's actions. Why does he stay at Nineveh? Was Jonah hoping that God would still send a judgment against Nineveh?

God engages Jonah again with a remarkable object lesson. The LORD causes a plant to grow and provide shade for Jonah's head. The purpose of the plant is to deliver Jonah from "evil." This is a key word play. The evil here simply refers to the misery of the hot Middle Eastern sun that Jonah experienced at Nineveh. But this same word was used to describe the condition of Nineveh as a whole in 1:2 as well as what the Ninevites repented of in 3:10. "Evil" meaning the severity of judgment that God had planned is also of what God relents in 3:10. By saving Jonah from the summer heat, God demonstrates that he is a God who is committed to acting against evil. Notice that Jonah's response stands in stark contrast to Jonah's response to God's graciousness toward Nineveh. Jonah is "exceedingly glad" (4:6). This is the second time in the book that God has "saved" Jonah. On the first occasion, Jonah erupted into a psalm of thanksgiving and now his joy is emphasized. Jonah rejoices because of the shade that the plant provides for him. There is nothing wrong with rejoicing and giving thanks for God's blessings. The problem, however, is Jonah's self-centeredness. God's blessings are not an end in and of themselves. The biblical model from the time of God's calling of Abraham (Gen 12:3) is that God's people are blessed to be blessings. In contrast to this, Jonah models an inward focus that forgets the role that God's people play in the wider world.

Thus, God has one more lesson for Jonah. The previous day had ended with Jonah enjoying the shade from the plant that God had sent for Jonah's pleasure. When the sun rose the next morning, God sent a worm to chew the plant and cause it to whither. As the day wore on, the sun and wind combined to scorch Jonah's head. In response Jonah feels faint and requests death. But once again God does not let go of Jonah. God sees through Jonah's surface response. Jonah is not simply uncomfortable because of the heat. He is angry. God questions him directly in verse 9, "Is it right/proper for you to be angry about the plant?" Jonah responds strongly "It is right/proper for me to be angry, even angry enough to die!" Notice the moral language. This is not merely a report of feelings. Both God and Jonah couch the conversation in moral categories of rightness. Jonah contends that he is entitled to being angry.

God uses Jonah's strong feelings as the platform for helping Jonah to see the situation from the perspective of God's heart and mission. In 4:10 God reminds Jonah that Jonah shows deep concern for the plant even though he had nothing to do with its growth and despite the reality that it existed for only part of a day. In other words, Jonah's self-centeredness constricts Jonah's perspective. There is nothing wrong with Jonah's concern for the plant. The problem is that Jonah's concern seems to end with the plant. In 4:11 the LORD invites Jonah to view the current situation from God's missional perspective. God reminds Jonah that Nineveh is a great city filled with more than 120,000 women and men who "do not know their right hand from their left hand" as well as large number of cattle. God's message is sublime. How can Jonah care about a plant that came and went over the course of a few hours and be oblivious to the needs of a historically great city filled with women and men who are woefully ignorant of God and with a multitude of animals?

This final verse in the book is important for unpacking the full implications of God's love and compassion. First, it reminds God's people that God is radically for humanity even for the enemies of God's people. Again the book of Jonah does not turn a blind eye to the atrocities of the Assyrians as the rest of the biblical narrative speaks a powerful word for justice and against oppression. Indeed, to live wickedly has consequences. But Jonah reminds us that God's heart is to extend salvation and blessing to the nations. Verse 4:11 also speaks poignantly to the lostness of people. It depicts the Ninevites as persons who lack knowledge. They acted in ignorance. Now we must not miss the dynamic of their repentance in all of this. God showed them mercy because they turned to him in response to Jonah's preaching. If they had not responded positively to the prophecy of Jonah, they likely would have received the judgment that Jonah had proclaimed. The narrative of the Bible is clear about God's response to wickedness and injustice. The force of the book of Jonah, however, is to declare decisively that God's mercy and compassion are available to all.

Second, 4:11 also emphasizes God's commitment to all creation. It is remarkable that God acknowledges the animals in Nineveh. Perhaps this merely reflects the reality that the Ninevites even put sackcloth on their cattle (3:7-8). But it more likely serves to remind God's people of humanity's role as stewards of creation. This can be demonstrated by reflecting on the creational themes throughout the book. In Jonah 1:1–16, God controls the wind and the waves and uses them to stop Jonah's flight away from his mission. Moreover, God twice uses elements of creation to "save" Jonah. In 1:17—2:10, God deploys a great fish to keep Jonah from drowning. In 4:6–8, God uses a plant as a teaching tool to attempt to cause a shift in Jonah's mindset. Last, the Ninevites sensed the connection with creation and the implications of judgment for their own animals. Thus, they expanded their acts of repentance and contrition to include even their animals.

When we consider God's concern with creation as well as his desire to extend love and mercy to the Ninevites, we find ourselves reflecting once again on God's purposes as seen in our reading of Genesis 1–11. Humanity's original mission was to serve as stewards of creation. In the wake of humanity's rebellion (Gen 3–11), the missional need shifts to God working to redeem his original agents of blessing (women and men) by calling into existence a new missional community beginning with the family of Abraham (Gen 12:1–3). This missional community exists to extend reconciliation and blessing to a lost humanity, but also continues to practice creational stewardship in line with God's original mission for humanity. The book of Jonah reminds the community of both.

The book ends abruptly without revealing Jonah's response to God. Does Jonah realign fully with the missional heart of God by accepting the full implications that God's covenant love for Israel extends even to Israel's most feared enemies? It is a powerful way to end the book because this rhetorical tactic by the writer of Jonah forces his readers to work out this question in their own contexts. We are forced to ponder, "What did Jonah do?" but more profoundly, "What would we do if we were in Jonah's shoes?"

Jonah was sent to Nineveh as an agent of blessing and not merely as a prophet of doom. Jonah was in Nineveh to advance God's mission in the world. The evil of the Ninevites was not up for debate. The oppressive policies and atrocities against humanity perpetrated by the Assyrians were real. The book of Jonah does not call on God's people to sugar coat real wrongs, but instead uses this extreme example to emphasize the greatness and vastness of God's grace and mercy. The book of Jonah pushes God's people to embrace fully the big picture of God's mission—the blessing of the nations, even those historically and even presently hostile to God's people.

Through this dynamic narrative, communities of faith are forced to face head-on several challenging messages. God loves all people including those whom we do not personally like. Outsiders may be more open to the voice of God than God's people. Correct or orthodox theology is never a substitute for a faithful obedience to God's mission in the world. God's people are conduits of God's grace and mercy to the nations in fulfillment of their missional vocation from Sinai ("kingdom of priests and holy nation" Exod 19:4–6).

The question, "What will Jonah do?" becomes personal and communal for us: What will I do to advance God's mission in my context? Who outside of our comfort/safety zone is God calling us to love?

Reading Philippians Missionally

Paul penned his letter to the Philippians to encourage and shape the Christ followers in Philippi for God's mission in the world. Reading Philippians missionally involves hearing the text as instructions to empower its hearers to incarnate the Gospel in Philippi and beyond. In Philippians Paul models an incarnational and missional approach to proclaiming the Gospel.

In his salutation, Paul refers to himself as "servant/slave of Christ Jesus" (1:1). This is the only place in his writings where he embraces the title "servant/slave" without further qualification. For example, in Rom 1:1 and Titus 1:1, Paul is "servant of God" or "servant of Jesus" but also "apostle". Paul's use of "servant" (Greek *doulos*) elsewhere is thus balanced by the title/function "apostle." In Philippians, Paul and Timothy are simply "servants of Messiah Jesus." This is important. The only other use of *doulos* in Philippians occurs at 2:7 "but emptied himself taking the form of a slave, being born in in human likeness." Verse 2:7 records Jesus' action/demonstration of not considering equality with God something to be clung to or exploited. As we will see, the service of others over self is one of the fundamental issues of ethos to which Paul will return multiple times in this letter.

The genitive of possession "of Christ Jesus" modifies "slaves." Paul/Timothy are slaves belonging to Christ Jesus. The status that they possess comes in their relationship with Messiah Jesus.

Perhaps this choice of language is chosen intentionally to contrast with the theme of citizenship developed through the letter (1:27 and 3:20). A group of the Philippian Christ followers were Roman citizens. This gave them important status and privilege in the first-century Greco-Roman context. Slaves stood at the opposite end of the social ladder. They were considered property. Any status that they possessed came only as a result of the identity of their master/owner. Unlike a citizen, a slave did not have any special rights and privileges. Paul is thus embracing a low status as he writes to the church at Philippi.

This low status immediately comes into contrast with the titles of some of the letter's recipients. Notice the presence of the titles: overseers/bishops and deacons. These are sometimes linked with Paul's co-workers mentioned in 4:2. It appears that there are conflicts within the church of Philippi among leaders (3:15–16; 4:2–3). Thus, Paul's choice of words for his own ministry is important. He considers himself to be a "slave of Christ." Jesus Christ himself willingly took on "the form of a slave" (2:7). This points to a path for the resolution of conflict. Paul's willingness to embrace a low status models a way forward for the Christ following movement in our day as we seek models of leadership within the body of Christ. What would a community look like whose members embodied the title "slaves of Christ Jesus"? How would our community of faith be different than it is today? What would it mean for leadership to willingly embrace this mantle and model it for the community as a whole? Answering these types of questions allow Paul's words to shape us for mission.

Paul's missional intentions continue in his introductory materials: Paul's thanksgiving (1:3–8) and prayer (1:9–11) for the Philippians, as well as the way in which he describes his personal circumstances (1:12–26). Couched in the forms of a thanksgiving, prayer, and personal update, Paul fills these familiar elements with missional content that prepare the reader for what is to come in the body of the letter (1:27—4:1) and in the concluding exhortations (4:2–23).

(RE)ALIGNING WITH GOD

In 1:3–8, Paul is full of gratitude to God for the Philippians. What is the reason for Paul's thanksgiving? The Philippians have been partners (a fellowship or shareholders)[2] with him for or in the Gospel. The partnership has existed from the beginning of Paul's relationship with the Philippians and it continues into the present. Note the significance of this statement: Paul and the Philippians are bound together for the Gospel. They have a common cause. Their bond is God's mission. It is the Philippians' steadfast commitment to the Gospel that brings Paul joy. Philippi served as a gateway city to Europe for Paul. The Philippians supported Paul's mission and helped him to take the Gospel to the next city. They remained his financial patrons during his imprisonment and beyond (2:25–30 and 4:10–20).

Paul's prayer (1:9–11) for the followers of Jesus in Philippi is profound and powerful. Its fulfillment in the lives of the Philippians would mark the dawn of a new ethos—an ethos shaped by Jesus Christ lived out for the glory and praise of God. Paul prays that the Philippians' lives would abound more and more in a love shaped by true discernment of the purposes of God. What are God's purposes? This is not merely a prayer to become more loving. This is a prayer for a love of the things that God loves. Paul is praying for the missional holiness of the believers in Philippi so that through their lives Jesus may be known to the world for the glory and praise of God.

In 1:12–26, Paul reminds the Philippians of his imprisonment. Paul does not do this to complain about his circumstances. Instead, he focuses on the missional advances that the gospel has made through his imprisonment. In verses 13–14 Paul recounts that he has gained the opportunity to proclaim the Messiah to the Roman imperial guard. Moreover, through his example and perseverance, despite his chains, brothers and sisters in Christ are preaching and proclaiming the word of God boldly and without fear. Paul harvests the good in his personal circumstances. He is able to endure mistreatment and even prison because his focus is on the advance of the Gospel. Paul recognizes that he can serve a role in it regardless of his present predicaments.

Even when Paul acknowledges the presence of preachers in the world who proclaim Christ out of false motives and in ways that caused troubles for Paul, he does not complain or appear forlorn. Instead, he rejoices because the Gospel advances regardless. Paul's vision is a big one. His central focus is God's mission, so he aligns his expectations and how he understands the

---

2. Grk *koinonia*

meaning of life in light of his missional commitment to the announcement of the Gospel across the Greco-Roman world.

Paul is facing death. He is not in prison for punishment but merely awaiting a trial before Caesar at which he'll be released or executed. Knowing this, Paul acknowledges the prayers of the Philippians and we learn of Paul's hope based on their prayers and his faith. His goal is not merely to survive. He recognizes fully that he may die. Paul's chief concern is that he serves as a faithful witness to the Gospel regardless of how his trial turns out. Moreover, if Paul, in fact, lives, he sees only the missional end of this, which for the Philippians means their upbuilding in preparing them for their participation in the mission of God (1:21–26).

Paul, thus, in his prayers and report of his own imprisonment models a gospel-centered life that overflows with love and concern for others. It is rooted in gratitude and demonstrates the possibility of living well in the face of suffering. This is a crucial point for the Philippians. With many Roman citizens among their number, they enjoy a relatively high status compared with the typical non-Roman living in the Empire. This status protected them. Following Jesus was risky. Participation in God's mission can be costly in terms of status and livelihood. Christ followers suffered persecution. Through his own suffering, and especially the manner with which he responds to it, Paul offers a witness to the Philippians to the very sort of life that Paul will call them to embody as citizens, not of Rome but of the gospel.

The principal exhortation in Philippians is found in 1:27 "Only live as citizens worthy of the gospel of the Messiah." The main body of Paul's letter is 1:27—4:1. After Paul makes this exhortation in 1:27–30, Paul then offers three examples of what this sort of lifestyle looks like: Jesus (2:1–18), Timothy/Epaphroditus (2:19–30), and Paul himself (3:1–16). Paul closes out this teaching section by calling for the Philippians to imitate these models as the means to living and standing as citizens of heaven (3:17—4:1).

The wording of the initial exhortation is important. The main verb (*politeuomai*) in 1:27a is an imperative that means "live as a citizens." Its noun cognate (*politeue*) is found in 3:20 "our citizenship is in heaven." In Paul's other writings, he uses the Greek word (*peripateo*) meaning "walk/live" in similar expressions (1 Thes 2:12; Col 1:10; Eph 4:1). Why does he use this particular exhortation "Live as citizens of the Gospel of the Messiah" in his letter to the Philippians?

First, the missiological setting of Philippi set the stage for this vocabulary. Philippi was a Roman colonial city where many veterans of the Roman army resided. Many of its residents (including some of the Christ followers) enjoyed Roman citizenship. This was a significant and important status in the Empire. Roman citizens enjoyed rights and privileges as a favored minority in the Empire. Being citizens of Rome was central to the ethos of Philippi. The Philippians were a privileged citizenry. Thus, by using the language of citizenship, Paul captures a meaningful word for Roman citizens and deploys it skillfully to call the Christians of Philippi to embrace a different sort of status and citizenship. Paul begins with what the Philippians understand as the epitome of life: living as a citizen of the Empire and subverts this by replacing allegiance to Rome as the highest calling with the ethos and vision of a different way of life: living as a citizen of heaven. A fundamental insight of the Book of Philippians is this: *the status that one embraces sets the limits of one's capacity to reach others with the Gospel.* Roman citizenship is a set of privileges that one enjoys and is able to exploit for his or her benefit. Gospel citizenship is a privileged relationship with God through Jesus that unleashes one to lay aside personal benefits for the sake of God's mission and for the good of others.

Second, Paul is clear that this is the key command in his letter. Most of our English translations begin v. 27 with "only." The idea here is this: *pay attention to this one thing* or *only one thing*. In other words, if the Philippians can embody this one exhortation, they will be living well. This is emphasized by the framing use of "our citizenship exists in heaven" (3:20) near the end of 1:27—4:1. Paul begins and ends this large block of teaching with a reference to citizenship. Paul is challenging the Philippians to rethink their notion of citizenship with its privileges in the Empire with a chance to embrace new citizenship with the Kingdom of God as God's missional people in the world.

Third, the nuance of the imperative "live as citizens of the Gospel of Christ" is emphatic. It stresses this way of life as a continuous action. We may capture this by translating the clause "live *continually* as citizens worthy of the Gospel of the Messiah." Paul is stressing that this calling is a moment-by-moment existence. It is not a one time or occasional activity. It is the essence of being Christ followers in Philippi. The shift is one of allegiance from being citizens of the Roman Empire to being and living as a citizens of heaven.

Fourth, Paul's goal is missional. Paul's wants the Philippians to embrace this new mode of life so that he may *hear* about the Philippian's Gospel shaped actions (1:27b–28). The principal witness according to Paul will be the Philippians "standing unified ("in one spirit") contending for the Gospel without being intimidated by foes. The stress on unity as a witness will weigh heavily in Paul's subsequent argument. The people of God in Philippi are to present a *corporate* witness to the world that is vital and powerful. The shift from living as citizens of the Empire to living as citizens of the Kingdom of Heaven is the key means of reaching the city of Philippi with the Good News about Jesus.

Last, Paul does not shy away from the reality of suffering and hardship that comes to the Philippian Christ followers because of the Gospel (29–30). This is not suffering in general or suffering due to ill-chosen actions. The suffering Paul is describing is suffering *because* they are allied with Jesus the Messiah. Paul's initial entry into Philippi stirred up opposition (Acts 16:16–40). The Philippians Christ followers are now experiencing similar troubles as Paul. If Paul's current troubles were with the Empire (1:12–26), it may be that the Philippians were also running into conflict with Roman citizens in Philippi who honored the Emperor alone as Lord. The confession "Jesus the Messiah is LORD" (2:9–10) is a bold and daring one in the context of an Empire that crushed all opposition. To have an allegiance above the state was risky. But profoundly, the Philippian's ability to stand together as the body of Christ serves as a sign to the very ones seeking to do them harm (1:28).

Now that we've described the principal exhortation that Paul offers in Philippians, we can unpack it more fully. The call to live as citizens of heaven is a radical shift in one's understanding of *status*. We can now see that Paul prepared his readers for this shift in his self-description at the beginning of his letter. We noted that Paul used "slave/servant" as his title for himself and for his co-worker Timothy. Now in 2:7 Paul uses it again as a title for Jesus. The use of *slave* language for both Paul (the founder of the church in Philippi) and Jesus (the crucified and risen Lord) is subversive in the Philippians context. It is a call to the Philippian Christ followers, many of whom had privileges as Roman citizens, to willingly embrace a lower status in imitation of Paul and Jesus for the sake of the advancement of the Gospel. The Gospel moves forward not by selfishly clinging to or exploiting one's own status, but by valuing and serving others.

(re)Aligning with God

Don't miss the profound challenge contextually to the Philippians of Paul's description of Jesus as a *slave*. Slaves sat at the bottom of the status ladder in Roman society. Paul's subversive use of *slave* is a key element in his teaching about living as citizens worthy of the Gospel. In 2:1–18, Paul offers Jesus as the first of three examples. At the center of this section is the Christ hymn (2:5–11). This poetic text unpacks what it means to embody the mind/attitude/intentions[3] of Jesus. Jesus is described positively for his own renunciation of status for the sake of advancing God's mission. Philippians 2:6 marvels at the reversal of expectations over the issue of Jesus' status. This text affirms that Jesus was divine and equal to God. Despite this reality, Jesus did not take this position of being equal with God as a privileged position to be exploited for his own gain. Jesus does not regard his *status* of being equal with God to be a collection of rights and prerogatives to be exploited for his own benefit. Instead, Jesus took the form of humanity. This announces the incarnation of Jesus into our world as a human. Notice this is announced first by the phrase "taking the form of a slave" (Grk *doulos*). This establishes the full force of Paul's exhortation to the Philippians about a new kind of citizenship. Their model is no longer the status quo of Roman social norms. It is Jesus. It is not merely that Jesus assumes the role and status of a slave. He identifies with it fully by embracing death on a cross. Don't miss the subversive power of this statement. Today's Christ followers are too familiar with thinking about Jesus' death on the cross that we can easily miss its message here. Jesus could have died an atoning death in a variety of ways. Why death on a cross? Crucifixion was reserved for the lowest classes of society. Roman citizens could not be crucified except as a penalty for treason. So, to the Philippians, Jesus' death on a cross demonstrated the *extent* to which Jesus was willing to renounce his status and identify with his adopted status of slave for the sake of God's mission.

The last half of the Christ hymn records the results of Jesus' willing embrace of a new status. Verse 2:9 announced dramatically that as a direct result of his humble embrace of low status, God highly exalted Jesus and gave him the name above all names. In other words, Jesus has his lowly status reversed. Jesus moves from the bottom of the status ladder to the highest possible one. He is LORD (2:11). This is no mere honorific title. There is no status above it. By identifying Jesus with the Name, i.e., Yahweh of Israel's Scriptures (cf. Isa 45:22–23), Jesus moves from the bottom of the

---

3. Grk *phroneo*.

status ladder to a status above Roman citizenship, above the Roman Emperor, and even above the Roman gods. Jesus alone is LORD, and all others will bow before him. The message to the Philippian believers is clear. They may cling to their status as Roman citizens, but if they willingly embrace a lower status, God will raise them up in Christ Jesus. The only status worth attaining is one given by God. The implication is also that any temporary loss of status for the sake of God's mission is infinitely worth it. As the Philippian Christ followers realign themselves for God's mission, they position themselves to reach others for the Gospel through their witness by moving from a way of life that values putting the self and its status first to focusing on lifting the status and honor of others (2:2–3). By doing so, the Philippians will "shine continually as stars in the world" (2:15). Stars have functioned as navigation points and signs for millennia. In like manner, the Philippians will serve as clues to the world about the true God. Such a life is nothing more and nothing less than a rediscovery of what God intended for humanity at creation (Gen 1:26–31). The status that Christ followers embrace establishes the limits of whom they can reach with the Gospel.

Let me illustrate by using a second example from Philippians that has some interface with what we found above. Scholars frequently describe Phil 2:19–30 as a travel report. It seems out of place as it falls between the sublime Christ hymn and Paul's autobiographical remarks in 3:1–16. Yet, when we read Paul's words about his coworkers, Timothy and Epaphroditus, carefully within the context of Philippians, we discover that they function as a critical word of exhortation and example for the Philippian Christ followers rather than a mere itinerary of their activities. In fact, 1:27—4:1 functions rhetorically as the central message of Philippians. Verse 1:27 exhorts the Christ followers, "Only live continually as citizens [of heaven] worthy of the Gospel. In this seemingly "dry" itinerary, Paul makes a couple of key points, which compare Timothy and Epaphroditus favorably to Jesus Christ. They are examples of self-sacrificial service. Timothy is lifted up as one who "genuinely cares" for the Philippians (2:20). This means that he is others-centered rather than self-centered (2:21, cf. 2:4). Timothy does not cling to his own rights and prerogatives, but works for the good of others. Epaphroditus is even more closely compared with Jesus because he came close to losing his life for the cause of Christ (2:30). Notice that Paul lifts up this type of behavior for commendation (2:29). Epaphroditus embodies the vocation of self-sacrificial love for the sake of the Gospel. This is the ethos that is in keeping with following the One who renounced status for the sake of reaching others with the Gospel. Paul is provocatively raising the bar on the missional potential of Christ-followers. The Philippians can and must model Jesus to one another and to the world for the sake of the Gospel.

Paul then moves to discuss his own conversion and offer himself as a final example for the Philippian believers to emulate. Paul's own conversion reflects not a self-emulation for his own moral failings or missing some standard. Rather, in Phil 3:4–6, Paul offers a list of his own achievements. Paul does not denigrate these accomplishments. His life was exemplary except for one element: he did not know Jesus the Messiah. His conversion served to reorient Paul with the true reality or as Paul says in 3:8 the "surpassing greatness" of *knowing* Messiah Jesus as Lord. This shift in perspective is crucial for Paul. It is no longer about his accomplishments, status, or value; life is about *being in Messiah*. This is not a merely passive activity but one that involves imitating the Messiah and intending the same values and outcomes as Jesus. This involves embracing the message of the cross for the sake of God's mission in the world. Paul envisions a new metric for prosperity that involves movement toward Christ and a relentless avoidance of self-aggrandizement. Paul surrendered those elements that gave him status in the world and found a new status in Messiah. This did not mean that Paul suddenly lost his zeal or rejected his years of Torah study as a Pharisee. Instead, these good things became tools and talents that God could then redeploy through Paul's new Messiah-centered life for the sake of others. To illustrate this shift concretely, observe in verse 6 that Paul writes, "as for zeal, I was a persecutor of the church." After his conversion, Paul describes his passionate pursuit of Jesus the Messiah by penning, "I am pressing on toward the goal of the upward calling of God in Messiah Jesus." In the Greek, the words for "persecutor" and "pressing on" are forms of the identical Greek verb *dioko*.[4] Paul does not suddenly cease being Paul. He simply becomes the ultimate version of Paul because of his relationship with Jesus the Messiah. This is a crucial insight for a missional reading of Philippians. Many times there is a tendency to denigrate the pre-Christian life as worthless "dung" based on what Paul writes in 3:8. Paul does state that he considers his pre-Christian life as loss, but this does not mean everything in his life was bad. It simply is a way of emphasizing how much radically better and valuable his life in Messiah is. As we engage the twenty-first-century world with the Gospel, we don't have to limit its reach to people with broken lives and obvious sin. We don't have to force talented

---

4. In 3:6, *dioko* occurs as a participle; in 3:14 (cf. 3:12), it is a present indicative.

and gifted people to jettison their pre-Christian life as worthless or all morally corrupt. We don't have to make faithful adherents of other religions feel that their well-intentioned attempts at piety apart from the knowledge of Jesus were completely lost years. Don't get me wrong. I am not questioning their lostness apart from knowing Jesus. But remember, Paul was morally upright, passionate about God, and a leader in Judaism's Pharisee sect. His enthusiasm for God never waned. He simply realized at a critical moment that Jesus Christ was truly Lord, and this recognition transformed Paul into the man that God truly dreamed for him to be. Paul models a full surrender, not only of our sins when we come to God, but also a surrender of the best of our gifts, talents, and passions. We don't surrender the latter because they are worthless or bad but because the fullness of knowing Messiah Jesus is infinitely better. For the Philippians, living as Roman citizens may have presented some good, but Paul is describing how in his own life he came to realize the ultimate life in Christ Jesus as a citizen of a different Kingdom— a citizen worthy of the Gospel. This full surrender that Paul describes in his own life becomes the model for the Philippians to follow in becoming the witnesses that God desires for them to be in the world.

So in 3:17 when Paul writes, "Join together in imitating my life brothers and sisters." We need to hear his words not as boastful or arrogant. Paul powerfully reminds his hearers that living well as citizens of heaven is a present possibility and not merely some future reality. The mode of living for the Messiah in the city of Philippi was possible in the now. Paul's life demonstrated this. But not only Paul's life but also other people whom the Philippians knew: Timothy and Epaphroditus (2:19–30). Paul ends 3:17 by writing, ". . . and observe carefully those who are walking thusly just as you have us for a pattern." It is worth remembering that Paul wrote this letter from prison (1:12–26). In fact, Paul did not know whether or not he would even survive his imprisonment (1:21). By calling on the Philippians to imitate his life, the lives of persons such as Timothy and Epaphroditus, and the life of Jesus (or more rightly the death of Jesus on the cross). This takes us back to the key missional teaching of the Book of Philippians: *the status Christ followers embrace establishes the limits of their capacity to reach others for the gospel.*

Paul, Timothy, and Epaphroditus all demonstrated that they were fully committed to the Gospel by breaking out of the status fixation of the first-century Mediterranean world. They were willing to lose face, embrace a lower status, and endure unjust punishment for the sake of reaching others with the Gospel. Living as citizens worthy of the Gospel meant embracing the ethos of Jesus the Messiah and becoming fully other-centered. Ironically, this mode of living is the true pathway to a prosperous life of joy, contentment, and ultimately vindication, not from mere mortals, but from God himself.

Paul concludes his letter by offering exhortations. What are the implications of living as citizens worthy of the Gospel? What does a renunciation of the need for status mean?

The first exhortation is a call to unity among church leaders. This may seem to be a let down after the profundity of Paul's description of living as a citizen of the Gospel, but don't miss the power of it. Missional impact requires a unified community that corporately reflects God's character to the world. Specifically, Paul directly addresses Euodia and Syntyche, who presumably were serving as leaders in the house church at Philippi. Paul deploys language similar to 2:2, 2:5, and 3:15 by calling them to embrace the same mind or intention in the Lord. What is this same mind? It is the other-centered attitude embodied in the incarnation of Jesus. It is to intend the same purposes and actions as Jesus. It is to put the concerns of others over the concerns of self. It is a call to renounce status and rights to the extent that they prevent Euodia and Syntche from serving one another and the Christ followers in Philippi for the sake of God's mission in the world.

The second exhortation is to be joyful. This is not a joy that comes from a detached view of reality or by cutting oneself off from deep relationships with others. It is not Pollyannish. Paul knows that the Christ following community in Philippi in experiencing the suffering that comes from persecution. Paul writes about joy while experiencing Roman imprisonment. God's people on mission will not be immune from hardship, but they are gifted with the opportunity to find joy *despite* and, yes, even *in* suffering. Joy is missional. "Let your reasonableness be known to all people." Moving from self-centeredness to a God-focused confidence allows us to be other-centered in our relationship with others. This does not mean that there will be no challenges in life. As Paul has already testified, there will be. For the Christ follower, however, joy remains a transformative reality. Joy is a satisfying sense of inner tranquility, happiness, and confident peace that empowers the Christ follower to navigate all of life's circumstances without the need to panic or act out of bitterness and rage. Living with this type of joy sends an extraordinary message to the watching world. This joy transcends one's physical circumstances, whether they be good, bad, or in between.

Elsewhere in Paul's writings, joy is part of the fruit of the Holy Spirit (Gal 5). Joy is the work of God, but this does not mean that there is no human side to experiencing God's joy. Here in Philippians, Paul unpacks how the Philippian Christians can practice a life of rejoicing. Phil 4:5b–6 describe this. Joy is rooted in the work of God. Paul summarizes this: "The Lord is near." This nearness probably points to two realities. First, the Risen Jesus is with us. Knowing Christ is the ultimate value Paul has taught (3:8). Paul enjoyed such a profound communion with Jesus that he could write, "Living is Christ" (1:21a). Second, Paul anticipated confidently the arrival of God's future on the day of Christ (1:6, 1:10). This day would be marked by the final resurrection of which Jesus' resurrection was the first fruit. In other words, a fundamental piece of experiencing joy is recognizing that the future is secure in Christ. Christ followers can embrace citizenship in the Gospel because it guarantees the future in ways that mere Roman citizenship could never dream possible. Flowing from this sense of a secure future, Paul reminds the Philippians to move away from worry and anxiousness. There is no need for these. Worry is unnecessary for the believer because God has already won the future. Rather than worry, Paul instructs Christ followers to release everything to God in petitions and requests grounded in a sense of gratitude for what God has done, is doing, and will do. Paul has already testified to the advance of the Gospel in Philippi (1:3–8) and around the Mediterranean due to Paul's imprisonment (1:12–14). With the Gospel moving forward, there will always be reasons to be thankful. The result of this is the true peace that only God can provide. This is a peace that undergirds joy and secures the inner thought life of the Christ follower.

Paul's exhortation to rejoice is, thus, the logical result of living a life worthy of the citizens of the Gospel. Ironically, the willingness to relinquish one's status and rights opens one up to the possibility of experiencing a true joy that would never be possible to one that hold's tight to one's status and rights in vain hope that such human constructs could bring lasting satisfaction.

Paul's third exhortation is for the Philippian Christ followers to live out a moment-by-moment relationship of ongoing transformation in Christ. Philippians 4:8–9 sketches out a mode of living and growing for Christ followers in Philippi. This way of life involves thinking and acting. Living in Christ is not a static existence of monotony. Paul understood the shifting sands of time and context. He knew both Greek and Jewish Christ followers all over the Greco-Roman world. Living as a citizen worthy of the

(re)Aligning with God

Gospel involved living out habits of mind and heart, as well as acting out these with our lips, hands, and feet. First, Paul calls the Philippians to fill their minds with virtue and excellence. Negative or impure thinking does not produce the fruit of the Kingdom. This exhortation lines up well with Paul's prayer in 1:9–11. Paul had asked God to make the Philippians overflow with a loved rooted in the purposes of God so that they would be able to discern best practices and habits for living out the Gospel. Gaining true discernment would lead to holy living. Part of cultivating habits of holiness begins with filling one's mind with the best and most virtuous thinking, rather than the base drivel that is easily available to the masses. Paul desires for Christ followers to rise above this so he reminds them of the necessity of filling their minds well. Second, Paul moves from right thinking to right living. These are related. Paul is not drawing some sort of contrast here. Rather, he envisions a holistic relationship between thinking and acting. Right thinking leads to right living. Not only are the Philippians to fill their minds with the best and most virtuous, they are also to put into practice all that they have learned from Paul. A missional Christian life is not simply a possibility—it can be a reality. It must become the norm for Christian living and not merely some exception. How do you live as a citizen worthy of the Gospel? Paul would say to follow his model. Notice the words that Paul uses to describe his example: the Christ followers in Philippi had *received* from Paul, *had learned* from Paul, *heard* Paul, *and saw* how Paul lived his life. Paul modeled a life that demanded explanation through his teachings, his words, and his deeds. The implication of Paul's words though is for the each Philippian to begin to serve as a model for others and, thereby, multiply the work begun by Paul in the city.

Finally, Paul calls for the Philippians to share their resources generously (4:10–20). It is remarkable the amount of space that Paul spends acknowledging and giving thanks for the gifts he has received from the Christ followers in Philippi. The Philippians had been patrons of Paul's missional activities from the beginning. In fact, they had been his only source of support at times. Paul acknowledges this past generosity and shows gratitude for it. A key element in Paul's thinking here is that God is faithful to supply the needs of God's people. He declares memorably, "I can do all things through him who gives me strength." Paul trusts deeply in God. Even in prison, he had received the food and supplies that he needed. In fact, this is the gift that Epaphroditus had carried to Paul.

Moreover, Paul believes that God will bless the Philippians, too. In verse 19, he writes, "My God will fill all your needs according to his riches in glory in Christ Jesus." Paul is subtle and careful in his writing. He is not begging for a handout from the Philippians. He is content with whatever he has and profoundly grateful for their support in the recent past. However, it is clear that Paul is presenting an opportunity for the Philippians to contribute more. Paul's message is straightforward: continue to give generously to my work in furthering the Gospel. Invest in God's mission in the world. The Philippians are a wealthy group of believers compared with the fledging churches across Greece and Asia Minor. Living as citizens worthy of the Gospel for them means funding the work of others with their material blessings. Giving does not mean a loss for the Philippians but an opportunity for God to meet their needs. Paul's implict call is for the Philippians to move from a tendency to hoard and hold on tight to resources to a consistent practice of giving. In the process, Paul models the importance of deep and heart-felt gratitude for the generosity of others.

To summarize, it is fruitful to deploy a missional reading of the Book of Philippians. By reading Philippians as a letter written to equip and empower the Philippians to engage in best practices regarding God's mission in the world, we have gained substantive insight into Paul's letter. The principal teaching point is Paul's exhortation for the Philippians to embrace a higher form of citizenship than mere Roman citizenship. He reminds them that they are now citizens of heaven. As such, they are to follow the examples of Jesus, Paul's coworkers, and Paul himself who pursued a cross-centered life and willingly embraced a lower status for the sake of God's mission in the full confidence that such a life will be vindicated when Christ returns to consummate fully the Kingdom of God. The missional takeaway is this: *the status that one embraces establishes the limits of one's capacity to reach others with the Gospel.* By embracing the status of a *slave*, the Philippians gain a position from which to engage anyone with the Good News about Jesus the Messiah.

PART THREE
Aligning Our Communities

7

Unleashing the Biblical Narrative: Implementing a Missional Hermeneutic in Our Communities of Faith

All followers of Jesus Christ need to locate themselves in the biblical narrative of God's mission from Creation to New Creation and live in light of it. This is the goal of realigning with God. If the Scriptures exist to convert readers to their perspective, then the sign of this conversion is the abiding of followers of Jesus in the Scriptural story.

In the previous two chapters we have reflected on the process of learning to read Scripture for the Church and for the World, for insiders/followers and outsiders/seekers. Now we will reflect on how to implement this vision of a missional reading within our existing communities of faith. We must begin by assessing the extent to which our community is already realigned.

Here is a test. Ask yourselves these questions:

- Are you cast in God's story or are you part of some other story?
- With what great stories does your own soul resonate?
- What movies or fictional works have shaped the way that you live your life?
- What has more influence on your life: the story of Scripture or the stories popularized by the surrounding culture?

William Shakespeare penned these oft-quoted lines for his comedy "As You Like It" (Act II Scene 7):

(re)Aligning with God

> All the world's a stage,
> And all the men and women merely players:
> They have their exits and their entrances;
> And one man in his time plays many parts,
> His acts being seven ages.

These words are pregnant with meaning and invite us to think deeply about our own role in the unfolding drama of the twenty-first century. As followers of Jesus we need to consider the trajectory of our own lives. What is our part? What role should we be playing?

Theologian Robert Jensen points to the Scriptures as the guide:

> Scripture's story is not part of some larger narrative; it is itself the larger narrative of which all other true narratives are parts. Biblical exegesis is reading the sides and prop lists and so forth for the drama that God and his universe are now living together. And so do not when reading Scripture try to figure out how what you are reading fits into some larger story; for there is no larger story.[1]

Lindbeck makes the same point writing that it is not that "believers find their stories in the Bible, but rather that they make the story of the Bible their story."[2]

Too often we can find ourselves shaped more by the stories of the World than by the story of Redemption as unfolded in the Scriptures.[3] Our age is one of increasing ignorance of the biblical message. This means that followers of Jesus have to be intentional in (re)teaching the Scriptures. But the teaching must move beyond simply a recitation of biblical facts as though knowledge of Scripture could be equated with preparation for Jeopardy or some other quiz show. Instead, a missional reading of the Scriptures is committed to helping women and men to understand and find their place in the grand narrative that God is writing from Creation to New Creation. A missional reading fosters transformational learning for a life of following Jesus faithfully into the world on mission. Reading the Bible missionally means making a shift from privileging information to experiencing transformation. Moreover, a missional reading seeks to make evident the manifold ways in which each part of the Scriptures seeks to convert its reader/

---

1. Jensen, "Scripture's Authority," 34.
2. Lindbeck, *Nature of Doctrine*, 118.
3. To be shaped by the world is to live under the influence of idolatry. See Hirsch and Hirsch, *Untamed*, 55–81.

hearer to its perspective. The goal of such a life is to unleash transformed people not merely to make a difference in the world but to share in God's work of crafting a different world.

We have argued for a GPS reading of the Scriptures. God's people are to live as a missional community that serves by reflecting and embodying the character of God to/for/in the world. The triad of mission, community, and holiness serves as compass points for an ongoing realignment with God's intentions for the world and humanity as revealed in the Biblical witness.

How Well Are We Playing Our Part?

The God of Scripture continues to seek women and men who are willing to align with God's creational intentions. Church planter and consultant Alex McManus uses the metaphor of clue to capture the essence of our lives as Jesus' followers.[4] In his thinking, each of us serves as a clue to the meaning of life. As persons created in God's image, we exist to point others to God. We are clues to the mysteries of the universe. When we serve the purposes imagined for us in the Scriptures, we live as the people whom God created us to be. When others encounter enough "clues," the clues lead them to God. The goal of a missional reading of Scripture is conversion. Followers of Jesus must be converted continually by the message of the text so that they may realign with God's work in the world. The goal of this realignment is the expansion of the Jesus following community in the world. We realign continually so that God can deploy us fully to carry the message of realignment to others.

Evaluating our Communities of Faith

After we reflect on our individual role, we must find our place within a community. There are no perfect communities of faith so we need to evaluate and realign continually. The purpose of this evaluation is to create a longing for what is possible by God's grace and the *faithful response* of God's people. This section is not intended to justify the fracturing of any existing faith communities or communions. The criteria below are meant to move communities toward a more wholistic biblical norm.

4. Private conversation.

(re)Aligning with God

Global Mission

A missional reading of Scripture challenges each local community of faith to assess its fidelity to the Scriptural vision of God's people as a *missional community that reflects God's character to/for/in the world.*

Communities of faith and individuals within them must take seriously a couple of key questions.

First, do we/I embody an OT missional outlook or a NT missional outlook? In other words, are we fully embodying the mission of God unleashed by the Risen Christ through the power of the Holy Spirit? Said another way, do we "go and send" disciples into the world on mission or do we wait upon the world to "come" to us?

As we saw in Part One God's Old Testament people are formed and shaped in their own land in the midst of the nations. Although there are rare exceptions like Jonah, the Old Testament does not model a missionary or "go to" ethos. The nations *come* to Israel if they are to receive its blessing. The coming of Jesus creates a tectonic shift in the tactics of God's people. The Great Commission sums up the New Testament vision of the mission of God's people post-Resurrection: Go and make disciples of all nations (Matt 28:18). This is not an isolated text. It encapsulates the model of Jesus' peripatetic ministry and of the apostolic mission.[5] We don't make disciples by waiting for them to come to worship. People become disciples through encountering Christ-followers in the world. It is about going and sending. Communities of faith need to envision themselves as apostolic outposts that deploy disciples for the sake of God's mission. The alternative is to create consumers of religious goods and services. The mark of the New Testament church is an outward focused "make disciples of the nations" centered understanding of mission. Christ has died. Christ is risen. Christ will come again. The future is secure and it will be beautiful and full of love. This is the Gospel. To be missional is to align ourselves and our resources to maximize the proclamation of this good news to all.

Second, we must take seriously the question: *Who is my mission?* This question must not be answered, "Everyone!" This is the easy and obvious response, but it is a dangerous one. I would humbly suggest that if we say everyone, then it is likely that in reality we mean "no one." There are over

---

5. For example, Acts 1:8 serves programmatically to envision the reach of God's mission to the ends of the earth. Or consider Paul's words in Rom 15:18–21 where he states clearly his self-understanding of mission as proclaiming the good news where Christ has yet to be named.

six billion people on our planet. Our mission cannot be everyone. Instead, the question "Who is my mission?" must evoke the names and faces of people. I suggest that we make this question our prayer. I believe that when we ask this question God will put the faces of persons currently in our life in our mind's eye. Sometimes God will put people whom we've not yet met, but the key is mission equals tangible flesh and blood people. This gives us focus. Asking, "Who is my mission?" forces us to think strategically about our context and our relationship with persons outside of the community of faith. It will help to clarify our priorities in terms of time and resources. It reminds us of the purpose of the Christ following movement. The Gospel transforms us so that we can serve as conduits of God's grace and mercy to others. The burning question for our communities of faith involves identifying the people and the places that God has called us to serve and then *going* rather than waiting and expecting outsiders to find their way to us. As we saw repeatedly in our survey of the New Testament, the Christ following movement's modus operandi is "go." It is also important to help Christ followers avoid bait and switch friendships. The persons whom God calls us to serve may never move toward the cross. But this does not mean that we abandon our *friendships* with them.

Last, related to both of these is the issue of the global Christian movement. The eighteenth-century English evangelist John Wesley proclaimed, "The world is my parish." He took the Gospel across Britain and sent Methodist missionaries to the Americas. Wesley himself did not permit geography to limit his reach as an itinerant evangelist. During his lifetime, he preached approximately 40,000 sermons and traveled 250,000 miles on horse. Methodist circuit riders carried the Gospel into the hinterland of the newly founded United States. The reality today is that geography is no longer relevant. Tim Tennent, current Asbury Seminary President, expresses the truth this way: "It's not the world is my parish; now it's the world is *in* my parish." Our local communities can have global impact by acting *locally*. Most major cities in the United States have significant recent immigrant populations. Churches near colleges and universities have the opportunity to reach out in love and service to students and scholars from across the globe. In Orlando, several local churches host Chinese scholars in their homes and offer English classes that include introduction to the Biblical narrative. Around the country, churches are learning to minister cross-culturally simply by engaging immigrant populations in their towns and cities. Christians in Minneapolis serve a burgeoning population of Somali refugees. This phenomenon is not confined to large urban areas. Churches in rural Georgia have learned to serve migrant agricultural workers. In other words, we can continue the mission of reaching the world by reaching out to those who are now in close proximity to us. This in no way detracts from a commitment to funding and supporting overseas mission work. But it takes communities of faith to make a global impact *locally*. This is a key to achieving a truly missional ethos. Moreover, it allows the easy participation of virtually everyone in every day mission work over and against needing to raise funds for costly "short term" mission trips.

Persons in Community

A missional reading of Scripture calls us to become missional *communities*. We learn to read Scripture to discover what it means to serve as God's people on mission. We engage the text to invite persons on the outside to become members of our community as they explore the life of faith. Missional communities exist to empower Christ followers to function fully as God's people in the world. They, likewise, exist to shape outsiders into insiders. In our recent past, the approach to community was "believe first and then belong." A missional approach encourages women and men to belong first and then believe.

The more disconnected *and* interconnected that our world becomes the more vital *authentic biblical community* becomes. God created humanity for *community*. God calls God's people to be part of God's new humanity: a missional *community*. This claim is rooted in Creation where God forged humanity to live together in shared dominion for the purposes of fulfilling God's aims for the world. The consistent biblical witness is that God's salvific aims remain tied to a *people* rather than to solitary individuals.

The most basic question is this: Who is my community? With whom do I and will I live my life? Do I belong to a group that loves me authentically and where I can use my gifts and talents fully for God's mission in the world?

Second, what kind of a community are we? Do we exist primarily to equip, send, and go into the world on mission, or are we a community that exists for some other purpose? If *mission* is not central to the perceived and lived-out DNA of the community, then it is not a missional community.

Third, we must reflect critically on any *barriers* intentional or unintentional that block others from access to our community. How open are the various components of our community to newcomers? How easy is it for an *outsider/seeker* to become an *insider/follower*? Are we so mono-cultural as to be impermeable to persons of different ages, political views, styles of dress, ethnicity, socio-economic status, or any of the elements that fracture the wider human community? Are we in the world enough to be a visible presence or is the chief barrier the fact that we meet primarily inside of a building separated from the world? Perhaps the most important question is this: What do we expect a person to become as a precondition to hearing the Gospel from us?

Finally, we must ask: What kind of community do we need to become to embody fully the Scriptural vision of a missional community that reflects God's character to/for/in the world? As we evaluate our community there must be a willingness to *change* in favor of becoming more welcoming to *outsiders* for the sake of God's mission.

Spirit Transformed

God desires to transform each of us into the man or woman whom God created us to be. This is the power of the Gospel. A missional community exists to reflect God's character. To reflect God's character requires the work of the Holy Spirit.

The key questions for moving forward are these: What kind of person do I need to become in order to function as a member of a missional community? How does my life need to change? Am I willing to surrender my life to the world imagined by the Bible?

This moves the conversation away from *personal* spiritual formation as an end in itself to a true mission-centered spiritual formation that steadfastly insists on including active engagement in God's mission in any definition of Christian maturity and discipleship. E. Stanley Jones, the great twentieth-century missionary to India, once said, "Christianity that doesn't begin with the individual doesn't begin; Christianity that ends with the individual ends." The questions in the preceding paragraph inspire hearers to dream about the new life that is available through following Jesus Christ into the world on mission. The purpose of the transformed life is to unleash women and men to serve as visible clues to the reality of the invisible God. When outsiders encounter enough clues they should find themselves at the cross with its invitation to the life that God intended for them to embrace and embody.

"Cross" Pollination

GPS works as a triad of themes in tandem. They can be separated for study, but they must be held together in practice as we've already implied. As we evaluate our communities it is not enough to be for mission, community, or holiness. God has called us as human beings to serve as a missional community that reflects and embodies God's character to, for, and in the world.

There is a missional element in the Spirit's work of transformation. A transformed life witnesses to *outsiders* the reality of God's kingdom. The work of sanctification is an ongoing one is the life of the Christ followers. It moves forward in both crisis moments and gradually through the processes of life. Transformed lives that reflect God's creational intentions are potent clues to the mysteries of God. This is why holiness cannot be separated from mission or community. God does not transform our character simply so that we can be drawn out of the world. God transforms our character so that we can follow Jesus into the darkest places on earth and serve as lights.

There is equally a communal element to the Spirit's transforming work. Reflecting God's character is inherently communal. Holiness begins with the individual, but if it ends with the individual then it is not a biblical holiness. Holiness is always social. We reflect God's character as a testimony for others of God's glory.

Lesslie Newbigin captures the essence of our argument when he wrote,

> How is it possible that the gospel should be credible, that people should come to believe that the power, which has the last word in human affairs is represented by a man hanging on a cross? I am suggesting that the only answer, the only hermeneutic of the gospel, is a congregation of men and women who believe it and live by it.[6]

The goal of a missional hermeneutic is a continual realignment with God for the sake of God's mission in the world. It is imperative that we assess ourselves and our communities honestly. The criteria outlined above demonstrate the need. The remainder of this chapter will reflect critically and practically on the role that a missional reading of Scripture plays in creating missional communities that embody God's holiness.

---

6. Newbigin, *Gospel in a Pluralist Society*, 227.

Unleashing the Biblical Narrative

How Do We Implement this Vision?

A missional approach to the Scriptures demands a thoroughgoing rethinking of the role that the Bible plays in our local communities of faith. It needs to reach from the pulpit to the small group to an individual's private reading. Mission, community, and holiness are themes that permeate all of the Scripture. To miss these elements is to misread the Bible in significant ways. We will sketch out programmatically a means of implementing a missional reading.

Subvert the Dominant Narratives of Your Context

The goal of biblical interpretation is conversion. The key part of this process is learning to find our place in the biblical story and helping others to do likewise. God desires to unleash a missional community to reflect and embody God's character before a watching world. True conversion involves the subversion of our pre-Christian stories so that they are reshaped and reconfigured within God's story. Short of this subversion, we may never fully embrace and find the true humanity that God wants us to experience through the life, death, and resurrection of Jesus Christ. As interpreters of Scripture for Church and World we must be teachers and preachers who boldly and cogently paint a new world for our hearers. The biblical text is our portal to the reality that God desires for us to embody. Our interpretive work must seek to recreate and revision the world of the text so that our hearers can imagine what their lives might look like if they became part of that world. This involves a direct engagement with the world (locally and globally) of our hearers. We must become better readers of Scripture, but we must also learn to exegete our culture. The clearest pathway to subverting pre-Christian narratives and offering the way of the Kingdom is learning to read Scripture against and for the culture.

Understand Our Context

Who are the people whom God has called us to reach? What are their stories? What worldviews are held? What causes matter to them? About what do they care? A missional hermeneutic must be attentive to these questions. Obviously we are committed to encountering the Scriptures in all of their richness, but if we hope to share its message with others we must be willing to engage people at a deep level as well. Biblical studies professors often use this quotation to remind students of the centrality of reading the Bible within its literary context: "A text without a context is a pretext for saying anything that an interpreter wants to say." But it is, likewise, true that a biblical message apart from a local context of people becomes a pretext for misunderstanding and wasted words. We must be committed to shaping our speech, metaphors, and images in light of the context to which we are communicating. When we combine a rich understanding of the biblical story with a deep connection with the people to whom God has sent us, we find ourselves in an environment in which we can truly speak to fellow humans about the biblical message of (re)alignment. We find ourselves with the crucified and risen Jesus calling Christ followers to join fully in God's mission and inviting those on the margins to become part of God's work of ushering in a different world.

Moreover, we must also gain a sense of the gods that bind the hearts and minds of the women and men in our ministry context. Only when we understand the idols that capture the hearts of the world will we be prepared to proclaim the Lordship of Jesus in ways that subvert the claims and practices of those idols. A missional hermeneutic recognizes that idols exist within both the church and world. They are easy to spot: sex, consumerism, power, family, security, pleasure, and freedom among others.[7] But these have different localized expressions. A missional approach to Scripture listens to the text in light of the idols that reign over our culture.

As interpreters of Scripture, we learn the culture by listening carefully to the stories of the outsiders to the Christ following movement with whom we become friends. We also can learn the culture by reading the books and magazines enjoyed by the masses, and by being conversant and familiar with the popular culture of our day. In a sense, learning to exegete our context involves becoming more *worldly* in the sense of giving careful attention in terms of time and activities to persons presently outside or on the fringes of the Christ following movement.

A key dimension involves learning to treasure people as people. Talk of mission can sometimes involve bait and switch. We encourage Christians to befriend non-Christians principally for evangelistic purposes. But when a conversion does not follow, we move along to another non-Christian. We need to move to a more relational model of engaging the world where we build lasting friendships regardless of whether our new friend turns to Jesus

---

7. Hirsch and Hirsch, *Untamed*. See also Keller, *Counterfeit Gods*.

as Lord or not. Authentic friendships will open up entire new networks of people whom we would otherwise never have met. This will profoundly shape the way that we read the Bible because we will unconsciously begin to see and hear the Scriptures through the eyes and ears of our new friends.

Preach the Big Picture of the Bible Regularly.

A foundation of a missional hermeneutic is the commitment to the whole of Scripture as *the story of God's mission in the world and our response to it*. The Christ following community needs to hear the biblical narrative as a whole proclaimed in a single message or teaching block. Just as many churches regularly preach series on their core values, communities of faith who desire to live out the biblical narrative need to hear it in its totality often. I would recommend beginning each year with a message that succinctly captures the overarching contours of the Bible.[8] Rehearing the story from Creation to New Creation provides the foundation for rooting the self-understanding of the community in God's mission. It expands our understanding of a life with God beyond the realm of personal spirituality. The big picture of the Bible reminds us and pushes us to embrace a broader vision for life.

Proclaiming the biblical narrative of God's mission sets the rest of the teaching and preaching ministry of the community within the broad contours of biblical theology. Instead of a disjointed approach to the Scriptures, all preaching and teaching can be understood within the big story. Too often sermons and small group lessons grapple with a tiny portion of Scripture without relating it to the whole. Teaching the big picture regularly allows for coherence and continuity within the community of faith. Jesus followers gain a more wholistic understanding of Scripture. This understanding keeps mission on the front-burner. It reminds all who hear that God created men and women to participate in something much bigger than themselves.

Such an approach initiates outsiders/seekers and recent converts to the contours of the Bible. In our post-Christian reality the biblical message must be (re)taught continually. A basic knowledge of the Gospel message can no longer be assumed. It is vital for the Christ following movement to

---

8. It is up to local communities of faith to discern when the beginning of the year is. For some this may mean January; others may reckon it with the beginning of a new school year.

move away from fragmented approaches to preaching and teaching to a holistic approach in which the preacher/teacher walks the tightrope between in depth study of discrete parts of the Scripture and the rooting of discrete texts within the broader contours of the Gospel.

We need constant reminders of the story into which we have been cast. The Gospel is counter-cultural, but for it to function as a critique of the dominant stories of the wider culture it must be proclaimed continually and boldly. A commitment to presenting the big picture regularly allows a natural forum for continual formation of followers of Jesus. It keeps the main thing the main thing to use a dictum of modern leadership. We compete against the 24/7 bombardment of the entertainment/marketing/sports complex central to Western life. Repetition and staying on message is crucial for implanting, nurturing and sustaining a missional ethos within our communities.

Teaching and valuing the grand narrative encourages individuals and groups to read the Scriptures from Genesis to Revelation. By supplying a framework for understanding the whole, communities who regularly teach the biblical story empower individuals to engage the Scriptures on their own. The big picture serves as a framework or rubric for understanding and assimilating the various discrete components of the Bible.

Teaching the Big Picture

Use Part One in this book to teach the broad contours of the Scriptural story from Genesis to Revelation. In my years of teaching at Asbury Seminary and in local churches and conference across the United States and Canada, I have found students and audiences most riveted and helped by sharing the theological outline of the Bible that I unpacked in the initial chapters of this book.

It is applicable to all ages and stages of faith development. The sooner people learn that the Bible is not some random series of unrelated stories and teachings the better. The new adult convert to the Christ following movement will be able to engage the Scriptures. Young people will have their worldview shaped decisively for God's missional dreams and intentions. Families will be transformed and unleashed as witnesses to the reality of a New Creation.

Unleashing the Biblical Narrative
Rediscovering the Old Testament

A key feature of this proposal is that it provides a framework for reading the Old Testament and the New Testament as Christian Scripture. It sets the New Testament within its full Biblical context *and* it opens up the Old Testament to serve as authoritative Scripture in its own right.

In the context of the Western world's biblical illiteracy, the Old Testament in increasingly neglected in teaching and preaching. At best, its stories are left for Children's education. At worst, it is viewed as irrelevant, or even offensive.

To be sure the Old Testament contains its share of difficult passages. It shares stories of violence and human foibles. We can find the best and worst of humanity in its pages. John Bright once wrote, "I find it most interesting and not a little bit odd that although the Old Testament on occasion offends our Christian feelings, it did not apparently offend Christ's 'Christian feelings'!"[9] The witness of Jesus, the Apostles, and the early Church was univocal on the significance of the Jewish Scriptures. They treated Israel's Scriptures as substantive, essential, and authoritative for the Christian life and for engaging the world missionally.[10] We must recapture the Old Testament in our day.

A missional reading of Scripture boldly reasserts the relevance of Israel's Scriptures for the Christ following movement. The book of Genesis serves as the harbinger of renewed engagement with the theology of the Old Testament with its narratives of Creation, Fall, and God's calling into existence a new humanity that will serve as agents of blessing to all people. The Old Testament is essential for understanding God's creational intentions for both the world as a whole and for women and men in particular. It describes poignantly and relationally the problem of lostness and brokenness that confronts us in our daily lives. A missional reading resists the temptation to focus exclusively on the New Testament. Apart from the witness of Israel's Scriptures, one risks distorting the mission and message of Jesus the Messiah as well as that of the Church as the *sent* people of God for the sake of *all* peoples. Toward this end, communities of faith seeking to shape identity around God's mission will consciously teach the whole of the Scriptures because of their necessity in forming a *sent* people to reflect God's character to/for/in the nations.

9. Bright, *Authority of the Old Testament*, 77.

10. See Paul's words in 2 Tim 3:16–17 as one example of how the Apostles viewed the Old Testament and its use for life and mission.

(re)Aligning with God

As followers of Jesus, we may find in the stories of the Old Testament easier points of contact between the Gospel and outsiders. First, as we noted, Genesis 1–11 has an international focus. It invites all people everywhere to find their story in the Scriptures. Second, the stories found in Israel's Scriptures are profoundly human. We encounter in them all of the foibles and peccadilloes that befall women and men as well as the major life altering train wrecks with which we are all too familiar. The Old Testament narrative includes stories of risk and adventure, joy and sadness, success and failure, and liberation and oppression. These are the themes that capture the imagination of us all as they represent the dreams and fears of all people. Last, the Hebrew Scriptures narrate the working of God in human history. The story of God's mission offers a counter-narrative to those of our day, and it demonstrates that history is truly moving toward some greater purpose than self-centeredness and the carnage that ensues when self-centeredness, as practiced by individuals, tribes, or nations, is implemented against those deemed outsiders.

Rethink Church Leadership

Our understanding of church leadership must undergo a paradigm shift. Pastors must be re-commissioned as resident missiologists and equippers.[11] This shift in self-understanding to resident missiologist is an explicit reminder that the pastor functions primarily for the sake of the *world* rather than for the *church*. Christendom models for ministry viewed faith communities as safe places and refuges from the world. Pastors served as religious experts, chaplains, and dispensers of religious goods and services. Recapturing the DNA of the early church means a return to the apostolic imperative of a mission centered paradigm for ministry. Mission must permeate the entire body of Christ—especially its leaders. As pastors shift to seeing themselves as resident missiologists, they will shift from being only *students of Scripture* to also becoming *students of culture*. They will function not only as *shepherds of a flock of believers* but also more and more as the *shepherd who leads the flock to find other lost sheep*. Moreover, they will view themselves less as *administrators of institutions* and more as *catalysts of missional movements*. Remember the first convert to a missional reading

---

11. This is a move away from seeing the pastor as resident theologian, chaplain, or CEO. All of these have been popular over the last generation.

must always be the interpreter him/herself. Many of you reading this book are clergy. It is vital that you lead from the front.

A missional approach to the Bible invites us to unleash all of God's people in mission. A missional reading of Scripture recognizes that the Bible affirms the need for leadership, but it rejects any understanding of ordination that stifles the full participation of all of God's people in God's mission in the world.

God created all people (women and men) for service as his visible representatives. As God called Abraham and ultimately forged a new humanity in the nation of Israel, God commissioned the nation as a whole to serve as a "kingdom of priests and a holy nation" (Exod 19:6; cf. 1 Pet 2:9). Yes, Israel had a system of set apart servants (priests and Levites), but God's vision did not restrict mission to this subset of the nation. Outsiders to the religious hierarchy could and did make significant contributions to the advancement of God's mission in the Old Testament. For example, the prophet Amos self-identifies himself as an outsider rather than risk any misunderstanding of his calling as involving professionalization (Amos 7:14–15).

The New Testament documents portray the body of Christ as an organism in which each believer plays a crucial role through the deployment of his or her gift for the sake of the *mission* of the whole (Rom 12, 1 Cor 12–14, Eph 4). In contrast, Christendom subverted the biblical witness by setting churches up as institutions in which paid professions "do ministry" on behalf of a group of mostly passive spectators (usually called the "laity") who function principally as the providers of the financial resources to fuel the mission of the Church.[12] Pastors need to have the courage to teach and implement the biblical model of a gift-based culture in which all Christ-followers are unleashed to deploy their gifts, talents, and passions for the sake of the Gospel. In this new environment, pastors need to function primarily as equippers rather than laborers. Here is a test: if the pastor has to be present for a ministry to function, the pastor has not created a gift-based culture within his or her congregation.

Perhaps most significantly there is a need to recapture the apostolic nature of the New Testament church. Ephesians 4:11 describes the following gifts given to communities of faith for the upbuilding of the body: apostles, prophets, evangelists, pastors, and teachers.[13] Most communities

---

12. Forgive the overstatement for the sake of the overall argument.

13. This list may be four or five distinct gifts as the grammar linking pastors and

of faith emphasize the role of pastor-teacher. This worked out naturally in a context in which the culture was "Christian." But in our day as Christian memory recedes, or as in many places has been lost all together, the pastor-teacher model privileges principally the current Church membership. In the New Testament vision of Ephesians 4, these categories are mission focused. Those with an apostolic vision continually seek to advance the Gospel into new places. Mission advances through men and women with an entrepreneurial spirit to reach new places and people with the Gospel. In our day these new places are likely the very neighborhoods in which our communities of faith meet. Those with prophetic leanings serve to call God's people to realign with the core mission and values of the Gospel. The evangelists engage the uninitiated with Gospel. The interplay of these gifts creates a dynamic environment for the advancement of God's mission through the unleashing of the full human resources of the body of Christ. Imagine the renewed effectiveness of the pastor-teacher in a context in which the apostles, prophets, and evangelists are functioning. Pastors and teachers function by shepherding God's people and training them in the faith so that they may serve faithfully in God's mission.

Overarching Principles for Implementing a Missional Hermeneutic

1) Our own *missional* reading of Scripture needs to arise out of our *missional praxis*. As we (re)learn to read the Bible as a means of (re)aligning with God, we will discover that the practice of mission will enhance our understanding of Scripture. There is no way forward unless we are actively and intentionally present in the world.

As we seek to implement a missional reading of the Bible, it is imperative that we actively engage in missional activity. There is something of a hermeneutical circle in this process. A missional reading ought to fuel the actual practice of mission; the practice of mission brings the Church back to the Scriptures.

How will the Church learn to engage the World with the Gospel in a clear and compelling way? I've argued for a reading of the Bible that is *missional*. But a *missional* reading has to arise out of actual *mission*. When we engage the world, we will encounter the need to read the

---

teachers is ambiguous enough to allow for reading pastors and teachers as one gift or as separate ones.

Bible in a way that informs our *missional* practice. A *missional* lifestyle is empowered by a *missional reading of the Scriptures*. When we are living life on *mission* for God we will find the Scriptures, both Old and New Testaments, a rich resource. The Ancient Israelites and the early Church encountered many of the challenges in their respective historical contexts as we in the modern Church. The Scriptures teach us how to live as people on mission in a world that does not yet know God.

In a brief section on *missional hermeneutics*, Carlos F. Cardoza-Orlandi argues that to be effective in mission Christ-followers need to accept that the Bible and its stories are used by many "outsiders." This is a crucial insight. The Old Testament is known and revered by at least two other major world religions: Judaism and Islam. In addition, there are countless persons in the West who still possess *residual* memory of Scripture, or they may read the Bible out of an interest in the person of Jesus apart from a Christian community.[14]

Take a minute for this to sink in: there are hundreds of millions of people who have at least a tangential interest in the Scriptures that God has given to humanity as a witness to his mission in the world. What an opportunity this is for believers! How often does it feel as though we are simply trying to establish a toehold in the world of evangelism, and all along there are countless persons who already have more than a passing interest in the Scriptures. In my own conversations with Muslims, Buddhists, and Jehovah Witnesses (these are the most common adherents to other religions that I encounter regularly), I have found a general openness to conversations about God and Scriptures.

On the other hand, this means that Christians need to be prepared for such encounters. We truly need to *know* the Bible ourselves as well as learn to be aware of the sorts of *alternative* readings that non-Christians tend to use.

For example, Muslims tend to focus on two critical issues in conversations about the Bible. First, they claim that the Bible used by Jews and Christians is riddled with errors. This is particularly true for *translations* of the Bible. Muslims assert the superiority and reliability of the Quran on the basis of its availability in its original language of Arabic. It is undiluted and unchanging truth in the original Arabic. Second, the Quran offers alternative versions of biblical stories. The most significant alternative reading is a common reading of *Surah* 4:157:

14. Cardoza–Orlandi, *Mission*, 67–70.

> (The Jews) said (in boast), "We killed Jesus the son of Mary, the Messenger of Allah," but they killed him not, nor crucified him, but so it was made to appear to them. And those who differ therein are full of doubts, with no (certain) knowledge, but only a conjecture to follow, for of a surety they killed him not.

This is a classic text that many Muslims deploy to deny the central event in Christianity: the atoning death of Jesus Christ. Muslims have a difficult time believing that God would permit such a prophet to die on a cross.

Christians who will converse with Muslims need to be aware of these sorts of interpretations and be so fully immersed in the Old and New Testaments that they can avoid these potential stumbling blocks.[15]

The very act of involvement in *mission* takes us out of the safety of our own communities of faith and places us in the marketplace of pluralism. It is a realm in which our Christian language will prove to be *indecipherable* or *naïve* at best and *contested* at worst. Yet, I believe that the way forward is a passionate and rigorous return to the principal source of our knowledge of Jesus—the Bible. Being on mission demands that we are intimately acquainted with the Scriptures in their totality. In the Bible, we encounter the *mission of God* to bring salvation and wholeness to the world, and we meet *humanity* in all of its potential, fallenness, and ambiguity. If we learn to read the Bible in light of our *missional practice*, we will be more discerning in our conversations with others and learn to speak in the language of persons created in God's image.

To do this, however, we need to read Scripture "as a resource for discernment and analysis, more than as a recipe book or a book of instructions."[16] Cardoza-Orlandi is not attempting to "deny the Bible's authoritativeness," rather he is calling for a deeper engagement with Scripture. A missional reading is not merely an attempt to discover new "can't miss" strategies for evangelism—rather its goal is *conversion*: a conversion of believers to commit themselves fully to participating in God's mission in the world and a conversion of non-believers as they encounter the life-giving and affirming message of the Gospel.

---

15. For those interested in additional reading on this, I recommend Glasser, "Cross-Reference Theology," 246–60.

16. Cardoza-Orlandi, *Mission*, 57.

2) Approaches to Scripture need to be integrated into *mission.*

When the locus of our reading occurs within the context of mission, our study of Scripture move beyond two well-meaning but ultimately self-referential approaches that dominate too much of our reading today.

The first is a reading of the Bible that is primarily for our own spiritual formation. I need to be careful here. It is absolutely vital that followers of Jesus Christ sustain themselves with a steady diet of Scripture. The danger, however, is that our reading can easily become self-centered. Our Bible study adds steadily to our own knowledge base, but we can lose touch with the missional intent of the Gospel. Reading for spiritual formation is not the end goal of Bible study, but a means for becoming the sort of profound person who can impact the World for God.

The second type of self-referential reading is an antiquarian focused one in which one studies Scripture merely to learn more about the background of the Bible. This would include the sort of reading that one finds in churches where one defines the mature believer as the one who knows the most about the Scripture (i.e., the person whom you would not want to challenge to a game of Trivial Pursuit Bible Edition), but it also would include certain academic approaches to Bible Study that students often encounter in a seminary setting. Such approaches focus on issues of historical background, historical-critical methods, etc., but in the end the focus is merely on the text's past historical meaning without pressing on to how a text informs life in the Church today. Please hear this criticism in its proper context. It is crucial that we investigate the biblical text from a variety of angles and approaches, but the goal needs to be hearing God's word for the mission of the Church in the present and not mere past-historical knowledge.

A missional reading provides a means to integrating other approaches to Scripture into a way of reading that informs and empowers the Church to live faithfully in the world. McManus writes, "A theological construct for interpretation finds success in the attainment of knowledge. The more you know, the more mature a Christian you are thought to be. And yet, knowledge of the Bible does not guarantee application of the Bible. To know is not necessarily to do. When the construct applied to the Bible is missiological, you engage the Bible to discover the response required of your life."[17]

---

17. McManus, *Unstoppable Force*, 72.

(RE)ALIGNING WITH GOD

Since the Bible is the story of God's mission to redeem a lost humanity and a broken creation, the only way to understand fully its message is to live out its story in our daily lives. The implications for education and growth in our communities are clear. For Christian education to be credible in the coming decades, it must shift its goals from merely transferring knowledge about the Christian faith to an approach that shapes Christ followers into agents of God's mission in the world. It will be about missiology as much as theology. A missional approach to Scripture serves to establish this *new framework* for learning. As communities of faith struggle to break the grips of the paradigm of serving as inward-focused dispensers of religious goods and services to serving as outposts for the sake of God's Kingdom, a missional reading provides a different outcome for learning. "Christian education" is no longer merely learning facts about the stories of the Scriptures or grasping the basics of the historical creeds of the church. The goal of learning in the Church now becomes a constant conversion to the message of Scripture so that each disciple can be shaped into the sort of person that she or he needs to become in order to participate fully in God's mission in the world. All learning can now be set in the context of the missional reality of the twenty-first-century Church.

3) Christians living *missional lifestyles* and reading the Bible as the testimony of the *mission of God* will be interested in asking different sorts of questions of the text. The questions will be ones that hinge on conversion and calls for realignment into the people whom God called us to be and become.

Mission pushes us out of our comfort zones. It makes it difficult to focus on self-referential reading. By engaging culture, we are forced to make sense of what it means to be God's witness in our world.

I live in Central Florida in the greater Orlando area. This part of the United States is profoundly diverse and serves as a bell-weather for the changing demographics of the country. On the street where I live I have neighbors from New York, Pittsburgh, northern Kentucky, Jamaica, Brazil, Puerto Rico, and Virginia. On any given day, I can hear various dialects of English as well as the sounds of Portuguese and Spanish. Within two miles of Asbury Seminary's campus in Orlando, one will find Hindu University and the Islamic Society of Central Florida. A few miles from my home is a beautiful new Buddhist Temple. Just north of Orlando is a Sikh temple.

What does it mean to read the Bible within such a diverse grouping of humanity? If we commit to serving as a missional community, we need to read the Scriptures for our *context*. The more time that I spend engaged with my neighbors, the more that I find myself reading Scripture for the sake of *outsiders* to the Gospel. It is inevitable. Being confronted with diversity moves us out of our usual questions. We must now wrestle not with reading Scripture for the sake of our own salvation, our own spiritual formation, and our own edification. We begin to read the Scripture for insights into our new friends. How does the Biblical witness equip me to represent the living Jesus to an *outsider/seeker* to the faith? How do I understand the biblical truth claims within the pluralism of my contemporary culture? What sort of person do I need to become in order to serve as Christ's ambassador? How does the biblical language serve as a model for communicating the Gospel in the twenty-first century? How would my friend hear this text? What would be confusing? What is present in the text that would be problematic for my friend to understand? What might be offensive?

As our communities of faith begin this new journey, let our prayer be that we truly awaken to embody our creational mandate to live as a missional community that reflects God's character to/for/in the nations.

Bibliography

Barram, Michael. "The Bible, Mission, and Social Location: Toward a Missional Hermeneutic." *Interpretation* 61 (2007) 42–58.
Bauer, David R. *The Structure of Matthew's Gospel: A Study in Literary Design*. Library of New Testament Studies 31. Edinburgh: T. & T. Clark, 1989.
Beeby, Harry Daniel. "A Missional Approach to Renewed Interpretation." In *Renewing Biblical Interpretation*, edited by Craig Bartholomew, Colin Greene, and Karl Möller, 268–83. Grand Rapids: Paternoster and Zondervan, 2000.
Bonhoeffer, Dietrich. *Creation and Fall: A Theological Exposition of Genesis 1–3*. Translated by Douglas Stephen Bax. Edited by John W. de Gruchy. Dietrich Bonhoeffer Works 3. Minneapolis: Fortress, 2004.
Briggs, Richard. *Reading the Bible Wisely: An Introduciton to Taking Scripture Seriously*. Revised edition. Eugene, OR: Cascade, 2011.
Bright, John. *The Authority of the Old Testament*. London: SCM, 1967.
Brueggemann, Walter. "A First Retrospect on the Consultation." In *Renewing Biblical Interpretation*, edited by Craig Bartholomew, Colin Greene, and Karl Möller, 343–47. Grand Rapids: Zondervan, 2000.
Cardozza-Orlandi, Carlos. "'Lampara es a mis pies tu palabra': Biblical Authority at the Crossroads." In *Engaging Biblical Authority: Perspectives on the Bible as Scripture*, edited by William P. Brown, 27–35. Louisville: Westminster John Knox, 2007.
———. *Mission: an Essential Guide*. Nashville: Abingdon, 2002.
Clifford, Richard J. *Proverbs: A Commentary*. Old Testament Library. Louisville: Westminster John Knox, 1999.
Craigie, Peter C. "The Poetry of Ugarit and Israel." *Tyndale Bulletin* 22 (1971) 3–31.
Cross, Frank Moore. *Canaanite Myth and Hebrew Epic*. Boston: Harvard University, 1973.
Currid, John D. *Ancient Egypt and the Old Testament*. Grand Rapids: Baker Academic, 1997.
Dawkins, Richard. *The God Delusion*. London: Bantam, 2006.
Dayton, Donald W., and Douglas M. Strong. *Rediscovering an Evangelical Heritage: A Tradition and Trajectory of Integrating Piety and Justice*. 2nd ed. Grand Rapids: Baker Academic, 2014.
Ekblad, Bob. *Reading the Bible with the Damned*. Louisville: Westminster John Knox, 2005.
Ford, William A. *God, Pharaoh, and Moses: Explaining the Lord's Actions in the Exodus Plagues Narrativei*. Milton Keynes: Paternoster, 2007.

Bibliography

France, R. T. *The Gospel of Matthew*. New International Commentary on the New Testament. Grand Rapids: Eerdmans, 2007.

Fretheim, Terence. *Exodus*. Interpretation. Louisville: Westminster John Knox, 1991.

———. *God and the World in the Old Testament: A Relational Theology of Creation*. Nashville: Abingdon, 2005.

Frost, Michael and Alan Hirsch. *Rejesus: A Wild Messiah for a Missional Church*. Peabody, MA: Hendrickson, 2009.

———. *The Shaping of Things to Come: Innovation and Mission for the 21st Century Church*. Peabody, MA: Hendrickson, 2003.

Glasser, Ida. "Cross-Reference Theology: The Cross in Conversation with Muslims." In *Fanning the Flame: Bible, Cross & Mission*, edited by Paul Gardner, et al., 246–60. Grand Rapids: Zondervan, 2001.

Goldingay, John. *Old Testament Theology: Israel's Gospel*. Vol 1. Downer's Grove, IL: InterVarsity Academic, 2003.

———. *Theological Diversity and the Authority of the Old Testament*. Grand Rapids: Eerdmans, 1987.

Gorman, Michael J. *Elements of Biblical Exegesis: A Basic Guide for Students and Ministers*. Revised and Expanded edition. Grand Rapids: Baker Academic, 2010.

Guder, Donald. "Missional Pastors in Maintenance Churches." *Catalyst* 31.3 (2005) 4–5.

Hirsch, Alan, and Debra Hirsch. *Untamed: Reactivating a Missional Form of Discipleship*. Grand Rapids: Shapevine Baker, 2010.

Jensen, Robert W. "Scripture's Authority in the Church." In *The Art of Reading Scripture*, edited by Ellen F. Davis, and Richard B. Hays, 27–35. Grand Rapids: Eerdmans, 2003.

Keller, Tim. *Counterfeit Gods: The Empty Promises of Money, Sex, Power, and the Only Hope that Matters*. New York: Dutton Adult, 2009.

Kitchen, Kenneth. *On the Reliability of the Old Testament*. Grand Rapids: Eerdmans, 2006.

Klein, William W., et al. *Introduction to Biblical Interpretation*. Revised edition. Nashville: Thomas Nelson, 2004.

Lindbeck, George. *The Nature of Doctrine: Religion and Theology in a Post-Liberal Age*. Louisville: Westminster John Knox, 1984.

McBride Jr., S. Dean. "Perspective and Content in the Study of Pentateuchal Legislation." In *Old Testament Interpretation: Past, Present, Future: Essays in Honor of Gene M. Tucker*, edited by James L. Mays, et al., 47–60. Old Testament Studies. Nashville: Abingdon, 1997.

———. "Polity of the Covenant People: The Book of Deuteronomy." *Interpretation* 41 (1987) 229–44.

———. "The Yoke of the Kingdom: An Exposition of Deuteronomy 6:4–5." *Interpretation* 27 (1973) 273–306.

McManus, Erwin Raphael. *An Unstoppable Force: Daring to Become the Church God Had in Mind*. Loveland, CO: Group, 2001.

———. "Talk Back." Origin's Regional Conference. Orlando, FL (Jan 19–20, 2005).

McNeal, Reggie. *Missional Renaissance: Changing the Scorecard for the Church*. San Francisco: Jossey-Bass, 2009.

Newbigin, Lesslie. *Gospel in a Pluralist Society*. Grand Rapids: Eerdmans, 1989.

Oswalt, John N. *The Bible Among the Myths: Unique Revelation or Just Ancient Literature?* Grand Rapids: Zondervan, 2009.

Russell, Brian D. "Psalms 1–2 as An Introduction to Reading the Psalms Missionally." *Encounters Mission Ezine* 33 (2010) 1–4. Online: https://encountersmissionjournal.

files.wordpress.com/2011/02/psalms_1-2_as_an_introduction_to_reading_the_psalms_missionally_33.pdf.

———. *The Song of the Sea: The Date of Composition and Influence of Exodus 15:1–21.* Studies in Biblical Literature 101. New York: Peter Lang, 2007.

Stark, Rodney. *The Rise of Christianity: A Sociologist Reconsiders History.* Princeton: Princeton University Press, 1996.

Steinbeck, John. *East of Eden.* Steinbeck Centenniel Edition. New York: Penguin, 2003.

Stone, Lawson G. "The Soul: Possession, Part or Person: The Genesis of Human Nature in Genesis 2:7." In *What about the Soul?: Neuroscience and Christian Anthropology*, edited by Joel B. Green, 47–61. Nashville: Abingdon, 2004.

Tennent, Timothy C. *Theology in the Context of World Christianity: How the Global Church is Influencing the Way We Think About and Discuss Theology.* Grand Rapids: Zondervan, 2007.

Thompson, David L. *Bible Study that Works.* Revised edition. Anderson, IN: Warner, 2011.

Traina, Robert A. *Methodical Bible Study.* Grand Rapids: Zondervan, 2002.

Traina Robert A., and David R. Bauer. *Inductive Bible Study: A Descriptive Guide to the Study of the Bible.* Grand Rapids: Baker Academic, 2010.

Wright, Christopher J. H. *The Mission of God: Unlocking the Bible's Grand Narrative.* Downers Grove, IL: InterVarsity, 2006.

———. *The Uniqueness of Jesus.* Thinking Clearly Series. Grand Rapids: Monarch, 2002.

www.ingramcontent.com/pod-product-compliance
Lightning Source LLC
Chambersburg PA
CBHW031428150426
43191CB00006B/443